By Knowledge & By Love

MICHAEL S. SHERWIN, O.P.

By Knowledge & By Love

CHARITY AND KNOWLEDGE IN THE MORAL THEOLOGY OF ST. THOMAS AQUINAS

THE CATHOLIC UNIVERSITY OF AMERICA PRESS
WASHINGTON, D.C.

The paper used in this publication meets the minimum requirements of American National Standards for Information Science—Permanence of Paper for Printed Library materials, ANSI Z39.48-1984.

Library of Congress Cataloging-in-Publication Data
Sherwin, Michael S., 1963–
By knowledge and by love : charity and knowledge in the moral theology of St. Thomas Aquinas / Michael S. Sherwin.—1st ed.
p. cm.
Includes bibliographical references and index.
ISBN 0-8132-1393-2 (hardcover : alk. paper)
ISBN-13: 978-0-8132-1871-7 (pbk)
1. Charity. 2. Knowledge, Theory of. 3. Love—Religious aspects—Christianity. 4. Christian ethics—Catholic authors. 5. Thomas, Aquinas, Saint, 1225?–1274. I. Title.
BV4639.S523 2004
241′.042′092—dc22
2004002868

To Our Lady of Knock
In silence she speaks

O Mater omnium credentium
in sinum pietatis tuae commendo
hodie et omnibus diebus vitae meae
corpus meum et animam meam,
omnesque actus meos,
cogitationes, volitiones,
desideria, locutiones, operationes,
omnemque vitam, finemque meum.

frater Thomas de Aquino

Contents

Figures

Abbreviations

Abbreviations for the Works of Thomas Aquinas

De caritate / *Quaestio disputata de caritate*

De malo / *Quaestiones disputatae de malo*

De spe / *Questiones disputatae de spe*

De veritate / *Quaestiones disputatae de veritate*

De virtutibus in communi / *Quaestio disputata de virtutibus in communi*

In divinis nominibus / *Super librum dionysii de divinis nominibus*

In ethic. / *Sententia libri ethicorum*

In metaphysic. / *Sententia super metaphysicam*

In physic. / *Sententia super physicam*

In sent. / *Scriptum super libros sententiarum*

Quodlibet. / *Quaestiones de quodlibet I–XII*

SCG / *Summa contra gentiles*

ST / *Summa theologiae*

Super romanos / *Expositio et lectura super epistolam Pauli apostoli ad romanos*

Super ioannem / *Lectura super ioannem*

Abbreviations for the Works of Aristotle

MP / *Metaphysics*

NE / *Nicomachean Ethics*

PS / *Physics*

Other Abbreviations

CCL / *Corpus christianorum series latina*

PG / *Patrologia graeca* (J. P. Migne)

PL / *Patrologia latina* (J. P. Migne)

Preface

One's first encounter with St. Thomas' theology of love can be disconcerting. His technical language can seem to render the rich reality of love lifeless. His analysis has nothing of the passion of St. Augustine's conversations with God in the *Confessions.* Augustine guides the reader through the city of love as a connoisseur of its joys. With Augustine as guide, the reader receives a wonderfully impressionistic collage of love's sights and sounds, its life and history. There are times, however, when the reader needs something other than this. In a time of crisis, it is not the impressionistic skills of the orator we value, but the precise skills of the draftsman who can draw a map of where we need to go. Painfully lost in the backstreets of our affections, we seek not a tour guide, but a cabby, someone who can lead us to the understanding we desire.

Early in my studies as a young Dominican, I discovered St. Thomas to be such a draftsman and guide. I did not make this discovery on my own. Many were involved in introducing me to Aquinas. This book would not have been possible without them. Those who first introduced me to Aquinas were my professors at the Dominican School of Philosophy and Theology at the Graduate Theological Union in Berkeley. Notable among these were the philosophers Antonio Moreno, O.P., and Vincent Guagliardo, O.P., both of whom now rest in the Lord. Among my professors in theology, Gregory Rocca, O.P., as my M.A. director, was a constant and energetic guide, as were Michael Dodds, O.P., and Luke Buckles, O.P. As those who first introduced me to the study of Aquinas' moral thought, Janko Zagar, O.P., and Edward Krasevac, O.P., deserve special mention. By their teaching, as well as their friendship, they instilled in me the desire to study Aquinas' moral theology more deeply.

One person more than any other, however, was involved in shaping this current project. In its original form, this book was my doctoral dissertation written for the University of Notre Dame. I wrote it under the wise and generous direction of Dr. Jean Porter. Without her patience and encouragement, as well as her insights into the thought of Aquinas, this work would never have been written. I also wish to thank the other members of my committee, Thomas O'Meara, O.P., Joseph Wawrykow, and Todd Whitmore, for their labors and insights. Two others who deserve special thanks are Romanus Cessario, O.P., and Guy Mansini, O.S.B., both of whom helped sharpen my grasp of Aquinas' theology of faith.

Special mention should be made of the warm hospitality extended to me by the members of the Congregation of Holy Cross at Notre Dame, especially the community at Moreau Seminary. On many occasions their friendship and example encouraged me to continue in the labor of writing this work. I note happily as well the inestimable influence of Ralph McInerny on my studies. Like so many others, I have benefited from the generous formation he quietly offers doctoral students during his Thomistic seminars, giving them the opportunity to share their ideas with senior scholars in an atmosphere of intellectual curiosity and liturgical celebration. Nowhere else have I found the spirit of Jacques and Raïssa Maritain as alive as it is at the Maritain Center under Dr. McInerny's direction. Another philosopher who has influenced the direction of my thought is David Solomon, whose seminar on the virtues situated the philosophy of virtue in its historical context and introduced me to the work of key authors such as Elizabeth Anscombe. I am keenly aware, in addition, that none of this would have been possible without the financial support of the benefactors of the Western Dominican Province, and the fraternal support of my religious superiors, especially John Flannery, O.P., who first sent me to undertake doctoral studies, and Daniel Syverstad, O.P., who shepherded me through them.

Another person who deeply shaped this study is Fr. Servais Pinckaers, O.P. During the year and a half I spent with him in Fribourg researching these pages, he was my constant guide. By the example of his patient charity as well as by his penetrating insights, he shaped me as well as my work. Fr. Pinckaers is truly one of those who, like the poet, has taken the road "less traveled by, and that has made all the difference." Lastly, I would like to thank my family, especially my parents, Harriet and Elton Sherwin. They were my first teachers in the faith and they were and continue to be the best of teachers, instilling in their youngest son a desire to study as well as live the faith that underlies their love.

Introduction

The saints are united to God
by knowledge and by love.
Thomas Aquinas[1]

When confronted with the question of love's relationship to knowledge, we might be tempted to say, along with a voice from a *Midsummer Night,* that "reason and love keep little company together nowadays."[2] Indeed, in reaction to the rationalism of modern thought, many would join their voices to the sentiment that "reason and love are sworn enemies."[3] Yet, even if we grant that the warmth of love has little in common with the cold calculations of rationalism, love seems nevertheless to remain deeply intertwined with knowledge. "Love talks with better knowledge, and knowledge with dearer love."[4] This hard-won insight from an older Shakespeare speaks more truly the classical perspective on love. For Augustine, nothing is loved that is not first known.[5] Deeper knowledge will either increase or diminish this love. Moreover, our judgments are deeply shaped by our loves.[6] These two aspects of knowledge and love seem to dance in uneasy tension within the human heart. The temptation is to focus on one aspect to the detriment of the other.

In the pages that follow, we shall explore one thinker's conception of

1. *Summa theologiae* (henceforth cited as *ST*) III 2.10: *"unio sanctorum ad deum [est] per cognitionem et amorem."*

2. William Shakespeare, *A Midsummer Night's Dream,* act 3, scene 1.

3. Pierre Corneille, *La Veuve (The Widow),* act 2, scene 3.

4. William Shakespeare, *Measure for Measure,* act 3, scene 1.

5. See Augustine, *De trinitate* 10.1 (*PL* 42, 971).

6. See Augustine, *De moribus ecclesiae catholicae* 15.25 (*PL* 32, 1322). See also Aristotle, *Nicomachean Ethics* 3.5 (1114a32–b1).

these twin features of love's relationship to knowledge. We shall explore Thomas Aquinas' understanding of the divine love poured into the human heart by God's Spirit (Rom 5.5). In other words, we shall study St. Thomas' theology of charity. Our primary goal will be to reveal the Thomistic understanding of charity's relationship to knowledge in human action. Even though the divine love of charity is our focus, this focus requires a preliminary study of natural human love. Since in Aquinas' view charity elevates the human will's natural love, to understand charity's relationship to knowledge one must first grasp the will's relationship to intellect and human love's relationship to human knowledge. Consequently, the core chapters of this work offer a close analysis of the relationship in Aquinas' thought between intellect and will (chapter two), knowledge and love (chapter three), and most fully, between charity and the infused cognitive virtues (chapters four and five). Lastly, we shall investigate what the Thomistic conception of charity's relationship to knowledge implies about how charity functions as a virtue (chapter six).

Other scholars have studied St. Thomas' understanding of charity's relationship to knowledge.[7] Why, therefore, does Aquinas' theology of this relationship merit yet another extended study? Answering this ques-

7. A. Forest, "Connaissance et amour," *Revue thomiste* 48 (1948): 113–122; Russell Hittinger, "When It Is More Excellent to Love than to Know: the Other Side of Thomistic 'Realism,'" *Proceedings of the American Catholic Philosophical Association* 57 (1983): 171–179; Albert Ilien, *Wesen und Funktion der Liebe bei Thomas von Aquin* (Freiburg im Breisgau: Herder, 1975); Raymond McGinnis, *The Wisdom of Love: A Study in the Psycho-Metaphysics of Love according to the Principles of St. Thomas* (Rome: Officium libri catholici, 1951); Elsbeth Michel, Nullus potest amare aliquid incognitum: *ein Beitrag zur Frage des Intellektualismus bei Thomas Von Aquin* (Fribourg, Switzerland: Editions universitaires de Fribourg, 1979); Charles J. O'Neil, "Is Prudence Love?" *Monist* 58 (1974): 119–139; William L. Rossner, "An Inclination to an Intellectually Known Good: the Question of the Existence of Intellectual Love," *Modern Schoolman* 52 (1974): 65–92; "The Process of Human Intellectual Love, or Spirating a Pondus," *Thomist* 36 (1972): 39–74; Pierre Rousselot, *The Intellectualism of Saint Thomas*, translated by J. E. O'Mahony (New York: Sheed and Ward, 1935); H-D Simonin, "La Primauté de l'amour dans la doctrine de saint Thomas d'Aquin," *Vie spirituelle* 53 (1937), suppl.: 129–143; C. A. J. Van Ouwerkerk, Caritas et Ratio: *étude sur le double principe de la vie morale chrétienne d'après s. Thomas d'Aquin* (Nijmegen: Drukkerij Gebr. Janssen, 1956); Daniel Westberg, *Right Practical Reason, Aristotle, Action, and Prudence in Aquinas* (Oxford: Clarendon Press, 1994), 245–260.

tion is the goal of these introductory remarks. The answer hinges on the recent work of a number of Catholic moral theologians. Specifically, these theologians, whom we can profitably call theologians of moral motivation, affirm that charity's act is antecedent to and independent of the conceptual knowledge proper to practical reason. The theory of charity advanced by these theologians is relevant to our study of Aquinas because some of them interpret Aquinas as having developed a similar view of charity. They affirm that in his mature work Aquinas presents charity's act as antecedent to and independent of practical reasoning.

The affirmation that the love of charity is independent of practical reason stands in stark contrast to the conclusions reached by a number of moral philosophers from the Anglo-American tradition of analytic philosophy. As part of a larger interest in virtue theory, these moral philosophers have looked anew at intellect and will and the relationship between knowledge and love in human action. In contrast to the theologians of moral motivation, these moral philosophers emphasize the dependence of love and virtue on knowledge and practical reasoning. The work of these moral philosophers raises questions concerning charity's character as a virtue. Specifically, if these philosophers are right, then the Catholic theologians who portray charity's act as independent of knowledge are confronted with a problem: namely, if charity is independent of knowledge and if the virtues require knowledge, then in what sense is charity a virtue? The conclusions of these moral philosophers also have implications for those who regard Aquinas as having developed a theology of charity similar to the one developed by the theologians of moral motivation. If they are correct, in what sense is charity a virtue in the mature thought of Thomas Aquinas?

The moral philosophers of the analytic tradition who consider the relationship between knowledge and love have developed a nuanced position. They recognize the role of the appetites (of the emotions and of the will) in shaping our moral knowledge, while at the same time affirming the dependence of the will and emotions on this knowledge. Thus, for example, Iris Murdoch asserts that "I can only choose within the world I can *see*, in the moral sense of 'see' which implies that clear vision is a result of moral imagination and moral effort."[8] Our choices depend on what we "see," while what we see is the product of our choices, of a chosen discipline cultivated and lived over time and within the fabric of one's whole life.[9] This means that reason and will do not stand in isolation from each other. "Will and reason then are not entirely separate faculties in the moral agent. Will continually influences belief, for better or worse, and is ideally able to influence it through a sustained attention to reality."[10] From this perspective, therefore, the human person "is not a combination of an impersonal rational thinker and a personal will. He is a unified being who sees, and who desires in accordance with what he sees, and who has some continual slight control over the direction and focus of his vision."[11] Murdoch is here describing what Martha Nussbaum calls the "priority of perceptions."[12] In describing the work of several influential scholars, Nussbaum affirms that they all portray love and the other "emotions" as having a "cognitive dimension in their very structure."[13] These scholars "make the acceptance of a certain belief or beliefs at least a necessary condition for emotion, and, in most cases, also a constituent part of what an emotion is."[14] Consequently, in their estimation, emotions are so closely linked to beliefs that "a modification of beliefs brings about a modification of emotion."[15] From this perspective, "love, pity, fear, and their relatives—all are belief-based in a similar way: all involve the acceptance of certain views of how the world is and what has importance."[16] A number of ethicists from the Anglo-American tradition, therefore, assert that the human person is a creature of both vision and desire. Pure desire requires clarified vision, while clear vision is the product of purified desire.

This mutual dependence has implications for one's theory of virtue,

8. Iris Murdoch, "The Idea of Perfection," in *The Sovereignty of Good* (London: Routledge, 1970), 37. (This essay was reprinted in Iris Murdoch, *Existentialists and Mystics, Writings on Philosophy and Literature,* edited by Peter Conradi [New York: Penguin, 1998], 299–336. In what follows, I employ the page numbers of the original edition.)

9. Ibid., 37.

10. Ibid., 40.

11. Ibid.

12. Martha C. Nussbaum, *Love's Knowledge: Essays on Philosophy and Literature* (Oxford: Oxford University Press, 1990), 37.

13. Ibid., 41.

14. Ibid.

15. Ibid.

16. Ibid.

something that many of these same scholars recognize. It implies, as Elizabeth Anscombe has noted, that in order to understand what it means to have a certain virtue, one must know the kinds of actions that embody that virtue. In her influential essay, "Modern Moral Philosophy," Anscombe explains that virtuous action presupposes some conception of the ideal "man" that functions as the norm according to which one acts. Just as with regard to the function of human teeth, there is an ideal number of teeth for humans to have (even though few may actually have this number), so too, "regarded not just biologically, but from the point of view of the activity of thought and choice in regard to the various departments of life—powers and faculties and use of things needed," there are an ideal number of virtues with an ideal set of specific characteristics for humans to have. The ideal "man" who has "the complete set of virtues is the 'norm'" according to which one strives to live.[17] Alasdair MacIntyre develops Anscombe's insight by underlining its social context: "One of the features of the concept of a virtue . . . is that it always requires for its application the acceptance of some prior account of certain features of social and moral life in terms of which it has to be defined and explained."[18] The social and moral features MacIntyre refers to here have a narrative structure. They place us within a specific narrative account of human life as ordered toward a specific goal. "I can only answer the question 'What am I to do?' if I can answer the prior question 'Of what story or stories do I find myself a part?'"[19] In other words, as MacIntyre states elsewhere, "one cannot understand the exercise of the virtues except in terms of their role in constituting the type of life in which alone the human *telos* is to be achieved."[20] From this perspective, the virtuous act presupposes and depends on knowledge. It presupposes that one knows something about the goal of a given virtue

17. G. E. M. Anscombe, "Modern Moral Philosophy," *Philosophy* 33 (1958): 14; reprinted in *Virtue Ethics*, edited by Roger Crisp and Michael Slote (Oxford: Oxford University Press, 1997), 40.

18. Alasdair MacIntyre, *After Virtue*, second edition (Notre Dame, Ind.: University of Notre Dame Press, 1984), 186.

19. Ibid., 216.

20. Alasdair MacIntyre, *Three Rival Versions of Moral Enquiry* (Notre Dame, Ind.: University of Notre Dame Press, 1990), 139.

and about which actions embody that virtue in the present context of one's life and social situation.

The work of these ethicists challenges us to confront anew Thomas Aquinas' theology of charity. If it is true, as the ethicists from the tradition of analytic philosophy claim, that human virtue presupposes knowledge of that virtue's object and of what constitutes actions in accordance with that virtue, what does this imply about St. Thomas' understanding of charity? Specifically, if virtue requires knowledge (as the moral philosophers claim), and if (as the theologians of moral motivation claim) in the mature theology of St. Thomas charity's act does not depend on knowledge, in what sense is charity a virtue? If charity in the mature theology of St. Thomas does not share this feature in common with the human virtues, what does charity share in common with them? In other words, if charity's act does not presuppose and require knowledge in the intellect, in what sense is charity recognizably a virtue, and in what sense is charity's act a human act? The theologians of moral motivation, therefore, confront us with a question of Thomistic interpretation: in the mature theology of Thomas Aquinas, what is charity's relationship to knowledge and what are the implications of this relationship for charity's status as a virtue?

In the chapters that follow we shall attempt to answer the first part of this twin question and to suggest an answer to the second part. First, however, we shall begin by considering more closely the work of some of those theologians who claim that charity's act is independent of practical reason: the theologians of moral motivation. Before doing so, we wish to underline that our study is fundamentally a work of Thomistic interpretation. We intend to study St. Thomas' theology of charity's relationship to knowledge. Our earlier introductory remarks concerning the insights of contemporary ethicists, and our subsequent analysis of contemporary moral theologians and of contemporary interpreters of St. Thomas, all serve to set the context of our treatment of Thomas' theology. They provide us with the twofold question that will guide our treatment of Aquinas' work: what is charity's relationship to knowledge, and what are the implications of this relationship for one's theology of charity as a virtue?

One final introductory comment is in order. It concerns my use of the first person plural throughout this study. Pascal once mused that scholars should rarely employ the first person singular in reference to their work because, "normally there is more in it which belongs to other people than to them."[21] Pascal's warning points to the collaborative aspect of any work of analysis. Every scholar is a weaver. His work is the product of his own art, but is nonetheless a tapestry woven from threads spun by many other voices. If the tapestry of voices is well woven it invites the reader to carry on the conversation. Thus, in order to emphasize the dialogical character of theological reflection, I have employed "we" and "our" throughout. It is not the imperial "we" I employ. It is, rather, a conversational or dialogical "we," by which I hope to invite the reader to join me in the work of analysis that follows. With this in mind, we can now begin.

21. Blaise Pascal, *Pensées,* n. 64 [édition Bossut, Suppl. II] (43) in *L'Oeuvre de Pascal,* edited by Jacques Chevalier, volume 34, *Bibliotèque de la Pléiade* (Paris: Editions de la nouvelle revue française, 1936), 836.

By Knowledge & By Love

CHAPTER I

Charity's Relationship to Knowledge

Charity's Act: Contemporary Efforts at Renewal

In its *Decree on the Training of Priests,* the Second Vatican Council turned its attention to the renewal of moral theology.

> Special care should be given to the perfecting of moral theology. Its scientific presentation should draw more fully on the teaching of holy Scripture and should throw light upon the exalted vocation of the faithful in Christ and their obligation to bring forth fruit in charity for the life of the world.[1]

The Council's call to present the Church's moral teaching from within the biblical conception of charity was a direct response to the limitations present in the perspective of the manuals of moral theology. These manuals were designed for a very specific task: the preparation of priests for the ministry of hearing confessions. In their day, these works were popular. They brought clarity and order to the confusing domain of human action, and provided wise and prudent guidelines for the compassionate care of souls.[2] Nevertheless, the dominant perspective held by the most influential manuals had several serious drawbacks.[3]

1. *Decree on the Training of Priests (Optatam totius),* n. 16 in *Vatican Council II: the Conciliar and Post Conciliar Documents,* New Revised Edition, edited by Austin Flannery (New York: Costello Publishing Company, 1984), 720.

2. Servais Pinckaers, *Morality: the Catholic View,* translated by Michael Sherwin (South Bend, Ind.: St. Augustine's Press, 2001), 37–41.

3. It is perilous to speak in generalities about the manuals of moral theology. There was not one monolithic type of moral manual. The Church contains within it various different traditions of moral reflection and the manuals, as the product of these

These manuals viewed the moral life primarily in terms of law and its application in particular acts. While this perspective was useful, it imported far-reaching changes in the Church's understanding of the moral life. "Once Christian moral life is placed within an ultimately legal frame of reference, moral norms, freedom, and conscience must be reinterpreted accordingly."[4] Influenced by the "Cartesian demand for geometrical clarity," the most influential manuals of theology employed a deductive understanding of the application of laws to particular cases in conscience.

[T]he casuistry of the neoscholastic manuals was presented as a deductive system. Moral principles were likened to mathematical axioms; their meaning was thought to be univocal. Behavior that was allowed or forbidden was likened to necessary conclusions deduced from first principles; judgments about rightness and wrongness were universally applicable. Based on a mod-

---

traditions, reflect their differences. Also, the perspectives of these traditions developed over time and the manuals were shaped by these developments. Nevertheless, there was a dominant perspective and this perspective shaped the most influential manuals. In what follows, it is not my intention to offer a full treatment of the various traditions and types of moral manual. Instead, the focus will be on the dominant perspective that most shaped the theologians of moral motivation who react against it.

4. Walter J. Woods, *Walking with Faith: New Perspectives on the Sources and Shaping of Catholic Moral Life* (Collegeville, Minn.: Michael Glazier Press, 1998), 452. For a concise outline of the new perspective introduced into Catholic theology by the manuals of moral theology, see Servais Pinckaers, *The Sources of Christian Ethics* (Washington, D.C.: The Catholic University of America Press, 1995), 267. For more on the manuals of moral theology, see Woods, *Walking with Faith,* 441–457; Charles E. Curran, *The Origins of Moral Theology in the United States: Three Different Approaches* (Washington, D.C.: Georgetown University Press, 1997), 12–167; James F. Keenan and Thomas A. Shannon, editors, *The Context of Casuistry* (Washington, D.C.: Georgetown University Press, 1995); Raphael Gallagher, "The Fate of the Moral Manual Since Saint Alphonsus," in *History and Conscience: Studies in Honour of Sean O'Riordan,* edited by Raphael Gallagher and Brendan McConery (Dublin: Gill and Macmillan, 1989), 212–239; "The Manual System of Moral Theology Since the Death of Alphonsus," *Irish Theological Quarterly* 51 (1985): 1–16; Albert R. Jonsen and Stephen Toulmin, *The Abuse of Casuistry: A History of Moral Reasoning* (Berkeley: University of California Press, 1988), 152–175; Louis Vereecke, "La théologie morale du concile de Trente à saint Alphonse de Liguori," *Studia moralia* 25 (1987): 7–25; "Histoire et morale," *Studia moralia* 12 (1974): 81–95; "Préface à l'histoire de la théologie morale moderne," *Studia moralia* 1 (1963): 87–120; "Le concile de Trente et l'enseignement de la théologie morale," *Divinitas* 5 (1961): 361–374. The last three cited essays also appear in Louis Vereecke, *De Guillaume d'Ockham à saint Alphonse de Ligouri* (Rome: Collegium S. Alfonsi de urbe, 1986), pages 15–26, 27–55, and 495–508 respectively.

ern scientific ideal, moral reasoning erected a coherent, ahistorical, and closed system of norms and precepts to guide everyday life.[5]

In principle, this "quasigeometrical system" of moral casuistry enabled one to offer solutions to difficult cases that could be "presented with a great deal of certainty and were universally applicable."[6] In the after-the-fact context of the confessional, the moral analysis of the manuals amounts to the following: it is the application of laws to particular cases in the courtroom of conscience in order to determine the moral status of an act and its degree of merit or sinfulness. Employed antecedently to action, this method applies laws to particular cases in the courtroom of conscience in order to determine the extent to which the law restricts one's freedom in a specific situation.[7]

As John Mahoney has noted, this method of analysis leads to several imbalances. It generates a preoccupation with sin; an almost obsessive concern for law; and a myopic focus on the individual and his or her specific acts.[8] Karl Rahner rightly protested that the moral life must be more than this. We are called to obey the law, but the Christian life is more than merely legal observance.[9] Besides cutting off moral theology

5. Thomas R. Kopfensteiner, "Science, Metaphor, and Moral Casuistry," in *The Context of Casuistry,* edited by James F. Keenan and Thomas A. Shannon (Washington, D.C.: Georgetown University Press, 1995), 212.

6. Ibid., 207.

7. Manualist authors generally do not offer theoretical explanations or descriptions of their own method. Their method, however, can be gleaned by looking at the structure and mode of analysis of their works. See, for example, Jean-Pierre Gury's *Compendium theologiae moralis* (Ratisbon: Georg Josef Manz, 1874). Charles Curran offers an analysis of Alphonsus Sabetti's method in *The Origins of Moral Theology in the United States,* 77–167. See also Pinckaers, *Sources of Christian Ethics,* 272.

8. John Mahoney, *The Making of Moral Theology: A Study of the Roman Catholic Tradition* (Oxford: Clarendon Press, 1987), 27–36.

9. Karl Rahner, "On the Question of a Formal Existential Ethics," in *Theological Investigations* (Baltimore: Helicon Press, 1963), vol. 2, 222–223: "The morally obligatory cannot and must not contradict these [universal] norms—this is clear. There can be nothing which actually ought to be done or is allowed in a concrete or individual situation, which could lie outside these universal norms, and to that extent everything which morally ought to be done in the concrete is also the realization of the universal norms. But is it not *more* than that? Is what is morally done *only* the realization of universal norms—is what ought morally to be done in the concrete case *merely,* as it were, the intersection of the law and the given situation? And conversely: if in a certain situation the universal

from the rich reality of Christ, grace and the virtues, the manuals' focus on law and its application to particular acts made it difficult to resolve several issues that regularly confront a confessor in his pastoral ministry. Two issues stand out in particular. The first concerns how to understand the moral status of Catholics of good will who chronically struggle with "sins of weakness." The second concerns how to understand the status of Catholics who sincerely strive to lead morally good lives but from a profound and abiding ignorance of moral truth are living in ways that are objectively contrary to the Gospel. In both sets of difficult cases the individuals are striving to lead holy lives, yet the first group habitually acts contrary to their moral knowledge, while the second group acts in ignorance of moral knowledge.[10] Is the moral status of these individuals before God best understood in relation to their external actions, or is there something about their relationship with God that the standard manualist focus on acts fails to convey? A number of moral theologians affirm that these cases are not fully nor accurately understood by focusing merely on these individuals' external acts. Responding to the Council's call to renew moral theology, these moralists have attempted to develop a theory of human action and moral analysis that offers a richer conception of the moral life and provides a more satisfactory description of the above sets of cases.

The manualists recognized that many factors could limit a person's ability to know the law or apply it correctly in concrete cases. The manualists were aware of the forms of ignorance and lack of freedom that can beset a person from causes not directly under the agent's control. The best of the manualists took care to identify the factors that can limit a person's moral responsibility. They also recognized that because of a person's invincible ignorance, his or her subjective relationship with God could still be good, although his or her actions were objectively

laws leave room for a free choice, i.e., if according to the universal norms several things are still 'allowed' and ethically possible in a determined situation, can we then do what we want, just because *ex supposito* we do not in such a case offend against any universal laws whose content could be materially formulated?" See Benedict Ashley, "Fundamental Option and/or Commitment to Ultimate End," *Philosophy and Theology* 10 (1998): 121.

10. See Ashley, "Fundamental Option," 119–120.

mortally sinful. Some manualists even affirmed that a person who acts from invincible ignorance could subjectively be engaging in meritorious action because he or she was acting from charity.[11]

But Josef Fuchs and others have rightly argued that it is not enough to recognize the disjuncture that can occur between the agent and his or her acts. What is needed is a more adequate psychology of action to explain how this disjunction occurs.[12] What is needed, they argue, is a moral psychology rooted in a conception of the moral life that no longer views individual acts as so many isolated stepping-stones toward human life's goal. Instead, what is needed is a psychology of action that views the moral life as analogous to natural growth. As John Mahoney explains, human acts are not so much steps, as "stages of personal growth, more like rings in a tree."[13] From this perspective, the focus shifts from acts to the person who performs these acts, "or, to be more accurate, to the person who is becoming more, or less, himself in and through his actions."[14]

To effect this shift in perspective, a number of theologians draw on the work of Karl Rahner and distinguish between the freedom to choose between different "categorical" objects and a deeper "transcendental" freedom, expressed in a person's "total self disposal," or "*option fondamentale.*"[15] They also join with Rahner in affirming that charity's act occurs on the level of one's transcendental freedom, and is that out

11. These authors were encouraged to advance this position by the authority of St. Alphonsus Liguori, who affirmed that, "not only does one who acts from an invincibly erroneous conscience not sin, he *probably acquires merit*" (emphasis in the original) (*Theologia moralis* [Rome: Typographia vaticana, 1905], vol. 1, n. 6).

12. Josef Fuchs, "Basic Freedom and Morality," in *Human Values and Christian Morality* (Dublin: Gill and Macmillan, 1970), 111.

13. Mahoney, *Making of Moral Theology,* 220.

14. Ibid., 220.

15. Karl Rahner, "Theology of Freedom," in *Theological Investigations,* volume 6 (New York: Seabury Press, 1974), 186. See also Karl Rahner, *Foundations of Christian Faith: an Introduction to the Idea of Christianity* (New York: Crossroad, 1985); "Freedom: iii. Theological," in *Sacramentum Mundi,* volume 2 (New York: Herder, 1969), 361–362; "Guilt—Responsibility—Punishment Within the View of Catholic Theology," in *Theological Investigations,* volume 6 (New York: Seabury Press, 1974), 197–219; "Justified and Sinner at the Same Time," *Theological Investigations,* volume 6 (New York: Seabury Press, 1974), 218–230.

of which one's "categorical" actions flow. In other words, charity's act is the graced elevation of one's fundamental option or self-disposal.[16] Since these moralists almost universally describe charity's act as the will's motivation—distinguishing it from the will's intentions or choices—they can aptly be described as developing a theology of moral motivation.[17] We should note, however, that the extent to which these theologians of moral motivation are accurate interpreters of Karl Rahner or the extent to which they develop positions in harmony with Rahner's core insights are issues open to question. Moreover, these authors often differ significantly among themselves. It is perilous, therefore, to generalize about the theologians of moral motivation. I assert only that some authors, especially Josef Fuchs and James Keenan, develop Rahner's views in a direction that unequivocally separates the will's motion on the level of one's transcendental freedom from one's practical reasoning or categorical acts. Specifically, Fuchs and those who follow his lead posit the existence of a morally significant motion in the will that is antecedent to, or at least independent of, practical reasoning and the objects of choice. Following Rahner, Fuchs describes the foundation of this voluntary motion as a person's "*basic* freedom or *transcendental* freedom."[18] The motion in the will that results from this freedom is what

16. See Karl Rahner, "The 'Commandment' of Love in Relation to the Other Commandments," *Theological Investigations,* volume 5 (New York: Crossroad, 1966), 439–459; "Reflections on the Unity of the Love of Neighbor and the Love of God," in *Theological Investigations,* volume 6 (New York: Seabury Press, 1974), 231–249; *The Love of Jesus and the Love of Neighbor* (New York: Crossroad, 1983).

17. See, for example, James Keenan's description of charity: "In a word, the contemporary phrase, 'moral motivation,' best expresses the charitable person who loves self and neighbor formally out of union with God" (James Keenan, *Goodness and Rightness in Thomas Aquinas's* Summa theologiae [Washington, D.C.: Georgetown University Press, 1992], 142).

18. Fuchs, "Basic Freedom and Morality," 96. Fuchs acknowledges his debt to Rahner explicitly, noting, however, that "fundamental option" was not Rahner's preferred term: "The theory of a 'fundamental option' goes back mainly to the development by the late Karl Rahner, S.J., of ideas borrowed from Jacques Maritain and Joseph Maréchal, S.J. Rahner's preferred term was not in fact 'fundamental option' but 'the human person's disposition of his self as a whole'" (Josef Fuchs, "Good Acts and Good Persons," in *John Paul II and Moral Theology: Readings in Moral Theology No. 10,* edited by Charles E. Curran and Richard A. McCormick, S.J. [New York: Paulist Press, 1998], 47).

Fuchs calls a person's "self-realization in basic freedom," or "basic free option."[19] This self-realization, which has popularly become known as one's fundamental option, is either "a total surrender of the self to the Absolute, or a refusal of such surrender."[20] The refusal of this self-surrender is the essence of mortal sin, while total self-surrender to the Absolute is, for these moralists, the essence of charity. Charity is a person's "basic free love of God," and consists in the "radical opening of the self to the Absolute."[21]

As we noted in the introduction, the theology of charity developed by the theologians of moral motivation is of interest to our current project because of the questions it raises concerning charity's character as a virtue. If, as the theologians of moral motivation claim, charity's act is a morally significant motion in the will occurring at a level distinct from one's concrete (categorical) knowledge, then in what sense is charity a virtue? In what sense does charity's act retain any of the characteristics proper to the acts of the other virtues? To grasp the full significance of these questions we must sketch a little more fully the psychology of action developed by the theologians of moral motivation.

The psychology of action proper to the theology of moral motivation provides an avenue for moving away from the manualists' over-concentration on individual acts, its proponents claim, because it recognizes two levels of freedom. There is the level of basic freedom and the level of freedom of choice. Free choice is exercised in particular (categorical) acts; our choices occur in response to (categorical) objects of cognition. Free choice is, therefore, the equivalent of what the manualists describe as the will's "freedom of indifference" before the objects of choice.[22] Al-

19. Fuchs, "Basic Freedom and Morality," 96 and 98.

20. Ibid., 97.

21. Ibid., 105 and 99. The relationship between what the theologians of moral motivation call the "basic free love of God" and the traditional distinction between the natural and supernatural love of God (i.e., charity) is complicated. A treatment of it is beyond the scope of our current project. We should note, however, that James Keenan wishes to distinguish between the love proper to one's basic freedom as existing in non-Christians, describing it as "benevolence," and charity, which is the love proper to Christians. See Keenan, *Goodness and Rightness,* 11, 14, 54–56.

22. See, for example, Gury, *Compendium theologiae moralis,* n. 11, p. 7: "*variae speciei*

though the will on the level of "free choice" is radically free before its objects, the will is nonetheless limited by the range of choices presented to it by reason. Consequently, "freedom of choice" is constrained by the various psychological limitations that plague us. Our knowledge and our ability to make clear judgments are limited, while our emotions are often disordered. As a result, freedom on this level is often profoundly restricted or entirely absent. Yet, from the perspective of the theology of moral motivation, freedom of choice is not the deepest level of freedom. There is also one's basic freedom. This freedom is not actualized by any particular object of cognition; thus, one's basic freedom is not restricted by the social and psychological limitations that afflict us. Moreover, proponents of this view argue that one's self-realization in basic freedom is not exercised in any particular categorical act.[23] Rather, one's free option is a process that accompanies and underlies one's particular acts. Thus, one's self-realization in basic freedom is not something that one can easily lose. It is on this level that a person is either morally good or bad before God.

According to this view, one is good or bad depending on how, in grace, one exercises one's basic self-realization, by whether one opens up to God or turns way from him. Consequently, Josef Fuchs describes charity as a "striving for self-realization" that underlies a person's categorical acts, rendering them morally good.[24] One's particular acts of free choice, whether they be objectively right or wrong, can be signs of one's fundamental option, pointing to whether one is loving from charity or not, but they do not cause this option nor are they necessarily in harmony with it.

The man who, because of his self-commitment in basic freedom, lives in grace and love will not come so easily to serious sin as another who has not made the basic decision of surrender to God. For he does not only have to

libertas datur; 1) libertas a necessitate, i.e., libertas indifferentiae seu electionis, quae est immunitas ab omni necessitate intrinseca antecedente, et est libertas proprie et stricte dicta." For an analysis of the manualist conception of the "freedom of indifference," see Pinckaers, *Sources of Christian Ethics*, pp. 327–353.

23. Fuchs, "Good Acts and Good Persons," 50.

24. Fuchs, "Basic Freedom and Morality," 98.

carry out the evil deed in free choice, but he has also to reverse, in basic freedom, his basic free attitude to God.[25]

One immediate implication of this perspective is a reappraisal of the traditional analysis of those who chronically commit sins of weakness, the first of our earlier mentioned types of difficult cases. The distinction between the levels of freedom (transcendental freedom and freedom of choice) enables Fuchs to explain how one who chronically falls into objectively sinful action is not necessarily "falling in and out of mortal sin."

Therefore it cannot be assumed that someone continually—'seven times a day'—changes from mortal sin to the love of God and *vice versa,* not only because of the bias of grace, but also because of the effective power of love. Where the specific acts—grave sins or acts of sorrow—seem to indicate the contrary, one has to deal with more or less free acts of choice without the involvement of self-commitment in basic freedom. That is to say, the person is presumably in a continuous state either of sin or of justification.[26]

The incontinent person, therefore, is not necessarily sinning mortally because he may still nonetheless be surrendering to God on the level of his basic freedom.

Fuchs next considers the implications of his theory for the second type of our difficult cases: those who live in apparent ignorance concerning the objectively sinful character of their actions and styles of life. Fuchs holds that the distinction between the two levels of freedom reveals that even in such cases, these individuals may not be sinning mortally.

A further consequence follows from the fact that acceptance or refusal of grace comes about through activation of basic freedom. We are thinking of those people whose way of life does not conform at all to the moral standard. This can be the outcome of a basic negative decision, that is, of rejection of grace. But what if the far-reaching lack of psychological and social formation—one thinks of 'a-social' people—leads one rather to think that such conduct is far from corresponding to true freedom of choice? Then it is indeed not impossible that such people, despite their outwardly immoral and a-social

25. Ibid., 104.
26. Ibid.

way of life, have not refused the grace of Christ in basic free self-activation, but have accepted it—or, after willed failures, have accepted it anew.[27]

Fuchs is affirming here that social and psychological conditions can leave a person in chronic ignorance of essential moral truth, and that, therefore, these conditions can limit their freedom of choice—freedom on the categorical level. For example, because of the culture in which one is raised, a couple might not know that pre-marital sex is objectively sinful. Nevertheless, on the transcendental level of one's basic freedom, they may nevertheless be morally good and in right relationship with God. In the view of its proponents, therefore, the theology of moral motivation offers a more satisfactory way to explain the moral status both of those who struggle with incontinence and of those who act from chronic ignorance.

The above quotations from Fuchs also reveal that on the level of free choice, the categorical level, Fuchs accepts a modern voluntarist view of practical reasoning: reason decides what should be done, and the will in the act of choice either accepts or rejects it.[28] As we have seen, however, Fuchs seeks to overcome the limitations of this view by positing a motion in the will that is antecedent to practical reason and thus not subject to its determining influence. The theologians of moral motivation, therefore, attempt to overcome the limitations of the manualist perspective, and the apparent psychological determinism that it implies, by positing the existence of a morally significant motion in the will that is not determined by any specific object of cognition and which transcends the level of prudential reasoning about means to ends. The person may fail on the level of his or her particular acts, but can remain in right relationship with God because on a deeper level of freedom he or she is still striving to surrender to God.

In the introduction we drew attention to the work of moral philosophers from the analytic tradition of philosophy who have turned their attention to the virtues. We noted that these moral philosophers claim that in order to engage in an act of virtue one must have some knowl-

27. Ibid., 110.

28. For a description of this modern view, see Murdoch, "The Idea of Perfection."

edge of the goal of that virtue and of what actions embody that virtue. This claim has implications for the theology of charity advanced by the theologians of moral motivation because, as we have seen, they portray charity's act as occurring in isolation from specific (categorical) knowledge. Before considering these implications more closely, we shall further note the work of one scholar who interprets Thomas Aquinas as having developed in his mature work a theology of charity similar to the one advanced by the theologians of moral motivation.

Thomas Aquinas and Charity's Relationship to Knowledge

In several recent studies, James Keenan has developed the work of Josef Fuchs in novel and influential ways.[29] His work is of interest to our current study because of the interpretation he offers of Thomas Aquinas' theology of charity. Keenan argues that St. Thomas in his mature thought develops a theology of moral motivation similar to the one advanced by Fuchs and his disciples. Specifically, Keenan maintains that in the aftermath of the Parisian controversies and condemnations concerning human freedom, St. Thomas develops a psychology of human action that establishes the will's "autonomy."[30] Keenan defines autonomy as the will's ability to engage in a motion that wholly "precedes and is independent of reason."[31] It is the will's ability to engage in an "an-

29. James Keenan, *Goodness and Rightness in Thomas Aquinas's* Summa theologiae (Washington, D.C.: Georgetown University Press, 1992); "Being Good and Doing Right in Saint Thomas' *Summa theologiae*" (Th.D. diss. Gregorian University, 1988); "The Problem with Thomas Aquinas's Concept of Sin," *Heythrop Journal* 35 (1994): 401–420; "Can a Wrong Action Be Good? The Development of Theological Opinion on Erroneous Conscience," *Église et Théologie* 24 (1993): 205–219; "Distinguishing Charity as Goodness and Prudence as Rightness: A Key to Thomas's *Secunda pars*," *Thomist* 56 (1992): 407–426; "A New Distinction in Moral Theology: Being Good and Living Rightly," *Church* 5 (1989): 22–28.

30. Keenan, *Goodness and Rightness*, ix–x: "During his second regency in Paris, precisely while writing *De malo* 6 and question nine of the *Prima secundae*, Thomas develops a new position concerning the will's autonomy. The will's autonomy is a necessary condition for understanding moral goodness." See also ibid. Keenan, *Goodness and Rightness*, 38–41 and 43.

31. Ibid., 55. See also ibid., 47: "As first mover, the will's movement is independent of

tecedent self-exercise."[32] St. Thomas came to recognize, Keenan contends, that unless the will has a morally significant act that is antecedent to and independent of practical reason, the will would not be free. The will's act would always be limited and determined by one's psychological disorders and social constraints. Recognizing this, St. Thomas, in *De malo* 6 and *ST* I-II 9, develops a theory of the will's primary motion *(exercitium),* which, in Keenan's view, Thomas portrays as independent of reason's primary act *(specificatio).*[33]

Furthermore, Keenan contends that after establishing the will's autonomy, Aquinas also develops an account of the moral goodness proper to the will's autonomous action. To understand what Keenan means, we must look briefly at the distinction he establishes between rightness and goodness. Following Fuchs and other contemporary ethicists, Keenan distinguishes between moral rightness and moral goodness.[34]

> Goodness means that out of love we strive to live and act rightly. Rightness means that our ways of living and acting actually conform to rational expectations set by the ethical community.[35]

At first sight it may seem that for Keenan goodness refers to persons, while rightness refers to actions. Keenan himself at times describes the distinction in this way.[36] This, however, is only part of the picture, since

and prior to reason's presentation of the object, and thus movement becomes the key for understanding the will."

32. Ibid., 50.

33. Ibid., 38–55.

34. Keenan draws upon the work of G. E. Moore who developed a fuller presentation of this distinction (See ibid., 5–6). See also W. D. Ross, *The Right and the Good* (Oxford: Clarendon Press, 1930). The distinction has been taken up by some Catholic moralists in their effort to move away from an excessive emphasis in moral theology upon individual acts. The moralists among this group who most influence Keenan are Joseph Fuchs, Klaus Demmer, Klaus Riesenhuber, and Bruno Schüller. For a brief account of the influence of this distinction on Catholic moralists, see Bernard Hoose, *Proportionalism: The American Debate and Its European Roots* (Washington, D.C.: Georgetown University Press, 1987), 41–67.

35. Keenan, *Goodness and Rightness,* 3.

36. For example, in appraising the philosophies of the past, Keenan asks, "If good people performed bad acts, and if bad people performed good acts, should there not be distinct moral descriptions for persons and acts?" (Ibid., 4–5).

in Keenan's view rightness also refers to persons.[37] Keenan explains that the divide between goodness and rightness is not located at the frontier between persons and actions, but rests within persons themselves. "The boundary between goodness and rightness is marked by the distinction between motivation and intention."[38] Intention is the first act of the will within the process of practical reasoning, while motivation, in Keenan's view, is an act of the will that is antecedent to reasoning. The divide, therefore, between goodness and rightness is a divide between motivation and practical reason. "The distinction between goodness and rightness is not between person and act, but between the heart and reason."[39] Persons are right if they reason in ways that lead to right action and if they themselves engage in right action. Persons are good only if being motivated out of love they strive to reason and act rightly. In the description of persons, therefore, rightness and wrongness focus upon practical reasoning, while goodness and badness focus upon motivation, an action antecedent to and distinct from practical reasoning.[40] In other words, employing Josef Fuchs' terminology, the distinction is between the transcendental and categorical levels of the human personality. Goodness pertains to the transcendental level of one's fundamental freedom, rightness pertains to the categorical level of one's freedom of choice.

With this distinction in hand, Keenan affirms that in his mature theology of charity St. Thomas partially establishes a distinction between rightness and goodness.[41] Specifically, Keenan contends that in his later

37. Ibid., 12: "rightness describes two dimensions of human living, persons and actions."

38. Ibid., 14.

39. Ibid., 143. For Keenan, "heart" is the image used by the biblical authors to express moral motivation. See ibid. 16: "In the Bible, the heart is designated as the locus of morality. The heart as moral motivation appears in the synoptic gospels in passages that emphasize the moral motivation of the Pharisees . . ."

40. Ibid., 7: "goodness is not consequent to rightness, but antecedent to and distinct from rightness."

41. Ibid., x: "to some extent the distinction between goodness and rightness is in the *Summa theologiae,* but . . . Thomas never thematizes it. Thomas, distinguishes charity from reason and, therefore, implicitly goodness from rightness. But, he never actually entertains the distinction between badness and wrongness."

works Thomas portrays charity's act as a purely formal striving that establishes our fundamental moral goodness.[42] We and our actions are "right" if they conform to the dictates of practical reason expressed through the virtue of prudence.[43] Yet, we are "good" only if these actions are *from* charity—only if they spring from, and are generated and informed by charity.[44] This goodness is what maintains and deepens the holiness and union with God poured into our hearts by the action of God's grace.[45]

Keenan portrays these supposed developments in St. Thomas' work as effecting a deep shift in Thomas' thought: while in his earlier works Thomas describes all of the will's acts as subsequent to and dependent on reason, in his later works he recognizes an act of will that is antecedent to and independent of reason.[46] Further, Thomas presents charity's act as the elevation of this antecedent voluntary motion. Ac-

42. Ibid., 142: "charity, which unites one to the last end, describes the self-movement of striving to grow in greater union with God, to integrate oneself better, and to seek the good of one's neighbor. These strivings, or formal interior acts, are antecedent to questions concerning specification, that is, they are antecedent to questions of intention and choice, or to questions pertaining to the proximate ends intended and the actual objects realized. In a word, the contemporary phrase, 'moral motivation,' best expresses the charitable person who loves self and neighbor formally out of union with God."

43. Ibid., 100–108.

44. Ibid., 133–135.

45. Ibid., 142: "Gratuitous charity perfects us in attaining the last end, and thus makes us right, but this is solely God's action, not ours. . . . But, as this chapter demonstrates, our response in charity is another function of the virtue and provides a distinctive moral description for how we humans strive. Charity as the response to gift is an expression of moral goodness, not rightness."

46. Ibid., 47: "As first mover, the will's movement is independent of and prior to reason's presentation of the object." Ibid., 50: "This *exercitium* is always antecedent to specification. The will must first be willing to consider any object offered by reason for its acceptance. That the will must first be willing means that the will must first move itself and reason. Without that antecedent willingness reason does not influence the will with its objects. By establishing this antecedent self-exercise of the will, Thomas distinguishes between God as final cause of the will, *quantum ad exercitium,* and reason as formal cause of the will's movement, *quantum ad specificationem.* This antecedent *exercitium* provides the foundation for Thomas's assertion that the will is free to move itself and reason." Ibid., 55: "[the will's] *exercitium* precedes and is independent of reason." See also James Keenan, review of *Right Practical Reason: Aristotle, Action, and Prudence in Aquinas* by Daniel Westberg, *Theological Studies* 56 (1995): 803.

cording to Keenan, therefore, St. Thomas in his mature work disengages will from reason and portrays charity's act as the graced elevation of the will's pre-rational motion.

James Keenan's detailed analysis of Aquinas' thought merits close consideration. Indeed, his interpretation of Aquinas has many more features and nuances than we have here addressed. Yet, a full treatment of Keenan's thought is beyond the scope of our current project.[47] This cursory account of Keenan's interpretation of Aquinas is meant only to show that Keenan poses questions that merit our attention. His interpretation challenges us to look anew at Aquinas' theology of charity and its relationship to knowledge. Specifically, from the perspective of the earlier cited ethicists who claim that a virtue's act presupposes and depends on knowledge, the notion that Aquinas disengaged charity from knowledge in his mature thought raises issues concerning charity's status as a virtue. If Aquinas truly develops an understanding of charity that regards charity's act as independent of reason, does he also similarly develop a new understanding of how charity functions as a virtue? If so, this would mean that Aquinas' mature theology of charity would be subject to the same limitations that constrain the theology of moral motivation.

Implications of the Theology of Moral Motivation

The claim that charity's motion—the motion that renders us morally good—is antecedent to and independent of reason appears to pose (at least) three interrelated difficulties. First, it seems to empty charity and moral goodness of conceptual content. As a purely formal striving, charity as an ethical concept would seem no longer to have explanatory power. From such a framework, one would no longer be able to describe the charitable life in terms of specific kinds of actions or a specific pattern of life. Secondly, this conception of charity appears to imply that

47. For critiques of Keenan's interpretation of the later Aquinas, see Lawrence Dewan, "St. Thomas, James Keenan, and the Will," *Science et esprit* 47 (1995): 153–175; and James C. Doig, "The Interpretation of Aquinas's *Prima secundae,*" *American Catholic Philosophical Quarterly* 71 (1997): 171–195.

knowledge of God is of little practical importance for moral goodness as theologians of moral motivation define it. If the motions of charity's love are pre-conceptual, doesn't this imply that charity's love cannot depend upon conceptual knowledge of God?[48] As a result, Christ (as the revelation of God), and the Christian community (as the place where one encounters Christ) would seem to have no essential importance for one's relationship with God. Paradoxically, although right behavior and moral virtue would depend upon knowledge of God, one's relationship with God would not. Thirdly, this view of charity would seem to have implications for the psychology of moral judgment. To assert that charity's motion is causally independent of practical reasoning, appears to imply that charity does not influence our judgments concerning right action. This would mean that what we love, at least on the level of spiritual love, would not affect what we choose to do. Each of these difficulties seems to arise inevitably once one embraces a psychology of action that locates one's response to God's grace in an action that is antecedent to and independent of reason.

In chapter 6 we shall return to these difficulties, addressing them in relationship to our analysis of St. Thomas' thought. Looking back over our analysis of St. Thomas, we shall assess the extent to which St.

48. In the pages that follow I frequently refer to "conceptual knowledge." Since this term means different things to different people, I should state here how I am employing it. In St. Thomas' works "*conceptio*" normally refers to the first act of the intellect by which we know real things. It is not directly the object of our thought, except when we choose to reflect on how we know what we know. Instead, it is that *by which* we know the object. Thus, strictly speaking, to refer to conceptual knowledge in relation to the intellect is somewhat redundant. Since the *conceptio* is the act of the intellect, all rational and intellectual knowledge is conceptual. (This is true even for angels and for God; thus, in St. Thomas' view, conceptual knowledge does not necessarily imply composition and division. See, for example, *ST* I 27.1; *ST* I 41.2 ad 4; *ST* 57.3 ad 2; *ST* 66.4 ad 3.) The phrase is helpful, however, because it enables us to underline that we are referring to a knowledge which is consciously accessible to us and can become the object of our further reflection. In other words, I employ conceptual knowledge to distinguish it from what some would call "pre-thematic" knowledge. For St. Thomas' understanding of how we can have conceptual knowledge of God, see *ST* I 12.13; *ST* I 12.13 ad 1; *ST* I 13.4; *ST* I 13.12; *ST* I 84.7 ad 3. For more on the character of conceptual knowledge in St. Thomas, see John O'Callaghan, *Thomist Realism and the Linguistic Turn* (Notre Dame, Ind.: University of Notre Dame Press, 2003), 31–32, 67–77, 165–175, 237–256.

Thomas in his mature work develops a moral psychology and theology of charity that make charity the act of a radically autonomous will. Specifically, we shall assess whether St. Thomas ever asserts the will's radical independence from reason and regards charity's motion as the graced elevation of this autonomy. This will then enable us to consider the implications of St. Thomas' theology of charity for charity's status as a virtue and whether and in what ways charity operates like other virtues. To determine this, however, we must first establish what St. Thomas holds concerning intellect and will and the knowledge and love that flow from them. This will be the task of chapters two through five. It is to this task that we now turn.

CHAPTER 2

The Will's Role in Practical Reasoning

At the outset of the *Summa theologiae* St. Thomas affirms that, "Since it is by our will that we employ whatever powers we have, the human person is said to be good, not by his good understanding, but by his good will."[1] This affirmation might give the reader the impression that for Aquinas moral goodness depends on an act of will that is structurally independent of practical reason and its objects. The first goal of this chapter will be to show that the contrary is in fact the case. We shall establish that Thomas Aquinas maintains throughout his career that every act of the will is informed by the intellect. For Thomas, the will is a rational appetite. The essence of the will's act is to be an inclination that follows some cognitive apprehension.

If Aquinas maintains, however, that every act of will follows some form of cognition, this seems to present a problem. Does this not imply intellectual determinism, or at least run the risk of reducing sin to ignorance? A second goal of this chapter, therefore, will be to show that far from leading to determinism, Aquinas' theory of the will as a rational appetite accounts for how the human person is both guided by reason and free in his or her actions. Intellect and will together form the dual principle of human action. At every stage of practical reasoning, the intellect is bringing the informing light of human intelligence to bear upon the particulars of human action, while the will is directing the intellect in the consideration of those particulars. The intellect specifies

1. *ST* I 5.4 ad 3.

the will's object, while the will moves the intellect to exercise its act. This last feature raises the issue of the ultimate foundation of practical reasoning. If the intellect specifies the will's object and if the will moves the intellect to specify, where does the process begin? Thus, the third and final goal of this chapter will be to sketch Aquinas' understanding of the natural principles underlying free choice and practical reasoning. This sketch will enable us to understand more deeply how for Aquinas human acts are informed by reason and executed by the will. It will also prepare us for our analysis of Aquinas' theory of love.

Acting from Knowledge

St. Thomas begins his analysis of human agency in the *Summa theologiae* by affirming that humans always act for an end, and that this implies some cognitive understanding of the end they seek to attain by acting. "Every agent necessarily acts for an end."[2] "In order that something be done for an end, some knowledge of the end is necessary."[3] He continues to affirm this even after the celebrated innovations he introduces in questions nine and ten of the *Prima secundae.* "In the order of agency *(ordo agibilium),* it is first necessary to have the apprehension of the end, then the desire *(appetitum)* for the end; then there is counsel about the means and then desire for those means."[4] This is true, Thomas believes, not only for the immediate goal of the agent's action (which Aquinas calls the proximate end), but also for the ultimate end of the act. Thomas explains that when we act there must be some ultimate end that is the first cause moving us to act. We must both have some knowledge of this end and believe that it is attainable, otherwise we would neither hope to attain it nor desire it as the goal of our actions.[5] As rational agents, this means that our actions presuppose some conceptual understanding of the ultimate end of human life. Each of us has some conception of human flourishing, some notion of happiness. We act in or-

2. *ST* I-II 1.2.

3. *ST* I-II 6.1; see also *Summa contra gentiles* (henceforth cited as *SCG*) II 23.6; *Scriptum super libros sententiarum* (henceforth cited as *In sent.*) III 26.2.4.

4. *ST* I-II 15.3.

5. See *ST* II-II 17.7.

der to attain this flourishing. When we reason about what we should do, we evaluate possible courses of action in relation to our conceptual understanding of flourishing, which in turn also implies some understanding of these particular actions themselves.

But in saying that humans always act from some cognitive understanding of human flourishing, Aquinas is not affirming that the human person's notion of human flourishing is always correct or even that he or she always has a clear understanding of this notion.[6] For example, one might incorrectly believe that human flourishing is chiefly attained in sense pleasures, but be unable to describe exactly what this flourishing would entail. Even if one were able, upon further reflection, to construct a clearer account of what happiness as bodily pleasure would entail, the point here is that one need not do so in order to act as a human agent. To act one need only have some general notion of human happiness. Nevertheless, Aquinas retains his initial affirmation. Humans may have a wrong notion of happiness, and their understanding of happiness may be very general. Yet, in order to act as rational agents they must have some cognitive conception of human flourishing.

In saying this, however, we have not yet said enough. When Aquinas says that human action requires knowledge of the end, one might assume that nevertheless the moral goodness of the agent does not. In other words, one might assume that for Aquinas, while action requires knowledge, the goodness of the agent depends only on an act of the will that accompanies our knowledge but is not dependent upon knowledge for its goodness. A careful reading of the Thomistic texts, however, reveals that Aquinas does not merely affirm that in human action knowledge accompanies the act of the will; he further maintains that knowledge is a necessary component of the will's own act. "The act of the will is nothing else than an inclination proceeding from an interior principle of knowledge."[7] The will is a rational appetite, and as such always acts from knowledge. "Every act of will is preceded by an act of the intellect."[8] As a result, the moral goodness of the will, and thus also of the agent him or herself, depends upon knowledge. This is a significant

6. See St I-II 5.8 corpus and ad 3.

7. *ST* I-II 6.4.

8. *ST* I-II 4.4 ad 2.

claim. For us to maintain this requires that we look more closely at what Aquinas himself says.

Already in his earliest works Aquinas describes the will as a rational appetite and explains what this means. "Rational appetite is one that follows the apprehension of reason. This is called the motion of reason and is nothing other than the act of the will."[9] He continues to refer to the will in this way well into the *Summa theologiae.*[10] Appetite, Aquinas elsewhere explains, is always an inclination toward something else: "it is evident that all appetite is for the sake of something. For it is foolish to say that someone desires for the sake of desiring, since to desire *(appetere)* is a certain movement tending toward something else."[11] A rational appetite differs from merely natural appetite because it is an inclination toward something apprehended by reason. The will's object is not merely the good, but the apprehended good.[12] He explains that

9. *In sent.* II 24.3.1. See also *SCG* III 149.5: *"cognitio praecedit voluntatis motum."*

10. *ST* I-II 6 prol.: *"voluntas est rationalis appetitus, qui est proprius hominis." ST* I-II 5.8 ad 2: *"cum voluntas sequatur apprehensionem intellectus seu rationis, . . ."* See also *ST* I-II 6.2 ad 1: *"voluntas nominat rationalem appetitum." ST* I-II 8.1: *"voluntas est appetitus quidam rationalis." ST* I-II 46.4 ad 1: *"voluntas est cum ratione; unde et dicitur appetitus rationalis." ST* I-II 66.4: *"voluntas autem est appetitus rationalis."*

11. *Sententia libri de anima* III 15.821. See Stephen L. Brock, *Action and Conduct: Thomas Aquinas and the Theory of Action* (Edinburgh: T and T Clark, 1998), 46.

12. Aquinas affirms this throughout his earlier works (*"obiectum enim voluntatis est bonum apprehensum"* [*Quaestiones disputatae de veritate* (henceforth cited as *De veritate*) 22.9 ad 6]) and continues to do so in his later writings (*"actus morales procedunt a voluntate, cuius obiectum est bonum apprehensum. et ideo si falsum"* [*ST* II-II 98.1 ad 3].). See also *In sent.* III 26.1.2: *"proprium autem motivum appetitivae virtutis est bonum apprehensum; unde oportet quod secundum diversas virtutes apprehendentes sint etiam diversi appetitus: scilicet appetitus rationis, qui est de bono apprehenso secundum rationem vel intellectum, unde est de bono apprehenso simpliciter et in universali." SCG* I 82.11: *"bonum apprehensum voluntatem sicut proprium obiectum determinet." SCG* I 95.3: *"cum enim voluntatis obiectum sit bonum apprehensum, non potest voluntas ferri in malum nisi aliquo modo proponatur sibi ut bonum." SCG* II 24.2: *"voluntas enim ad agendum ex aliqua apprehensione movetur: bonum enim apprehensum est obiectum voluntatis." SCG* III 73.3: *"bonum apprehensum movet voluntatem ut eius obiectum." ST* I 19.1: *"natura intellectualis ad bonum apprehensum per formam intelligibilem, similem habitudinem habet, ut scilicet, cum habet ipsum, quiescat in illo; cum vero non habet, quaerat ipsum. Et utrumque pertinet ad voluntatem. Unde in quolibet habente intellectum, est voluntas." Compendium Theologiae* 1.128: *"bonum apprehensum est obiectum voluntatis." ST* I-II 13.5 ad 2: *"cum obiectum voluntatis sit bonum apprehensum, hoc modo iudicandum est de obiecto voluntatis, secundum quod cadit sub apprehensione." ST* I-II 20.1 ad 1: *"actus exterior est obiectum voluntatis, inquantum proponitur voluntati a ratione ut quoddam bonum apprehensum et ordinatum per rationem." ST* I-II 77.1: *". . . ex*

"some knowledge must precede the will," even if it be imprecise and general, because, "otherwise, if [the object] were completely unknown, it would not be desired."[13] Aquinas continues to hold this view in the *Secunda pars* of the *Summa theologiae.* "The motion of the will follows the act of the intellect."[14] "The will cannot desire a good that is not previously apprehended by reason."[15] Consequently, "the will tends to its object according as it is proposed to it by reason."[16] Aquinas affirms this view of the will in other later works as well. For example, in the *Disputed Question on the Virtues in Common,* he affirms, "It is necessary that the animal or rational appetite incline toward its appetible object from some preexisting apprehension."[17]

In the *Prima secundae* of the *Summa theologiae,* Aquinas asserts the intellect's structural priority over the will at every level in the process of free action. He begins by considering the three elicited acts of the will that are directed to the end, namely, volition, enjoyment, and intention.[18] He asserts that volition *(velle)* "flows from an apprehended form," such that in order for the will to will anything it must be "apprehended as good."[19] For this reason, the intellect moves the will with regard to the "determination of the act."[20] Next, Aquinas tells us that enjoyment of the end *(fruitio finis),* which is attained fully at the completion of the act, is an act of the will that also presupposes an act of the intellect.[21] Indeed, Aquinas affirms that perfect enjoyment is only possible in creatures endowed with intellects.[22] Intention too, we are told, presupposes an act of the intellect. "Intention signifies an act of the will, presupposing an ordinance of reason ordering something to the end."[23]

---

parte obiecti voluntatis, quod est bonum ratione apprehensum." Quaestiones disputatae de malo (henceforth cited as *De malo*) 6: *"obiectum movens voluntatem est bonum conveniens apprehensum." Quaestio disputata de virtutibus in communi* (henceforth cited as *De virtutibus in communi*) 6: *"aliquod bonum apprehensum oportet esse obiectum appetitus animalis et rationalis." Quaestiones de quodlibet i–xii* (henceforth cited as *Quodlibet.*) 3.12.2: *"obiectum autem voluntatis secundum propriam rationem est bonum apprehensum." Lectura super ioannem* (henceforth cited as *Super ioannem*) 13.1: *"voluntas movetur ab exteriori obiecto sicut a bono apprehenso."*

13. *In sent.* I 6.1.3 Ex.
14. *ST* I-II 10.1 sc.
15. *ST* I-II 19.3 ad 1.
16. *ST* I-II 19.10.
17. *De virtutibus in communi* 6.
18. *ST* I-II 8 prol.
19. *ST* I-II 8.1.
20. *ST* I-II 9.1 ad 3.
21. *ST* I-II 11.1 ad 3.
22. *ST* I-II 11.2.
23. *ST* I-II 12.1 ad 3. See also *ST* I-II 12.1 ad 1 and *ST* I-II 12.3 ad 2.

Aquinas then considers the elicited acts of the will that are directed toward the means, namely consent, choice, and use. He explains that consent presupposes and follows reason by being the application of appetite to reason's decision in counsel.[24] Choice, which differs from consent when consent has approved more than one option,[25] also presupposes an act of intellect. In choice, "reason precedes the will and orders its act," preceding the will in the act of "decision or judgment."[26] Lastly, Aquinas contends that use *(usus),* which is "to apply an active principle to action," presupposes reason's act of referring this principle to action.[27] Aquinas offers a concise summary of reason's structural priority in the movement from volition to consent (or choice) as follows. "The order of action is this: first there is apprehension of the end; then desire of the end; then counsel about the means; then desire of the means."[28] In each stage of the will's elicited acts, therefore, the free act of the will presupposes an act of the intellect.[29]

The structural priority of the intellect at each level of the will's action is in line with Aquinas' definition of the human act. When investigating whether humans act for an end, Aquinas defines the human act as one that flows from a deliberated will *(ex voluntate deliberata),* by which he means that the human act is one that flows from a will under the direction of reason's consideration of the end and the means to that end.[30] Indeed, Aquinas regards the human act as synonymous with the moral act. The moral act, the act for which the agent is morally responsible, is one that flows from a deliberated will.[31] We began this chapter with

24. *ST* I-II 15.3.

25. *ST* I-II 15.3 ad 3.

26. *ST* I-II 13.1 and ad 2.

27. See *ST* I-II 16.2 and *ST* I-II 16.1 ad 1.

28. *ST* I-II 15.3.

29. Aquinas, however, introduces two decisively important caveats to the above description of reason's priority. First, he tells us that the will inclines toward the last end naturally (*ST* I-II 15.3). Second, he asserts that the rational component of the will's commanded acts presupposes an antecedent act of the will; a vicious circle is avoided only because the will's first act on the level of exercise is from God and not from the direction of reason (*ST* I-II 17.5 ad 3). These two features require close scrutiny. We shall discover, however, that the intellect's structural priority remains even here: although reason does not direct the will's first natural inclination, this inclination still presupposes the informing presence of the intellect. In other words, although the intellect does not (efficiently) cause the will's first motion, it nonetheless informs this motion.

30. *ST* I-II 1.1. See also *ST* I-II 1.1 ad 3 and *ST* I-II 1.2 ad 3.

31. *ST* I-II 1.3.

Aquinas' assertion that, "since it is by our will that we employ whatever powers we have, the human person is said to be good, not by his good understanding, but by his good will." Aquinas never backs away from this assertion, but he later explains that since the goodness of the will depends on the goodness of its object, and since the will relates to its object through reason, "the goodness of the will depends on reason."[32] Thus, although we are called good through our good will and not by our good understanding, nevertheless the will is good because of the goodness of the object toward which it tends.

Aquinas' description of reason's priority inevitably raises the issue of determinism. When Aquinas emphasizes so strongly the will's dependence on reason, how does he avoid intellectual determinism? David Gallagher poses the problem succinctly.

> [If the will's motion] depends on reason's perception of a good object, the will can seem to be necessitated by its object much the way a person, when he opens his eyes, necessarily sees whatever object lies before him. Thus when reason presents a good the will would seem constrained to will it.[33]

Once Aquinas describes the will as a rational appetite structurally dependent upon the intellect, how does he avoid concluding that the will necessarily moves toward whatever the intellect apprehends as a fitting good? Does not Aquinas' theory imply that the intelligible object moves the will the way a visible object moves an open eye, instantly and irresistibly? It is to this question that we now turn.

Free Choice in Practical Reasoning

St. Thomas undertakes his analysis of free choice in several different works, written at various periods of his life. Over the course of his life Aquinas did indeed develop and clarify his theory. Nevertheless, as several scholars have convincingly shown, the central elements of his explanation of human freedom remain constant.[34]

32. *ST* I-II 19.3.

33. David Gallagher, "Thomas Aquinas on the Causes of Human Choice" (Ph.D. diss., The Catholic University of America, 1988), 2.

34. Gallagher, ibid., 291–307, and "Free Choice and Free Judgment in Thomas

First, throughout his career, Aquinas both underlines how the will differs from the other appetites and acknowledges what the will shares in common with the other appetites. As a *rational* appetite, will differs from (merely) natural appetite by being an inclination that follows cognition, while it differs from sensitive appetite by being an inclination that follows intellectual cognition and by doing so from one's free decision. Yet, as an appetite of a creature with a determined nature, the will shares in common with other appetites that it naturally and necessarily inclines toward certain things. It inclines toward universal good and those goods that are naturally ordered toward the agent's attainment of universal good. Second, Aquinas affirms in both his earlier and later works that the intellect has a certain causal priority over the will and that the intellect moves the will by presenting the will its object. Third, Aquinas maintains consistently throughout his works that although on one level reason moves the will, on another level the will moves reason: the will has a role in shaping reason's practical judgments. Lastly, Aquinas affirms in his earlier and later works that God is the ultimate ground of the will's causal motion. God is both the cause of the will's natural inclination and the first efficient cause of the will's subsequent efficient causality.

In his later works, however, Aquinas does develop his theory of human action in important ways. Besides presenting his earlier views more clearly, he (1) introduces the distinction between specification and exercise; (2) develops an account of the central role played by the intellect's "consideration" of the object and the will's influence upon this consideration; and (3) analyzes explicitly the will's self-motion. In the following three sections, our task will be to sketch the main features of Aquinas' theory and to show that the development that occurs in Aquinas' thought serves to integrate intellect and will more deeply together in the genesis of human action. As Aquinas matured in his thought—a maturation no doubt fostered by the Parisian controversies of the 1270s

Aquinas," *Archiv Für Geschichte Der Philosophie* 76 (1994): 247–277; Daniel Westberg, "Did Aquinas Change His Mind about the Will?" *Thomist* 58 (1994): 41–60; Lawrence Dewan, "St. Thomas, James Keenan, and the Will," 153–175. The analysis that follows is deeply indebted to Gallagher's analysis.

over human freedom—he came to delineate more clearly the respective roles of intellect and will in practical action.[35] We shall draw our sketch of Aquinas' theory and its development by presenting two analyses of choice that Aquinas offers: one in an earlier work, the *De veritate* (written between 1256 and 1259), and one in a later work, the *De malo* (probably written near 1270).[36] This will enable us in a subsequent section to trace Aquinas' understanding of the natural principles that underlie free choice in practical reasoning.

De veritate and Free Choice

In question 22 of the *De veritate,* St. Thomas considers the nature of the will. Thomas maintains that all things incline toward their proper good, and that this inclination is simultaneously an inclination toward God as the ultimate end and as the ground of goodness. He further affirms that a hierarchy exists among these inclinations, or what he also calls appetites.[37] This hierarchy, Aquinas explains, is based on agency, on

35. For an historical analysis of these controversies and the condemnations of 1270 and 1277 that they occasioned, see Ferdinand Van Steenberghen, *La philosophie au xiiie siècle* (Louvain: Publications universitaires-Paris: Béatrice Nauwelaerts, 1966), 357–488; John Wippel, "The Condemnations of 1270 and 1277 at Paris," *Journal of Medieval and Renaissance Studies* 7 (1977): 169–201.

36. On the dating of *De veritate,* see Jean Pierre Torrell, *Saint Thomas Aquinas, volume 1: the Person and His Work* (Washington, D.C.: The Catholic University of America, 1996), 54–74, 334; on the dating of *De malo* 6, see Torrell, ibid., 201–207; 336; H. M. Manteau-Bonamy, "La liberté de l'homme selon Thomas d'Aquin (la datation de la Q. Disp. *DE MALO*)," *Archives d'histoire doctrinale et littéraire du moyen âge* 46 (1979): 7–33; Otto Pesch, "Philosophie und Theologie der Freiheit bei Thomas von Aquin in quaest. disp. 6 *De malo*," *Münchener theologische Zeitschrift* 13 (1962): 1–25. Kevin Flannery has recently advanced the remarkable suggestion that *De malo* 6 was actually written before the *De veritate,* making it one of Aquinas' earliest works (Kevin Flannery, *Acts Amid Precepts: the Aristotelian Logical Structure of Thomas Aquinas's Moral Theory* [Washington, D.C.: The Catholic University of America Press, 2001], 247–249). While I am in sympathy with Flannery's efforts to show the essentially Aristotelian structure of Aquinas' theory of action, where intellect and will work closely together in every human act, I do not believe that the existing evidence (not even the internal evidence he offers) supports his proposed early date for the *De malo.* As Flannery himself recognizes, however, his argument that Aquinas never held that the will is autonomous from the intellect does not depend on *De malo* being an early work (see ibid. 143).

37. For Aquinas' treatment of the general inclination of all creatures toward their good, where he explains that this inclination is simultaneously directed toward God, see *De veritate* 22.1 and 2.

the extent to which a creature has within itself an internal principle of motion under its own control and by which it moves itself and other things.[38]

St. Thomas describes the hierarchy of inclinations in terms of nearness to God.[39] The closer a creature is to God, the greater agency it exhibits. Among the creatures of the visible creation, humans exhibit the highest form of agency. Humans not only have an inner inclination and an inner moving principle, they also have dominion over this inclination and the actions that flow from it.

Rational nature, being the closest to God, does not merely, like inanimate things, have an inclination to something, nor, like sentient nature, merely have a mover of this inclination that has determined it as something extrinsic; beyond this, it has its own inclination within its power so that it does not necessarily incline to any appetible thing it apprehends, but can incline or not incline. And so its inclination is not determined for it by anything else than by itself.[40]

Unlike subrational creatures, humans have an inclination that is under their control. This inclination is the will. In later articles Aquinas investigates the nature of the will's control and probes the role of reason in it. First, however, he considers the manner by which the will acts from necessity.

St. Thomas begins by distinguishing two types of necessity. First, there is necessity of force, whereby something is made to act contrary to its natural inclination. Second, there is the necessity of natural inclination itself. This is an inclination that exists in a thing because of the very nature of the thing. Thus, we say that "God necessarily lives," because to live belongs to the very nature of God. It is according to this second type of necessity that the will necessarily wills certain things.[41] To explain this Thomas notes that what belongs to a genus must be present in the species of that genus. He offers the example of the human species in relation to the genus animal. Humans not only have what belongs to them as a species, i.e. rationality, they also retain what belongs

38. See *De veritate* 22.4 and *De veritate* 24.1.

39. *De veritate* 22.4.

40. Ibid.

41. *De veritate* 22.5.

to animals as animals. For example, humans also have physical senses. Aquinas affirms that an analogous relationship exists between nature and will.

Nature and will stand in such an order that the will itself is a nature, because whatever is found in things is a nature. There must accordingly be found in the will not only what is of will but also what is of nature. It belongs to any created nature, however, to be ordained by God for good, naturally tending to it. Hence even in the will there is a certain natural appetite for the good corresponding to it. It further belongs to the will to tend to something according to its own determination and not from necessity. This is proper to the will as will.[42]

Aquinas next explains that just as the will's natural inclination is the foundation of the will's free motion, so too the object of the will's natural inclination is the foundation of the objects that the will freely chooses. Aquinas is referring to the ultimate end, happiness. "Among the objects of appetite the end is the foundation and principle of the means to the end, because the latter, being for the sake of the end, are not desired except by reason of the end."[43] Thus, the will naturally wills not only "the last end, happiness," but also "whatever is included in it, such as to be, to know truth, and the like."[44] From this foundation the will is then able to will other things by its own "self disposal and without any necessity."[45]

St. Thomas discerns three levels on which the will is free of necessity: in relation to its act, its object, and its ordination to its end. In relation to its act, the will is free to act or not to act "with regard to anything at all."[46] In relation to its object, although the will necessarily wills the end, it is free to will whatever means it chooses. The will always naturally wills good in general, but not necessarily this or that particular good. "It is like sight, which naturally sees color but not this or that particular

42. Ibid. This distinction enables Aquinas to explain more precisely the relationship between will and natural appetite. The will is distinct from natural appetite strictly considered, in other words, from an appetite that is "only natural." Considered broadly, however, will is not distinct from natural appetite but includes it (*De veritate* 22.5 ad sc 6).

43. *De veritate* 22.5.

44. Ibid.

45. Ibid. See also *De veritate* 23.4.

46. *De veritate* 22.6.

color. For this reason whatever the will wills it wills under the aspect of good; yet it does not always have to will this or that good."[47]

In relation to the will's ordination to the end, the interplay between intellect and will is more complicated. Aquinas summarizes this freedom by stating that the will can "will good or evil."[48] Not only is the will free to choose this or that true means to the end, it can also choose a false means to the end. Aquinas affirms that this freedom does not merely result from the will's ability to choose the means to an end; it must also depend on reason's ability to misapprehend the relationship of a proposed means to the end. "From a correct appetite for the last end inordinate desire for something could not follow unless reason were to take as referable to the end something that is not referable."[49] Aquinas offers the example of fornication.

One who naturally desires happiness with a right appetite *(appetitu recto)* would never be drawn to desire fornication except in so far as he apprehends it as a human good, seeing it as something pleasurable and thus referable to happiness as an image of it.[50]

On the other hand, "where there is no failure in apprehending and comparing, there can be no willing of evil even when there is a question of means, as is clear among the blessed."[51]

Aquinas seems to stumble at this point in his analysis. While it may indeed be true that choice of the wrong means always implies an error on the part of reason, this does not explain how the will is free with regard to the choice of these wrong means. In other words, Aquinas has still not explained the will's role in moral error. Indeed, even his explanation of the will's role in choosing legitimate means to an end remains sketchy. Aquinas has thus far stated that although the will necessarily inclines toward the ultimate end, it is free to choose among intermediate ends that stand as means to this end: the will necessarily wills good in general, but not this or that particular good. He affirms this, but he does not yet explain how this occurs.

47. *De veritate* 22.6 ad 5.

48. *De veritate* 22.6.

49. Ibid.

50. Ibid.

51. Ibid.

St. Thomas pays closer attention to the will's role in practical reasoning in subsequent articles of the *De veritate.* After recognizing that intellect and will are two distinct powers, he considers how each moves the other. "In a way the intellect moves the will, and in a way the will moves the intellect and the other powers."[52] Thomas understands this in terms of efficient and final causality. "Two things are to be taken into account in any action, the agent and the reason for acting."[53] For example, in local motion the end moves by being the reason for acting, while the efficient cause produces the motion by moving the subject from one point to another.

Aquinas maintains that in the rational creature the end, or "reason for acting," can only be a cause of motion by preexisting intentionally in the agent. This it does by existing in the agent's intellect, "for it belongs to intellect to receive something by way of an intention."[54] The example Aquinas often gives is that of a builder working on a house. The builder does not build a house without first having some conception of the house in his intellect.[55] "Hence the intellect moves the will the way an end is said to move, by conceiving beforehand the reason for acting and proposing it to the will."[56] In other words, "the intellect rules the will, not by inclining it to that toward which it tends, but by showing it that toward which it should tend."[57]

The will, on the other hand, moves the intellect and all the other powers as the efficient cause of the action. Aquinas adduces two reasons for this. First, the will is an inclination, and in all other creatures we see that inclinations are the principles by which agents move other things after the manner of an efficient cause. Second, the intellect's object (truth) is primarily an intentional or cognitive reality existing in the mind; but knowledge of the truth is not by itself a cause of action. The good, however, which is the will's object, primarily exists in things. This points to the will's agency because action is applied to things. Thus, "the will has

52. *De veritate* 22.12. See also *De veritate* 22.13 ad 2.

53. *De veritate* 22.12.

54. Ibid.

55. See *De veritate* 23.1.

56. *De veritate* 22.12.

57. *De veritate* 22.11 ad 5. Aquinas fails to see here that the act of showing the end is not an act of final causality, but of formal causality. As we shall see, Aquinas later rectifies this mistake.

the function of moving in the manner of an agent cause; not, however, the intellect."[58] The intellect has the function of moving "as an end does" by showing the will its object. The will is able to apply this agency even to itself and the intellect, because as spiritual powers intellect and will are able to reflect back upon their own acts and upon the acts of the other powers. This enables the intellect to understand itself, the will and all the other powers, while it enables the will to will itself to will, the intellect to understand, and the other powers to engage in their proper actions.[59] Thus, even in the *De veritate,* Aquinas maintains that in practical reasoning the will is the agent cause of its own action and of the intellect's action, while the intellect moves the will by presenting the will its object—the end.

St. Thomas further probes the relationship between intellect and will when he considers the will's proper acts: willing, intending and choosing.[60] Thomas describes all three of these acts as presupposing reason. They differ by relating to reason in different ways. First, there is to will *(velle).* The will wills something when reason presents something that is simply good *(bonum absolute).*

[The will's act] is to will in so far as reason proposes to the will something good absolutely, whether it is something to be chosen for itself, as an end, or because of something else, as a means. In either case we are said to will it.[61]

This quotation reveals that for Aquinas *velle* is the primal act of will that underlies every act of will, whether one is intending an end or choosing a means.[62] *Velle* can even exist as the simple act of willing an end before one either intends it through some means or chooses those means.[63] The second act of will is to intend *(intendere).* To intend adds to the no-

58. *De veritate* 22.12.

59. Ibid.

60. In his later works Aquinas adds enjoyment, consent and use to this list of the will's elicited acts. See *ST* I-II 8 prol.; *ST* I-II 15.1; *ST* I-II 16.1.

61. *De veritate* 22.15.

62. Servais Pinckaers, "L'acte humain suivant saint Thomas," *Revue thomiste* 55 (1955): 399. Dennis Bradley, *Aquinas on the Twofold Human Good: Reason and Human Happiness in Aquinas's Moral Science* (Washington, D.C.: The Catholic University of America Press, 1997), 343.

63. *De veritate* 22.14.

tion of willing the aspect of willing an end through some means.[64] Third, there is the act of choosing *(eligere)*. Choice pertains to the means. "To choose is an act of the will in so far as reason proposes to the will a good as being the more useful to an end."[65]

All these acts presuppose the presence of cognition. Willing presupposes cognition of something as simply good; intending presupposes cognition of a good understood as attainable through some means; choosing presupposes the cognitive judgment that a particular good is the best means to attaining an intended end.[66] Nevertheless, Aquinas maintains that in these actions the will is still free from necessity in the ways listed above. In willing and intending, the will is free to act or not to act; in choosing, the will is free to choose this or that.

St. Thomas' analysis of choice is particularly important for understanding his conception of the relationship between intellect and will in action. Thomas regards choice as the locus of *liberum arbitrium,* which is perhaps best translated as "free decision." *Arbitrium* is a classical Latin word signifying the decision of an *arbiter.* One who had *liberum arbitrium* was free to act from his or her own decisions, in contrast to those who were bound to live according to the decisions of others.[67] Christian authors of the Latin West introduced the term into theology to signify that an agent was acting freely and thus worthy of praise or blame. Since Aquinas contends that *liberum arbitrium* most properly signifies the act of choice itself, understanding the relationship between intellect and will in choice is crucial to understanding the respective roles of reason and will in human freedom.

Aquinas maintains that choice depends upon both reason and will. "Choice contains something of will and something of reason."[68] When one assembles the different assertions that Aquinas makes concerning choice throughout the *De veritate,* one discovers that he advances three central positions. He asserts that, although in the act of choice (i) the

64. *De veritate* 22.15.

65. Ibid.

66. See *De veritate* 22.13 ad 16 and *De veritate* 24.1 ad 20.

67. See *Thesaurus Linguae Latinae* (Leipzig: Teubneri, 1900), 404, 410, 415–416; Charlton Lewis and Charles Short, *A Latin Dictionary* (Oxford: Clarendon Press, 1962), 151.

68. *De veritate* 22.15.

will always depends on reason, nevertheless (ii) choice is essentially an act of the will in which the will is always free to choose among the various things that reason presents to it. Moreover, (iii) in the act of choice itself, the judgment of reason is always in harmony with the choice of the will. As we shall see, this last feature suggests that, in the act of choice, the will has a role in shaping the judgment of reason. We shall consider each of these three positions, beginning with the first.

Aquinas considers *electio* to be the Latin equivalent of Aristotle's *prohairesis*. Aquinas recognizes that in book six of the *Nicomachean Ethics* Aristotle is uncertain whether *prohairesis* is primarily an act of intellect or of appetite.[69] Aquinas subsequently notes, however, that elsewhere in the *Ethics* Aristotle sides with the primacy of appetite, "defining choice as a desire for what has previously been deliberated *(desiderium praeconsiliati)*."[70] Hence, Aquinas embraces Aristotle's description of choice as "intellective appetite," viewing it as "an act of the will as ordered to reason *(actus voluntatis in ordine ad rationem)*."[71]

What does it mean for the will to act "as ordered to reason"? Aquinas maintains that, although "the will does not necessarily follow reason, nevertheless choice is not an act of the will taken absolutely, but in its relation to reason."[72] This is so, he explains, because there are present in the act of choice components of action that properly belong to reason: "the comparing of one thing with another or the putting of one thing before the other." Choice contains these cognitive elements because the will chooses "under the influence of reason, such that reason presents to the will something that is not merely useful, but is more useful in relation to the end."[73] This is the peculiar characteristic of the act of choice: it is the act of will in which "reason presents to the will a good that is more useful in relation to the end."[74]

This description of reason's role in choice raises anew the issue of intellectual determinism. If reason's role in choice is to present the more useful good to the will, in what sense is the will free not to choose it? Specifically, how could a will inclining toward a given end choose a less-

69. Ibid.

70. *De veritate* 24.6.

71. *De veritate* 22.15.

72. Ibid.

73. Ibid.

74. Ibid.

er means to that end when reason presents it with the more useful means? In the *De veritate* Aquinas does not view the issue in these terms. In fact, Aquinas maintains that the priority of reason over the will in choice is what enables choice to be a free act. In other words, the presence of reason in choice is what makes choice be a free decision: it makes *electio* be *liberum arbitrium.* This is so, he explains, because of reason's unique ability to reflect on its own act. Aquinas contends that an agent is able to act freely only if the agent's cognitive judgments are under his or her control.[75] Yet, judgment is under a person's control only if he can "judge about his own judgment."[76] This reflexive ability belongs uniquely to reason. "To judge about one's own judgment belongs only to reason, which reflects upon its own act and knows the relationships of the things about which it judges and of those by which it judges."[77] Because of this, "the root of freedom is located in reason."[78]

Nevertheless, although the root of freedom is located in reason, in Aquinas' estimation the act of freedom is located in the will.[79] This fact leads us to Aquinas' second core contention in the *De veritate:* choice is essentially an act of the will in which the will is free to choose among the various things reason presents to it. Aquinas offers two arguments to justify his assertion that choice is an act of the will. His first argument focuses on the nature the object. The object of choice is the means to an end. A means, however, is a useful good and good is the object of the will.[80] His second argument focuses on the nature of the act. Aquinas contends that even though choice is not an act of the will taken absolutely but as ordered to reason, it is nonetheless an act of the will.

Choice is the final acceptance of something to be carried out. This does not pertain to reason but to will; for, however much reason puts one ahead of the other, there is not yet the acceptance of one in preference to the other as something to be done until the will inclines to the one rather than to the other.[81]

75. *De veritate* 24.2.

76. Ibid.

77. Ibid.

78. Ibid.

79. *De veritate* 24.6 ad 3.

80. *De veritate* 22.15. Aquinas offers a similar argument to defend that *liberum arbitrium* essentially resides in the will as ordered to reason (*De veritate* 24.6).

81. *De veritate* 22.15.

The crucial feature of this argument is Aquinas' assertion that choice is the final acceptance of one thing over another. The will "does not necessarily follow reason," because even after reason has "put one thing ahead of another"—in other words even after reason has considered one thing to be the better means to the end—the agent has not yet accepted this consideration as a principle of action until the will accepts it in the act of choice, whereby it inclines toward it instead of toward another. This means that "the will in some way moves reason by commanding its act."[82] The will in some way shapes the final judgment of reason.[83]

To understand how in St. Thomas' estimation the will shapes the judgments of practical reason, we have to recognize that in the *De veritate* Thomas distinguishes the judgment of choice *(iudicium electionis)* from three other types of judgment.[84] First, the judgment of choice differs from theoretical judgments, because theoretical judgments do not lead to action.[85] Second, the judgment of choice differs from the natural judgment proper to synderesis. Synderesis is a natural *habitus* existing in the practical intellect whereby the intellect habitually contains universal knowledge of the goods to be pursued and of the evils to be avoided. This knowledge can be regarded as a type of universal judgment naturally present to the mind concerning good and evil in human action. This natural judgment is distinct from the judgment of choice because choice concerns particulars, while synderesis concerns universals. "Judgment is twofold: about universals, and this pertains to synderesis, and about particulars, which belongs to the judgment of choice, and this pertains to free decision *(liberum arbitrium)*."[86]

The judgment of choice belongs to the domain of free decision because while the most universal judgments of synderesis arise naturally

82. *De veritate* 24.6 ad 5.

83. "The will does indeed act in accord with the judgment of reason, but this judgment itself has been arrived at under the influence of the will. Thus the judgment itself is somehow in the power of the agent" (Gallagher, "Thomas Aquinas on the Causes of Human Choice," 66).

84. David Gallagher offers an excellent analysis of these three types of judgment in "Thomas Aquinas on the Causes of Human Choice," 62–64, from which I draw in the pages that follow.

85. *De veritate* 24.1 ad 17.

86. *De veritate* 16.1 ad 15.

and occur outside of the agent's direct control, judgment of choice is under the agent's control. Specifically, although one may know in general that an act is wrong, one may nonetheless judge in the act of choice that this particular instance of that general thing is good. Aquinas once again offers the example of fornication: "those who wish to fornicate, although they know in general that fornication is evil, nevertheless they judge this present act of fornication to be good for them and they choose it under the aspect of good."[87] The agent knows from a universal judgment rooted in synderesis that fornication is always evil. Yet he is able to act against this universal knowledge because of a particular judgment. This particular judgment is the judgment of choice.

Aquinas recognizes, however, that human action entails a further complexity. He notes that the judgment of choice is not the only form of practical judgment that concerns particulars. There is also the judgment of conscience.

> The judgment of conscience and the judgment of free decision *(liberi arbitrii)* differ in a certain respect and are similar in a certain respect. They are similar in that they are both about a particular act, for the judgment of conscience [also] belongs to the way of inquiry *(via examinans),* and in this respect both the judgments of conscience and of free decision differ from the judgment of synderesis. The judgments of conscience and of free decision differ from each other, however, because the judgment of conscience consists purely in knowledge, while the judgment of free decision consists in the application of knowledge to affection: this judgment is the judgment of choice.[88]

Both the judgment of conscience and the judgment of choice concern particular practical actions and flow from a discursive examination of particular components of these actions. The judgment of conscience, however, only concludes in knowledge, while the judgment of choice concludes in action: the action that results when "knowledge is applied to affection." For example, one may know with the universal knowledge supplied by the judgment of synderesis that taking what belongs to another is wrong; one my also know with the particular knowledge supplied by the judgment of conscience that this particular horse belongs to

87. *De veritate* 24.2.
88. *De veritate* 17.1 ad 4.

another and taking it would be wrong. Nonetheless, one may take the horse. In other words, even after one has judged in the judgment of conscience that a particular act is wrong, one may still freely choose to do it from an intervening judgment that affirms, despite the judgment of conscience, that this act is good for me here and now. When this occurs one is acting from the judgment of choice.[89] Aquinas' description in the *De veritate* implies that unlike the judgment of conscience, the judgment of choice is shaped by one's affections.[90] The cognitive component of the judgment of choice still belongs to reason and in some sense has priority over the will: "it is knowledge applied to affection."[91] Nevertheless, the judgment reached by reason is shaped by the will's own act: the will's action makes the judgment a free decision.[92] This does not occur in an act of will that is prior to choice, but in the will's very act of choice.[93]

The difficulty that the reader confronts in the *De veritate* is that Aquinas never explains how this happens. He never explains how in the judgment of choice the will is simultaneously dependent on reason and free to choose. David Gallagher suggests that Aquinas' intention is to affirm that the cognitive component of the act (i.e., the judgment) is somehow "embodied in the choice" itself. This judgment is "identical with the choice in the sense that it arises in the act of choice itself and

89. Ibid. See Gallagher, "Free choice and Free Judgment," 256.

90. In the *De veritate* Aquinas seems to hold that error occurs in the judgment of conscience from ignorance of facts (see *De veritate* 17.2). As we shall see, in his later works Aquinas now recognizes that error can occur in the judgment of conscience as the result of one's voluntary action (see *ST* I-II 19.6).

91. There has recently been some controversy over whether *judicium conscientiae* and *judicium electionis* are in fact two distinct cognitive judgments. Ralph McInerny affirms that they are; Theo Belmans has vigorously denied this, asserting that *judicium electionis* only signifies the appetitive act that accompanies the judgment of conscience. See Theo Belmans, "Au croisement des chemins en morale fondamentale," *Revue thomiste* 89 (1989): 246–278; Ralph McInerny, "The Right Deed for the Wrong Reason: Comments on Theo Belmans," in *Aquinas on Human Action: A Theory of Practice* (Washington, D.C.: The Catholic University of America Press, 1992), 220–239; Theo Belmans, "Le 'jugement prudentiel' chez saint Thomas, réponse à R. McInerny," *Revue thomiste* 91 (1991): 414–420.

92. *De veritate* 24.6 ad 3.

93. "The freedom of the judgment comes from the will, not an act of the will prior to choice, but the will's act in the very choice" (Gallagher, "Free Choice and Free Judgment," 256).

can be seen as the articulation of the choice."[94] This further implies that the priority of reason in the act of choice is not temporal but structural.[95] Daniel Westberg maintains that this is indeed Aquinas' studied view of choice. Westberg asserts that choice unites cognition and volition. "That is, the conclusion of the [practical] syllogism is not merely the judgement of reason, about which the will makes a separate choice, but is the judgement which expresses the combination of the agent's intellect and will."[96] Servais Pinckaers reads Aquinas' analysis of choice in the *Summa theologiae* in the same way.

> This refined analysis, which delineates what belongs to each of our spiritual faculties in choice, does not allow us to place a real separation between practical judgment and voluntary choice as occupying temporally distinct moments, as if we first judge what we should do and then choose to do it. For St. Thomas, practical judgment and voluntary choice are indissolubly united in one single psychological act.[97]

Hence, although it is easier to describe the genesis of action as a temporal back and forth between intellect and will, in reality the intellect's primacy is not temporal but structural: the will follows what reason judges, but the judgment itself is the product of the will's choice. Yet, is this Aquinas' view in the *De veritate*? Gallagher believes that it is; but as Gallagher himself recognizes, Aquinas does not demonstrate anywhere in the *De veritate* how this happens. In his later works, however, Aquinas delineates more clearly the respective roles of intellect and will in the act of choice.

De malo and Free Choice

Question 6 of the *De malo* is a compact presentation of St. Thomas' mature description of human choice. In it he retains all the positive fea-

94. Gallagher, "Thomas Aquinas on the Causes of Human Choice," 64.

95. Ibid., 66.

96. Westberg, *Right Practical Reason*, 151.

97. Servais Pinckaers, "Notes explicatives," appendix I in *Les actes humains: Somme théologique I-II 6–17* Nouvelle Edition (Paris: Editions du cerf, 1997), volume 1, 352. See also Servais Pinckaers, "La structure de l'acte humain suivant saint Thomas," *Revue thomiste* 55 (1955): 393–412.

tures present in his earlier account. In common with all natural appetites, the will wills some things naturally and necessarily. It necessarily wills happiness and the constitutive parts of happiness: to be, to live, and to know. Nonetheless, the will is free to will or not to will and to will this or that particular thing. Moreover, in the act of choice the will plays a role in shaping reason's judgment concerning what should be done here and now. All these features were present in his earlier account and they continue to be present in his mature thought. What has changed, however, is his manner of explaining these features. He has now found a way to offer a more satisfying description of the relationship between intellect and will in choice. He also considers more deeply the implications of this relationship.

The first innovation that St. Thomas introduces into his account is to describe intellect and will as a single principle of action. "Just as other things contain within them a principle that underlies their proper acts, so also do humans. This active or motive principle in humans is properly intellect and will."[98] He describes this dual principle by analogy with natural form and inclination.

> Just as in natural things there is found a form, which is a principle of action, and an inclination following the form, which is called the natural appetite, and from these action results, so in the human person there is found an intellective form and an inclination of the will following the apprehended form, and from these action results.[99]

Form and inclination together function as the human person's "active or motive principle." This analogy, while it enables Thomas to show what humans share in common with other things (that they act through their form and inclination), also enables him to highlight how humans differ from merely natural things.

> But there is this difference, that the form of the natural thing is a form individualized by matter, and therefore the inclination following it is determined to one, but the form intellectually grasped is universal, under which many can be comprehended. Hence since acts are concerned with singulars, among

98. *De malo* 6. See also *ST* I-II 6.1 ad 1; *ST* I-II 75.2.

99. *De malo* 6. Aquinas first introduces this analogy in *SCG* IV 19. See also *ST* I-II 8.1.

which there is none that is equal to the potentiality of the universal, the inclination of the will remains indeterminately related to many; for example, if an architect conceives the form of a house universally, under which houses of different shapes are comprised, his will can be inclined to build a house that is square or circular or of some other shape.[100]

The notion that no particular act is able to fill the potentiality of the universal grasped by the intellect was present in the *De veritate.* In the *De veritate,* however, Aquinas does not explain how this universal potency enables the will's inclination to remain "indeterminately related" to many different things. In *De malo* 6, Aquinas provides an explanation of this when he draws upon the second innovation he introduced into his mature thought, the celebrated distinction between specification and exercise.

St. Thomas explains that a power of the soul is moved in two ways. It is moved in one way by the subject in which it resides, while it is moved in another way by its object. Thomas offers the example of sight. "In one way on the part of the subject, as sight by a change in condition of the organ is moved to see more clearly or less clearly; in another way, on the part of the object, as sight now sees white, now sees black."[101] Aquinas maintains that the second type of motion determines the intelligible character of the act. It makes the act be of one type instead of another, an act of seeing black instead of seeing white. Aquinas calls this motion the specification or determination of the act. Citing Aristotle, he holds that an act is specified by its object.[102]

Aquinas describes the first type of motion as pertaining to the "very exercise of the act." Going beyond the content of the example he offers, Aquinas asserts that exercise has two facets. First, it controls whether the act is done or not done; second it controls whether the act is done more or less effectively. Aquinas affirms, as he had in the *De veritate,* that reason moves the will in one way and will moves reason in another. Here, however, to explain how this happens, he revisits his earlier account of the types of causality exhibited between reason and will. To

100. *De malo* 6.
101. Ibid. See also *ST* I-II 9.1.
102. Cf. Aristotle, *On the Soul* 2.4 (415a18–21).

shed light on the character of this causality he once again turns to the example of natural motion.

In natural things the specification of the act is from the form, but the exercise itself is by the agent that causes the very motion; but a mover acts for the sake of an end; hence it remains that the first principle of motion so far as concerns the exercise of the act is from the end.[103]

In other words, things both *move* toward their goal and move toward it *in a certain way*. The example Aquinas often uses to explain this is the motion of heavy and light objects. The natural motion of fire differs from the natural motion of a stone. Their respective substantial forms account for this difference. Yet, the movement itself (i.e., the exercise of the act) is not caused by their forms, but by something else. In the case of heavy and light objects it is the agent that generated the form of the object that causes the object's upward or downward motion.[104] On one level this generator is some natural thing. Natural agents, however, only act for ends toward which they themselves have been ordered by the Author of nature. Thus, the ultimate agent of these natural motions is God acting through the instrumental causality of some natural agent.[105]

Aquinas applies this analysis to his treatment of intellect and will. He determines the type of causality exhibited by intellect and will by considering the nature of their respective objects.

If we consider the object of the will and the intellect, we find that the object of the intellect is the first and primary principle in the genus of formal cause, for its object is being and truth; but the object of the will is the first and primary principle in the genus of final cause, for its object is the good, under which are comprehended all ends just as under the truth are comprehended all apprehended forms.[106]

Aquinas elsewhere defines truth as the conformity between intellect and thing.[107] Thus, the object of the intellect is the form of the thing. It is the intelligible species or "whatness" *(quidditas)* of the thing.[108] For example, when we know a tree, the form of the tree exists in the intellect immate-

103. *De malo* 6.

104. *ST* I-II 26.2; *ST* I-II 76.1.

105. *ST* I 103.5; *ST* I 105.5.

106. *De malo* 6.

107. *ST* I 16.2.

108. *ST* I 84.7; *ST* I 85.2.

rially. This, however, is an example of theoretical knowledge. The situation is different in practical knowledge. In theoretical knowledge the intellect receives into itself the form of some already existing thing.[109] In practical knowledge, however, the form first exists in the intellect and then is placed in things. The agent conceives the form in his intellect and then applies the form to art or action.[110] For example, in the case of architecture the builder first conceives the house in his intellect and then applies that form to matter by constructing the house according to that form. In human action, the same principles apply. The agent first conceives the act in his mind; the form or intelligible species of the act first exists in his intellect. He then applies this form to action by doing the act.

Aquinas recognizes that in art and action, as in natural generation, the form is the end of the action. In each case the goal of the act is to generate the form. Thus, the final cause and the formal cause are linked. For example, the formal cause of natural generation is the substantial form of the generator. Since, however, the goal of the generation is the reproduction of the generator's own form, the form is also the end of the generation. This means that the final cause of the generation preexists in the agent as the formal cause. Analogously the same thing occurs in human action. The form of the act is the end of the act. The goal the agent seeks to attain is to produce an action that is "conformed" to the form in his intellect. The form as it exists in the act is the final cause of the action, but as it preexists in the intellect it is the formal cause of the act.

In his earlier works Aquinas recognized that the form of the act preexists in the intellect. Yet he failed to recognize that, as existing in the intellect, the form does not function as the final cause but as the formal cause. If the form as it exists in the intellect were the final cause of the action, practical reasoning would end in thought. Yet, practical reasoning ends in action. The intellect acts as the formal cause of the act, because the form of the act exists in the intellect. As the end of the act,

109. The intellect receives a form already existing either in reality or in the imagination. The central point here is that in theoretical reasoning the goal is not to make some form exist outside the mind, but to understand the form that already exists either in things or in our imagination. See *ST* I 79.11.

110. *ST* I 79.11.

however, the form exists in the completed action itself. This conclusion follows necessarily from Aquinas' insight into the difference between the true and the good. Truth primarily exists in the intellect as something formal, while good primarily exists in things.[111] Thus the good existing in the intellect as something true primarily has the character of something formal. Note also that Aquinas does not say here that the will acts as the final cause of the act. Instead, he affirms that the will's object is the end. Aquinas explains that agents act for an end. Since the will's object is the end, the will must be the efficient or agent cause of the act.[112] In his mature thought, therefore, Aquinas delineates more satisfactorily the types of causality that the intellect and will exert. The intellect acts as a formal cause and the will acts as an efficient cause.

This advance enables Aquinas to explain with greater precision how intellect and will move each other. "Good itself, inasmuch as it is an apprehensible form, is contained under the truth as a particular truth, and truth itself, inasmuch as it is the end of the intellectual operation, is contained under the good as a particular good."[113] Consequently, as he explains in the *Summa theologiae,*

> the will moves the intellect as to the exercise *(exercitium)* of the act, since even the true itself, which is the perfection of the intellect, is included in the universal good, as a particular good. But as to the determination *(determinationem)* of the act, which the act derives from the object, the intellect moves the will, since the good itself is apprehended under a special notion as contained in the universal notion of the true.[114]

The object of one power and the power itself in a certain respect both fall under the object of the other power. Thus, whenever an agent engages in practical reasoning his intellect and will are simultaneously acting on each other: intellect knows the will and specifies its object, while the will moves the intellect in the act of specifying the object. Aquinas applies these insights to show how the will is free in the act of choice. He begins by considering the freedom of the will on the level of the exercise of the act.

The cornerstone of St. Thomas' analysis of the will's freedom of ex-

111. *ST* I 16.1.
112. *De malo* 6; *ST* I-II 9.1.
113. *De malo* 6.
114. *ST* I-II 9.1 ad 3.

ercise is his affirmation that the will moves itself. Already in *De veritate* Thomas recognized that the will moves itself and all the other powers.[115] He did not, however, investigate the implications of this assertion. To assert that the will moves itself seems to violate the Aristotelian principle that "whatever is moved is moved by another."[116] Thomas begins, therefore, by clarifying his position: in affirming the will's self-motion, he does not mean to imply that the will is simultaneously in potency and in act with respect to the same thing. Instead, being in act in one way, the will is able to reduce itself from potency to act in another way.[117] For example, from the fact that one wills health in general, one moves oneself to will to take a particular medicine.[118] Aquinas maintains that the intellect's specifying role in the will's self-motion is a key element in the will's freedom on the level of exercise. Aquinas notes that the will moves itself through the act of counsel, which for Aquinas is a cognitive act of a very specific kind. "Since the will moves itself by counsel, and counsel is a kind of non-demonstrative inquiry open to opposite courses of action, the will does not move itself of necessity."[119] Unlike demonstration that moves reason to assent necessarily, counsel always entails a comparison of opposites, either of which could be effected. Consequently, since the will moves itself through counsel, there is nothing to fetter the will's act on the level of exercise.[120] Aquinas explains more fully what this means in his treatment of specification.

In his analysis of specification St. Thomas makes three key points. First, he introduces the notion of the fitting good *(bonum conveniens)*. He explains that the object that moves the will is good apprehended as fitting *(bonum conveniens apprehensum)*. *Conveniens* adds to the general notion of goodness an explicit reference to the agent in a particular situa-

115. *De veritate* 22.12.

116. Aristotle, *Physics* (henceforth cited as *PS*) 7.1 (241b34–36); See *Sententia super physicam* (henceforth cited as *In physic.*) VII 1.885.

117. *De malo* 6. See also *De malo* 6 ad 20; *ST* I-II 9.3 ad 1.

118. *De malo* 6.

119. Ibid.

120. See *Sententia super metaphysicam* (henceforth cited as *In metaphysic.*) IX 4.1820. See also *ST* I-II 14.3 and 5. The inclusion of counsel in the will's own act of exercise seems to circularize Aquinas' description of practical reasoning and to raise the problem of the ultimate ground of freedom. We shall address this issue in a later section.

tion.[121] Something is fitting not merely by being apprehended as good, but by being apprehended as good for the agent here and now. Consequently, if something is proposed to the will as good but not as fitting *(conveniens)*, the will is not moved by it.[122]

The second key feature of Aquinas' account concerns particularity. Aquinas underlines that deliberation *(consilium)* and choice *(electio)* are about particular things. This emphasis enables Aquinas to explain more fully the will's freedom on the level of exercise. It enables him to explain how happiness necessarily moves the will on the level of specification but not on the level of exercise. Happiness defined as "a state made perfect by the gathering together of all good things," is the only object of thought apprehended as fitting according to all its particulars.[123] Thus, if one thinks about happiness one cannot help but will it: one cannot will its opposite. Nevertheless, Aquinas adds that "as concerns the exercise of the act" happiness does not necessarily move the will, because "since even the very acts of intellect and will are something particular," a person can will not to think about happiness. The passage reads as follows.

Since deliberations and choices are about particulars, which is what action is about, it is required that what is apprehended as good and fitting be apprehended as good and fitting in particular and not merely in general. If then something is apprehended as a fitting good according to all the particulars that can be considered, it will move the will necessarily, and for this reason the human person of necessity desires happiness, which according to Boethius is 'a state made perfect by the gathering together of all good things.' Yet, I say 'of necessity' with respect to the determination of the act since one cannot will the opposite, but not with respect to the exercise of the act, because one may now not will to think about happiness, since even the very acts of intellect and will are something particular.[124]

Some have interpreted this passage to mean that the will's act on the level of exercise is antecedent to and independent of reason. For example, James Keenan interprets this passage to mean that although on the level

121. See *ST* I-II 9.2.

122. *De malo* 6.

123. Ibid.: *"status omnium bonorum congregatione perfectus."* Aquinas takes this definition from Boethius, *De consolatione philosophiae* III pr. 2 (*PL* 63, 724a; *CCL* 94, 38).

124. *De malo* 6.

of specification the will's act is subsequent to reason's judgment and is bound to follow it, on the level of exercise the will's act is antecedent to reason's judgment and independent of reason's action.[125] According to this interpretation, Aquinas affirms this when he states that even when one is considering happiness, "one may now not will to think about happiness." One is free not to think about it because the will is free not to enter into reason's specification.

What this interpretation fails to recognize is that Aquinas' argument presupposes the recognition that on the level of human action every act of exercise presupposes an act of choice. Aquinas states explicitly that he is referring to happiness as an object of "deliberation and choice," as an object that one can "think about." The reason that the will is free to will not to think about happiness is because although *happiness* is a "fitting good according to all its particulars," the *act of thinking about* happiness is not. In this life, thinking-about-happiness is a particular act. As such it is not good according to all its particulars. Thus, it can be specified as not fitting here and now. (For example, thinking about happiness when one should be sleeping or helping a neighbor in distress is not a fitting good.) In other words, on the level of specification as long as the intellect thinks about happiness the will cannot not will it. On the level of exercise, however, the level at which the will moves the intellect to think about happiness, the will is free not to will this act. The will is free on this level because the exercise of the act of thinking about happiness presupposes an antecedent specification concerning that particular act, a specification that itself also involves an act of exercise on the part of the will.[126]

The third key feature of Aquinas' account of specification concerns his new emphasis on "consideration" and the will's influence on it with respect to particular things that are not good in all respects (i.e., all goods other than happiness itself). Aquinas holds that if there is a good

125. Keenan, *Goodness and Rightness*, 47.

126. This last statement once again raises the specter of an infinite regress at the heart of agency. Aquinas avoids this regress, as we noted above, by asserting that God places principles of knowledge and inclination at the heart of intellect and will. We shall look more closely at these principles in a later section.

that is not good according to all of its particular aspects, then it will not move the will of necessity even on the level of specification. This is so, he explains, because even while one is thinking about it one can view it as not fitting in some respect.[127] This fact raises a new question. If one is deliberating about goods that are not good in every respect, what leads the will to incline toward one limited good over another? Stated more precisely, on the level of specification what draws the will toward "this particular aspect of what is presented to it instead of another aspect?" Aquinas lists three causes, one that is rooted in the object, another rooted in the intellect and a third rooted in a person's character, as shaped by nature, by a *habitus,* or by a sudden passion.

The first way that the will responds to one aspect of the act instead of another concerns the objective character of that aspect. The will inclines toward it because that aspect objectively outweighs the other. Aquinas gives the example of a medical procedure that brings health but is unpleasant to experience. When one chooses health, one's will is inclining toward and choosing what is beneficial to one's health over what is pleasurable. Aquinas describes this as "the will being moved according to reason." Note, however, that it is the objective status of the act itself—e.g., receiving a beneficial but unpleasant medical treatment—that moves the will. Reason judges correctly and the will follows this judgment. Stated more accurately, reason and will unite in the act of judging and choosing the true good to be done here and now. Thus, when Aquinas describes the action as "according to reason," what he means is that it is according to right reason.

Next, Aquinas affirms that the will can incline toward one thing instead of another because a person thinks about one circumstance to the exclusion of all others. Aquinas affirms that this happens whenever "from some internal or external cause," reason fixates on one aspect instead of another. Presumably, at least in some cases, the fact that reason considers one aspect instead of another is due to the will's exercise. Aquinas is more explicit elsewhere about the will's ability to direct reason's consideration toward one particular aspect of an act instead of an-

127. *De malo* 6.

other. Aquinas refers to an ignorance that is "directly and *per se* voluntary." This is an ignorance that arises in reason from a person's own free engagement *(sua sponte),* when one chooses to be ignorant "in order that he may sin more freely."[128] A case in point is when a person freely chooses to hate God by directing reason's "consideration" away from God's goodness and toward the painful effects of his just punishments.[129] This feature of Aquinas' later works reveals that Aquinas has apparently modified his earlier view of conscience. In the *De veritate* he seems to hold that reason engages in the judgment of conscience in isolation from the will. Here, however, we see that Aquinas recognizes our ability, through our wills, to shape the judgment of conscience.[130] In the *De malo,* however, Aquinas does not explicitly refer to the will's role in this one-sided consideration. He merely affirms that reason sometimes focuses on one aspect of a thing instead of another, no matter what the objective status of that thing may be. In such cases, the will's choice of the object results from some type of cognitive ignorance, resulting either from an act of the will or from some other cause. Reason considers one aspect to the exclusion of all others and will chooses according to this myopic vision.

The third cause that leads the will to incline in one way rather than another flows from what Aquinas describes as a person's disposition *(dispositio hominis).* Quoting Aristotle, Aquinas notes that a goal appears to each person according to his or her character. "As each one is, so does the end seem to him or her."[131] Aquinas describes this as happening in three ways: from nature, from *habitus,* and from passion. He explains that when some particular thing is naturally specified as good and fitting, then it is not "subject to the will," and the will "chooses it naturally and necessarily." Aquinas lists "to be, to live and to know" as particular goods of this sort. They are always apprehended as fitting, and the will naturally and necessarily chooses them.

When particular things are specified as good and fitting because of a *habitus* or a passion—as when the will of an angry or intemperate per-

128. *ST* I-II 76.4. See also *ST* I-II 9.2.

129. *ST* II-II 34.1.

130. *ST* I-II 19.6.

131. *De malo* 6: *"qualis unusquisque est, talis finis videtur ei."*

son is moved in ways that it would not be if he or she were calm or temperate—the will is not moved of necessity because the will has the power to remove this *habitus* or passion. In other words, we can, through our wills, shape whether or not something appears fitting *(conveniens)* because our character is something we freely choose. In Aquinas' estimation, therefore, there are two ways that the will can shape reason's judgment concerning the process of specification: it can move reason to consider one particular instead of another and it can choose to develop a person's character in such a manner that things appear one way instead of another. Stated more accurately, a person, through his will, can (a) direct his intellect to consider one aspect of an act instead of another, or he can (b) through his will develop his character in such a manner that, through the habitual dispositions of his reason and will, he habitually perceives an act in one way instead of another. This further implies a third way that the will moves reason. It implies that the will can also move reason to consider all the relevant features of the act, and thus lead the agent to act according to right reason.[132]

Free Choice in *De veritate* and *De malo* 6: Evaluation

When one reviews all that St. Thomas says about reason and will in the *De veritate* one discerns a clear concern to affirm both the rationality

132. One curious feature of Aquinas' later works is that he never explicitly explains the relationship between conscience and the particular judgment of choice that leads to action. As we noted above, Aquinas recognizes that the will shapes even the judgment of conscience. Yet, what is the relationship between this judgment and the judgment of choice? Ralph McInerny has argued convincingly that Aquinas' mature description of the incontinent person demonstrates that Aquinas still distinguishes between conscience, a judgment of particulars that does not necessarily lead to action, and the judgment of choice, that results in action. When the incontinent person acts against the judgment of conscience he or she is replacing the *dictamen rationis* formed by conscience with another *dictamen rationis,* shaped by passion. In the virtuous person, however, "the judgment of conscience all but elides into the judgment of choice." See McInerny, *Aquinas on Human Action,* 225–231, and "Prudence and Conscience," *Thomist* 38 (1974): 291–305. (The quotation concerning conscience eliding into choice is from McInerny, *Aquinas on Human Action,* 230.) The relevant texts from Aquinas are *ST* I-II 19.5; *ST* I-II 19.6; *ST* I-II 77.2 ad 4 and *Sententia libri ethicorum* (henceforth cited as *In ethic.*) VII 3.1345ff. See also Bradley, *Aquinas on the Twofold Human Good,* 346, and Odon Lottin, *Morale fondamentale* (Tournai, Belgium: Desclée, 1954), 223–228.

and the freedom of human action. The human person, when acting in a fully human way, always acts from knowledge and in freedom. The principles that enable him or her to do so are reason and will. Both principles work together to enable the agent to act knowingly and freely. As we have seen, however, Aquinas' analysis of intellect and will in the *De veritate* has two principal limitations: he fails to grasp the true nature of reason's causal influence upon the will, and he fails to explain how the will shapes reason's practical judgments. In the *De malo,* Aquinas overcomes these limitations.

In the *De veritate* St. Thomas fails to describe with sufficient clarity the nature of reason's causal influence on the will. He asserts that the intellect moves the will the way an end is said to move something. Yet, when he actually describes this causal action he instead offers a description of formal causality: "the intellect moves the will the way an end is said to move, by conceiving beforehand the reason for acting and proposing it to the will."[133] In an earlier article he describes the intellect's act even more succinctly. The intellect moves the will not by inclining it but by "showing it that toward which it should tend."[134] If we turn to Aristotle's treatment of formal causality, we discover that "presenting" and "showing" belong to the formal cause. Nevertheless, Aristotle also equates the form with the end in natural generation and in art.[135] The generation of the form is the goal of generation and of art. Yet, although the form is the end, it preexists in the artist potentially, just as in natural generation it preexists potentially in the seed.[136] Consequently, by supplying the form and by being the place where the form preexists, reason is acting as the formal cause. In the *De veritate* and his other early works, Aquinas has not yet grasped this point, or, at least he has not yet expressed this insight clearly in his writings. He has not yet explained that "showing the end" is an act of formal causality.

By the time Aquinas writes *De malo* 6, he expresses clearly the true nature of the formal cause. His analysis of natural generation supplies

133. *De veritate* 22.12.
134. *De veritate* 22.11 ad 5.
135. *PS* 2.7 (198a24–27); see *In physic.* II 11.242.
136. Aristotle, *Metaphysics* (henceforth cited as *MP*) 7.7 (1032a–1032b23).

him with the needed analogy. Although in natural generation the form of the offspring is the end of the action, as preexisting in the parent the form is the formal cause of the act. Similarly, in human action, the informed act is the end of the act, but as preexisting in the intellect of the agent it is the formal cause of the act. Thus, the intellect acts as the formal cause, but not as the final cause. Moreover, since agents act for an end, and since the end is the object of the will, the will must act as the efficient or agent cause of the act. The analogy with natural generation seemed also to have suggested to Aquinas the distinction between specification and exercise that he introduces in his later works. Just as in natural things the specification of an act is from the form, but the exercise of the act is from the agent that causes the motion, so too in human acts the form in the intellect specifies the act, and the will of the agent causes *(exercet)* the act to occur.

The second principal limitation present in the *De veritate* concerns the will's influence upon the judgment of reason in the act of choice. As we have seen, St. Thomas affirms that the will shapes the judgment of choice, but in the *De veritate* he does not explain how this happens. In the *De malo* and his other later works Thomas develops a more satisfactory account. Aquinas turns to the notion of consideration *(consideratio)* and explains how the will shapes the way reason considers the object. Reason can consider the same object in a number of different ways. Consequently, according to different considerations the object can appear either good or bad. Since, however, the will moves the powers of the soul, including the intellect, to exercise their acts, the will can move the intellect to consider one aspect of the object instead of another. In addition, the will can shape how reason perceives that aspect of the object. As we have seen, Aquinas affirms that we perceive things according to our character, which we form by our own actions. Since we can control our emotions and shape our dispositions through the action of our will, our wills can also shape how reason perceives any aspect of an object it considers.[137] In other words, in practical reasoning the will can

137. We should also note that in providing this explanation Aquinas explicitly connects his analysis of free choice in practical reasoning to his theory of the virtues and the emotions. Aquinas gives this feature of the moral life closer attention in the *Summa*

both direct what reason considers and shape how reason perceives what it considers. (Stated more accurately, the agent acts through considering one aspect of the act over another and does so through the interrelationship existing between intellect and will.) Thus, what Aquinas had left unexplained in the *De veritate,* he now in the *De malo* explains more fully.

Our analysis of St. Thomas' earlier and later descriptions of free choice enables us to draw two important conclusions. First, a basic continuity exists between the earlier and later versions of his theory of free choice. Second, the development that occurs in the theory integrates more fully the interaction between intellect and will in practical reasoning. Thomas clarifies the way in which the intellect moves the will (as the formal cause) and the way in which the will moves the intellect (as the efficient cause). This development enables Aquinas to express more clearly views he had held from the beginning. Throughout his career Aquinas maintains that the will is a rational appetite: the will always follows some intellectual cognition. Thus, in the act of choice, the will inclines toward what reason judges as good. Nevertheless, since the will moves the powers of the soul—including reason—as the agent cause of their acts, the will has a role in shaping the rational judgment that specifies the will's own act of choice. Aquinas states this feature of his account more fully in the *Summa theologiae:*

> The human person can will and not will, act and not act; again, he or she can will this or that, and do this or that. The reason for this is found in the very power of reason. For the will can tend to whatever reason can apprehend as good. Now reason can apprehend as good not only *to will* or *to act,* but also *not to will* and *not to act.* Again, in all particular goods, reason can consider an aspect of some good, and the lack of some good, which has the aspect of evil: and in this respect, it can apprehend any single one of these goods as electable or avoidable.[138]

Aquinas here highlights more fully how the act of freedom is in the will, while the root of freedom is in the intellect. The will follows reason's

---

theologiae in his treatment of the emotions and the virtues. It is there that he introduces his theory of love. We shall give these elements of Aquinas' thought closer scrutiny in the chapters that follow.

138. *ST* I-II 13.6.

judgment on the level of specification, but because reason can judge limited goods in numerous ways, and because reason's act of consideration is under the will's control on the level of exercise, the will can shape reason's judgments. The will, therefore, both follows reason's judgment and shapes the rational consideration that leads to this judgment.

Natural Principles of Practical Reasoning

To understand how one avoids an infinite regress in the description of practical reasoning, where every cognitive act presupposes a voluntary act and vice versa, St. Thomas appeals to the level of nature and the action of the Author of nature. The grounds of free choice are the natural principles of cognition and appetite that underlie the intellect and will, placed there by the God who creates and sustains each person in existence. Thomas' treatment of the natural principles underlying practical reasoning becomes crucially important in the face of two opposite objections that are often leveled against the above description of his theory of choice. On the one hand, some hold that if we regard the will as having a role in shaping reason's practical judgments we inevitably fall into voluntarism and moral relativism.[139] On the other hand, others maintain that if we regard the will's act as always presupposing an act of the intellect we inevitably fall into psychological determinism.[140] An analysis of Aquinas' conception of the natural principles underlying free choice will enable us to respond to these two concerns. It will also allow us to distinguish Aquinas' theory of practical reasoning from the two theories of practical reasoning that spring from these concerns.

St. Thomas maintains that human action, as one type of created motion, shares features in common with all created natural motions. Thomas affirms that God, as the author of nature, determines each

139. See Belmans, "le 'volontarisme' de saint Thomas d'Aquin," *Revue thomiste* 85 (1985): 181–196; the response of Servais Pinckaers, "A propos du 'volontarisme' dans le jugement moral," *Revue thomiste* 85 (1985): 508–511; and Belmans' rejoinder, "Au croisement des chemins en morale fondamentale," 246–278.

140. Keenan, *Goodness and Rightness,* 29–34. See also theorems 1–4 and remarks in Emmanuel Kant, *Critique of Practical Reason,* translated by T. K. Abbott (New York: Prometheus Books, 1996), 31–50.

thing to be and to act according to the nature he has given it. Humans are no exception. Humans are naturally determined to act according to their nature. In Thomas' view, however, this does not mean that humans are not free.

Whatever belongs to nature must be preserved in subjects that have intellect. Now it is common to every nature to have some inclination; and this is its natural appetite or love. This inclination, however, exists differently in different natures, existing in each one according to its mode. Consequently, in the intellectual nature natural inclination exists in the mode of will; in sensitive nature, it exists in the mode of sensitive appetite; while in a nature devoid of knowledge, it exists only as the tendency of the nature to something.[141]

Nature inclines each thing to its proper end in the way (the mode) that is proper to it. The mode of inclination proper to the rational creature—the mode of inclination belonging to the will as the rational appetite—is a mode that entails free decision *(liberum arbitrium)*. God, as the author of nature, has established the will to be an inclination that moves the human person to his ultimate end through the person's free decision. In other words, humans are determined by nature to be free.

St. Thomas accounts for this paradoxical fact by analyzing the natural principles that underlie intellect and will. In the *Summa theologiae,* when Thomas asks whether the will is moved by anything naturally, he responds by describing the will's natural motion in relation to the natural motion of the intellect: "the motion of the will follows the act of the intellect. But the intellect understands some things naturally. Therefore the will also wills some things naturally."[142] For Aquinas, natural here signifies what is proper to each thing's substance. As such, something that is natural is not a matter of choice. Instead, it is a necessary feature of the very substance of a given creature. Leopards do not choose to have spots; they have them naturally and necessarily. In a like manner, the motions of intellect and will flow from natural principles; they flow from principles that occur necessarily in every act of knowing and willing. The intellect knows certain things naturally, while the will inclines toward certain things naturally.

141. *ST* I 60.1.
142. *ST* I-II 10.1 sc.

As we have seen, Aquinas affirms that the will naturally inclines toward the good in general, as toward its own proper object, as well as toward all the goods toward which the other powers of the soul naturally incline, goods that together constitute the integral good of the human person. The practical intellect, for its part, also naturally knows the good in general and apprehends it as something to be pursued. Moreover, parallel to the will's natural inclination toward the goods of human flourishing, practical reason also apprehends these goods as goods to be pursued.[143]

Aquinas explains practical reason's natural knowledge by analogy with theoretical reason. He maintains that the first thing that the theoretical intellect apprehends in any act of knowing is being. With this knowledge there naturally arises in the intellect knowledge of the primary indemonstrable principles of theoretical reasoning, the first of which is what philosophers have come to call the principle of non-contradiction: namely, that the same thing cannot be and not be at the same time and in the same respect.[144] This principle and the other principles of theoretical reason—such as "every whole is greater than its part" and "things equal to the same thing are equal to one another"—are habitually present in the intellect in the theoretical *habitus* that Aquinas simply calls *intellectus*.[145] Similarly, the first thing that the practical intellect apprehends is good.[146] With this knowledge there naturally arises in the practical intellect the primary principles of practical reason, the first of which is "good is to be done and pursued and evil is to be avoided."[147] As with the theoretical principles, the principles of practical reason are habitually present in the intellect. They are present in the practical *habitus* called synderesis.[148]

143. *ST* I-II 94.2.

144. Ibid.

145. *ST* I-II 57.2.

146. For a full account of Aquinas' theory of the good and its relation to being, see Jan Aertsen, *Medieval Philosophy and the Transcendentals: the Case of Thomas Aquinas* (New York: E. J. Brill, 1996), and Jean Porter, *The Recovery of Virtue: The Relevance of Aquinas for Christian Ethics* (Louisville, Ky.: Westminster/John Knox Press, 1990), 34–99.

147. *ST* I-II 94.2.

148. *ST* I-II 94.1 ad 2; *ST* I 79.12; *De malo* 16.6 ad sed contra 5. See also *ST* II-II 47.6 ad 1 and ad 3. Discussion of naturally known principles of reason might lead one to assume that Aquinas holds an entirely deductive theory of reasoning based upon a priori

Particularly important for our analysis is the symmetry that St. Thomas establishes between the natural principles of intellect and will.

> Since good has the nature of an end, while evil has the nature of a contrary, all those things toward which the human person has a natural inclination, reason naturally apprehends as good, and consequently as works to be pursued and their contraries as evils to be avoided. Therefore, the order of the precepts of the natural law is according to the order of the natural inclinations.[149]

Thomas delineates what these natural inclinations are and describes the precepts that correspond to them. In doing so, he provides a list virtually identical to the one he offered during his analysis of the will: humans naturally incline toward *being, living* in society, *knowing* the truth about God, and procreating and caring for offspring.[150] Just as the will naturally inclines toward good in general (happiness or the ultimate end) and toward all the goods that constitute human flourishing, so too the practical intellect naturally knows the general notion of the good and appre-

principles. Aquinas is careful to explain, however, that we acquire all our knowledge through the senses. The proper object of the human intellect in this life is the forms of material things, which it knows immaterially but always in relation to a sense image. The human mind even understands spiritual or universal concepts, such as God or justice, in and through some sense image of the imagination (*ST* I 85.2 ad 2; *ST* I 88.2). Thus, in Aquinas' view, although knowledge of the first principles is not the product of reasoning but is contained habitually in synderesis, knowledge of these principles becomes actively present to us only through our contact with the material world: "for first principles become known through the natural light of the agent intellect, and they are not acquired by any process of reasoning but by having their terms become known. This comes about by reason of the fact that memory is derived from sensible things, experience from memory, and knowledge of these terms from experience. And when they are known, common propositions of this kind, which are the principles of the arts and sciences, become known" (*In metaphysic.* IV 6.4). See Thomas Hibbs, "Against a Cartesian Reading of *Intellectus* in Aquinas," *Modern Schoolman* 66 (1988): 56–62. See also Jean Porter, "What the Wise Person Knows: Natural Law and Virtue in Aquinas' *Summa theologiae,*" *Studies in Christian Ethics* 12 (1999): 57–69.

149. *ST* I-II 94.2.

150. In *ST* I-II 94.2, Aquinas refers to "the conservation of one's being and nature," "the union of male and female and the education of offspring," and "to know the truth about God, and to have those things that make life in society possible." In other places, he lists these goods as follows: *ST* I-II 10.1: "knowledge of truth, which befits an intellectual creature, to be, to live and other such things;" *De malo* 6: "to be, to live, and to understand;" *In perihermeneias* I 14.24: "to be, to live, to understand, and other similar actions."

hends the things that constitute human flourishing as goods to be pursued.

Aquinas' description of the symmetry between the natural principles of action provides the context for understanding his conception of the ultimate foundation of practical reasoning. At each place in Aquinas' works where he considers the problem of a possible circularity in practical reasoning—since reason's consideration seems to presuppose will's inclination and vice versa—Aquinas drops to the level of nature. In each of these accounts, he limits the causal action of one power upon the other by affirming that the primal motion of one is not caused by the other but by nature and ultimately by God.

In his earlier works Aquinas is concerned to limit the will's action on the intellect. For example, both in the *De veritate* and in the *Prima pars* of the *Summa theologiae,* when Aquinas affirms that the will moves the intellect with regard to the execution of the intellect's act, he considers the objection that since the will's act presupposes an act of the intellect this implies an infinite regress.[151] In his response, he recognizes that the will's act presupposes an act of the intellect, but he affirms that this does not imply an infinite regress because the will is not the cause of the intellect's first act. The intellect's first act is from nature *(De veritate),* and from a higher intellectual principle, namely God *(Prima pars).*[152] In these responses, Aquinas does not say that the intellect is the cause of the will's first motion. He merely affirms that the will is not the cause of the intellect's first motion.

In his later works, Aquinas is concerned to limit reason's causal action on the will. For example, in *ST* I-II 17.5, when he affirms that reason commands the acts of the will, he considers the objection that since reason's act of commanding presupposes an act of the will, this implies an infinite regress. Aquinas responds by saying that reason only commands those acts that are subject to reason, but "the first act of the will is not due to the direction of reason, but to the instigation of nature, or of a higher cause."[153] Thus, reason commands all of the will's acts, except the

151. See *De veritate* 22.12 obj. 2 and *ST* I 82.4 obj. 3.

152. *De veritate* 22.12 ad 2; *ST* I 82.4 ad 3.

153. *ST* I-II 17.5 ad 3.

will's first act that is instilled in it by nature, while the will moves the intellect to engage in all its acts except the intellect's first act that is instilled in it by nature.[154] That Aquinas means to retain in his later works this symmetry between intellect and will on the level of their natural principles is evident in his analysis in *De malo* 6 of the primal source of the will's first action. He does not limit his comments to the will alone, but refers to both intellect and will: "what first moves the will and the intellect is something above the will and the intellect, namely God."[155] He says virtually the same thing towards the end of the *Prima secundae.*

> Man is the lord of his act, of willing or not willing, on account of the deliberation of reason, which can be bent toward one or the other. Yet, if man is also to have dominion over whether to deliberate or not to deliberate, this too would have to be from a preceding act of deliberation, and since this cannot go on to infinity, it must arrive at a point where the free decision of man is moved from an exterior principle, which is above the human mind, namely God.[156]

In Aquinas' view, therefore, the ultimate ground of free choice and of practical reasoning are the natural principles instilled in the intellect and will by God himself.

St. Thomas regards the natural principles of both the intellect and will as participating in the eternal law of God.[157] As such, they can be regarded as the twin sources of the natural law.[158] In Thomas' view, a law is a promulgated precept of reason issued for the common good by the

154. Aquinas' analysis in *ST* I-II 17.5, presupposes his earlier analysis in *ST* I-II 9.4 and 5, where he considers that the will cannot be the ultimate cause of its self-motion. The will's self motion consists in this: by actually willing the end, the will moves itself—through the aid of counsel—to actually will the means. This self motion must be a relative self motion, because it presupposes a primary volition: the act of willing the end. If we say that the will moved itself to will this end, then by definition this end is a means to some further end that the will must now be actually willing. Thus, the question arises once again: what is the cause of the will's actual volition of this new end? The intellect's natural knowledge of truth cannot be the cause of this volition, because knowledge of itself does not cause the will to exercise its act. Thus, on the level of exercise, the will's motion must be caused by something other than itself. This something can only be God.

155. *De malo* 6.

156. *ST* I-II 109.2 ad 1.

157. *ST* I-II 93.6.

158. Bradley, *Aquinas on the Twofold Human Good,* 323ff.

one who has care of the community.[159] Since God cares for the community of creation and since he instills the principles of practical reason into the human intellect in order to direct the human person to promote the common good, these principles have the character of law. They are the first principles and primary precepts of the natural law.[160]

Strictly speaking, since a law is an ordinance of reason, natural law properly exists only in the intellect. Nevertheless, in Aquinas' view the natural inclination of the will participates in a certain way in the natural law: the will's natural inclination enables the principles of practical reason to function. It is what enables them to regulate human behavior.[161] In other words, although the precepts of the natural law exist in the intellect, these precepts are able to regulate human action only because of the natural inclinations present in the will. The natural principles of intellect and will, therefore, together underlie and regulate human action.

It is here, in the context of the principles of the natural law, that St. Thomas is able to avoid the charge of voluntarism and moral relativism. Although Thomas maintains that the will has a role in shaping the judgments of practical reason, this does not plunge his theory into moral relativism because the will's own action is rooted in and flows from the natural inclinations instilled in it by God.

At the same time, however, Aquinas' theory avoids the pitfalls of an often overlooked form of determinism. We have already seen that because of the intellect's orientation toward universal truth and the will's orientation toward the good in general, the human person is always able to specify any particular act as a limited good and thus as not good for the agent here and now. This spiritual openness to universal truth and goodness in the face of the limited goods of this life provides the psychological foundation of human freedom. If we halt our analysis on this level, however, we run the risk of seeing freedom as merely the ability to sin: merely the ability in the concrete to act contrary to our habitual

159. *ST* I-II 90.4.

160. *ST* I 79.12; *ST* I-II 94.1 ad 2. See Daniel Westberg, "The Relation of Law and Practical Reason in Aquinas," in *The Future of Thomism*, the American Maritain Association (Notre Dame, Ind.: University of Notre Dame Press, 1992), 279–290.

161. *ST* I-II 91.2 ad 2.

knowledge about our true good. Implicit in such a description of freedom is the view that although we are always "free" to sin, to be morally good we must become bound: we must submit to the impersonal determinations of practical reason.

Yet, as we have seen, although Aquinas establishes a powerful analogy between the principles of theoretical reason and of practical reason, he does not regard the judgments of practical reasoning as operating like a scientific or mathematical deduction. Moral decision-making is not simply a matter of deducing conclusions from principles. This is so, Thomas maintains, because while theoretical reason has as its object necessary things, practical reason considers contingent things: it deals with future possibles that might or might not occur.[162] This means that while the primary precepts of the natural law never change and are always applicable, the secondary and more particular precepts hold only for the most part and can change in particular situations.[163] This contingency at the heart of human agency highlights the creative, unforeseen aspect of morally good action. In any given situation there are innumerable means one can choose to attain the ends toward which the principles of intellect and will direct us. "The end does not always necessitate in the human person the choosing of the means, because the means are not always such that the end cannot be gained without them."[164] Aquinas is not merely referring to the human person's freedom to sin by acting contrary to his or her natural knowledge and inclinations.[165] More

162. Thomas Hibbs, "Principles and Prudence: The Aristotelianism of Thomas's Account of Moral Knowledge," *New Scholasticism* 61 (1987): 275. Aquinas recognizes two ways in which something can be derived from the natural law. On the one hand, certain general principles can be deduced as conclusions from more general principles (Aquinas gives the example of deducing the conclusion that "one must not kill," from the principle that "one should not harm anyone."). On the other hand, more detailed precepts can be derived from the natural law as certain determinations of general principles (Aquinas offers the example of the forms of punishment: the natural law precept that evil doers should be punished can be determined in numerous ways in the concrete). See Hibbs, ibid., 277.

163. See *ST* I-II 94.4 and 5.

164. *ST* I-II 13.6 ad 1.

165. We shall consider the nature of moral error more closely in our analysis of St. Thomas' theory of love in the following chapter.

deeply, he is asserting our spiritual freedom to do the morally good act in many different ways. In Aquinas' view, human action has more the character of a free artistic expression than of a necessary scientific deduction.[166] We enjoy a freedom akin to that of the artisan who applies general forms to particular things, choosing freely among the particular elements at his disposal.[167] Just as a builder can make many good homes with the same form but constructed from very different materials, so too the human agent can freely apply the same formal principles to (morally good) actions that differ greatly in their particulars.

The creative character of moral goodness points to the central role of a community in the development of human freedom. It highlights the role of moral education in virtue: in order for one to apply properly the principles of natural law in particular situations one must be educated in a life of virtue. The goods toward which the natural law inclines us are social goods, and as such they become known to us as embodied in a particular community. The principles of the natural law and the spiritual openness of the intellect and will make freedom possible, but freedom is something that must be achieved in and through a community that teachers us the ways of (freely creative) morally good acts.

Much more could be said about the relationship between freedom and the community. Here, however, our focus is on the way the principles of the natural law both orient us toward certain types of action and underlie our capacity to do those actions in unique and unforeseen ways. Aquinas thus avoids moral relativism while simultaneously avoiding two distinct forms of determinism.[168] The freedom of the will in rea-

166. See *ST* I-II 95.2 and Mark Jordan, "The *Pars moralis* of the Summa theologiae as *scientia* and as *ars*," in *Miscellanea Mediaevalia: Scientia und Ars im Hoch- und Spätmittelalter* vol. 22/1 (New York: Walter de Gruyter, 1994), 470–471.

167. *ST* I-II 95.2. Hibbs, "Principles and Prudence," 277–278. Aquinas gives special attention to our freedom in the choice of contingent goods in his commentary of Aristotle's *Perihermeneias*, which Aquinas regards as partly an effort to "save the roots of contingency" (*Expositio libri peryermenias* I 14.24). See Thomas Hibbs, "Transcending Humanity in Aquinas," *American Catholic Philosophical Quarterly* 66 (1992): 193, and Laurence Dewan, "St. Thomas and the Causes of Free Choice," *Acta philosophica* (Rome) 8 (1999): 95–96.

168. In the final analysis, this creative freedom for the good is a participation in God's own creative freedom (*ST* I 103.6; *ST* I 23.8 ad 2). For an analysis of how this notion of freedom differs from later scholastic conceptions of freedom, see Pinckaers, *Sources of Christian Ethics*, 327–399.

soning occurs neither antecedently nor consequently to reason's judgment. It occurs within and throughout the genesis of practical judgment itself. In the decision to act, the intellect is always structurally antecedent to the will. Nonetheless, the practical intellect only acts in and through the action of the will. For Aquinas, therefore, "the act of choice *(electio)* is at the same time both a judgment and a willing, a spiritual synthesis implying both light and power, rational determination and efficient motion."[169] As such it is both rational and free.

169. A. D. Sertillanges, *La philosophie morale de saint Thomas d'Aquin* (Paris: Aubier, Editions Montaigne, 1942), 27.

CHAPTER 3

Knowledge and Love in Human Action

After having considered the character of the will's relationship to intellect in practical reasoning, we are now in a position to study more closely the will's proper act, which is love. A full account of the Thomistic psychology of love is beyond the scope of this project.[1] Instead, our goal in this chapter is to study St. Thomas' description of love's relationship to knowledge in human action. We shall consider the relationship between knowledge and love in Thomas' accounts of happiness (*ST* I-II 1–5), of the principles of practical reasoning (*ST* I-II 8–18), and of the virtues (*ST* I-II 49–67). We shall attempt to demonstrate that throughout his analysis, Thomas remains faithful to two apparently contradictory Augustinian assertions: that love depends on knowledge

1. For fuller treatments of St. Thomas' psychology of love, see María Celestina Donadío Maggi de Gandolfi, *Amor y Bien: Los Problemas del Amor en Santo Tomás de Aquino* (Buenos Aires: Universidad Catolica Argentina, 1999); Albert Ilien, *Wesen und Funktion der Liebe bei Thomas von Aquin* (Freiburg im Breisgau: Herder, 1975); Raymond McGinnis, *The Wisdom of Love: A Study in the Psycho-Metaphysics of Love according to the Principles of St. Thomas* (Rome: Officium libri catholici, 1951); Avital Wohlman, "l'élaboration des éléments aristotéliciens dans la doctrine thomiste de l'amour," *Revue thomiste* 82 (1982): 247–269; Jordan Aumann, "Thomistic Evaluation of Love and Charity," *Angelicum* 55 (1978): 534–556. Two influential studies that have shaped subsequent treatments of Thomas' theory of love are Pierre Rousselot, "Pour L'histoire du problème de l'amour du moyen âge," in *Beiträge zur Geschichte der Philosophie des Mittelalters. Text und Untersuchungen* (Münster, 1908) B. 6, H. 6: 1–104; H. D. Simonin, "Autour de la solution thomiste du problème de l'amour," in *Archives d'histoire doctrinale et littéraire du moyen âge* 6 (1931): 174–272. For a clear-sighted assessment of Rousselot and his critics, see Avital Wohlman, "Amour du bien propre et amour de soi dans la doctrine thomiste de l'amour," *Revue thomiste* 81 (1981): 204–234.

(for we cannot love what we do not know),[2] but that moral knowledge depends on well-ordered love as the principle that moves all the powers of the soul to act.[3] How St. Thomas is able to reconcile these two apparently contradictory assertions is something we shall consider in the pages that follow. First, however, we shall begin by tracing an important evolution in Thomas' theory of love.

Development of St. Thomas' Theory of Love

In chapter two we noted that St. Thomas in his later works more clearly delineates the types of causality exercised by the intellect and will in the genesis of human action. The intellect functions as the formal cause of the act, while the will functions as the efficient cause. In order to illustrate this difference, Thomas introduces his celebrated distinction between specification and exercise. When we turn to Thomas' analysis of love, we discover a similar development in thought and terminology. In his early work, Aquinas employs the language of form to describe the nature of love. Love, he tells us, is a form received into the appetite analogous to the form received into the intellect in the act of cognition. In his mature work, however, Aquinas reserves the language of form to the intellect and now describes love as a pleasing affective affinity *(complacentia)* or an inclination. As with the distinction between specification and exercise, we should avoid the common tendency to exaggerate the significance of this development. As we shall see, there is a fundamental continuity between Aquinas' earlier and later theories of love. Nevertheless, Aquinas did clarify his understanding of the relationship between intellect and will, and this clarification influenced his mature description of love. Specifically, it served to integrate the acts of knowledge and love more closely together in mutual dependence and interaction.

2. Augustine, *De trinitate* 10.1 (*PL* 42, 971): *"nullus potest amare aliquid incognitum." De trinitate* 10.1 (*PL* 42, 973): *"non enim diligitur nisi cognitum."*

3. Augustine, *De moribus ecclesiae catholicae* 15.25 (*PL* 32, 1322).

Love in the *Commentary on the Sentences*

In the *Sentences,* Peter Lombard introduces his analysis of charity in the context of his treatment of the Incarnation.[4] Following the Lombard's lead, it became standard for those commenting on the *Sentences* to offer their own analyses of charity at this point in their commentaries. Unlike other commentators, however, St. Thomas in his *Commentary on the Sentences* prefaces his treatment of charity with an analysis of "love in general."[5] In this analysis Thomas defines love as "a certain transformation of the affection into the loved object."[6] In his classic study of the Thomistic theory of love, H. D. Simonin notes that in the *Commentary on the Sentences* the language of form is a central feature of Thomas' analysis.[7] Aquinas employs the language of form to explain each of the principal characteristics of love.

First, love belongs to the appetitive power and arises in the appetite as the result of an object's action upon the appetite.

> Love pertains to the appetite. Now, the appetite is a passive power; hence, the Philosopher affirms (*De anima* 3) that the appetite moves as a moved mover. Now, every passive power is perfected by being informed by the form of an active power, and through this motion it is brought to its term and rests. The intellect before it is informed by an intelligible form doubts and inquires, but when it has been informed ceases to inquire and becomes fixed in this form, and then the intellect is said to adhere to the thing firmly. Similarly, when the affect or appetite is entirely imbued with the form of the good, which is its object, it takes pleasure in it and adheres to it as being affixed to it, and then it is said to love it. Hence, love is nothing other than a certain transformation of the affection into the loved object *(transformatio affectus in rem amatam).*[8]

4. Peter Lombard, *Libri iv sententiarum, liber* III *(De incarnatione verbi), distinctio* 27: *"De caritate dei et proximi, quae in christo est et in nobis."*

5. *In sent.* III 27. See Guy Mansini, *"Duplex amor* and the Structure of Love in Aquinas," in *Thomistica,* edited by E. Manning (Leuven: Peeters, 1995), 159.

6. *In sent.* III 27.1.1.

7. H. D. Simonin, "Autour de la solution thomiste du problème de l'amour," *Archives d'histoire doctrinale et littéraire du moyen âge* 6 (1931): 181: *"S'il considère l'amour comme la réception et la possession d'une forme déterminée ce n'est pas là simple manière de parler, ce n'est pas un de ces* obiter dicta *qui échappent aux plus grands philosophes. C'est chez lui une conception bien arrêtée et qu'il entend exploiter à fond."*

8. *In sent.* III 27.1.1.

From this perspective love is primarily the term of an appetitive motion *(terminatio appetivi motus)*.[9] It is the terminus of the change *(informatio)* caused in the appetite by the loved object.[10] Love is the form of the beloved existing in the appetite and in which the appetite rests.

A union of affection exists between lover and beloved, a union that generates mutual indwelling between them. Aquinas once again appeals to the concept of form to explain these features of love: "since everything that acquires the form of a thing is made one with it, love makes the lover one with the beloved."[11]

> Because love transforms the lover into the beloved, it draws the lover into the interior of the beloved and vice versa, with the result that nothing remains in the beloved that is not united to the lover: just as the form enters deeply into the one informed by it and vice versa, so too the lover in a certain way enters the beloved.[12]

The lover rests in the interior of the beloved by having the form of the beloved in his affections. Aquinas further applies his theory of form to account for the traditional view that love causes ecstasy. "Since nothing can be transformed into something else without in a certain way receding from its own form (because each thing has only one form)," love causes the lover to be "separated from himself as he tends toward the beloved."[13]

Importantly, Aquinas recognizes that although love is the terminus of a motion, it is also the principle of a further motion. Indeed, love is the principle of all that the lover subsequently does. Just as natural motions begin from some principle that is at rest, so too "all affective motion proceeds from the term and rest of love."[14] Once again Aquinas explains this by appealing to the notion of form.

9. *In sent.* III 27.1.2.

10. *In sent.* III 27.1.3.

11. *In sent.* III 27.1.1.

12. *In sent.* III 27.1.1 ad 4: *"ex hoc enim quod amor transformat amantem in amatum, facit amantem intrare ad interiora amati, et e contra; ut nihil amati amanti remaneat non unitum; sicut forma pervenit ad intima formati, et e converso; et ideo amans quodammodo penetrat in amatum."*

13. *In sent.* III 27.1.1 ad 4: *"sed quia nihil potest in alterum transformari nisi secundum quod a sua forma quodammodo recedit, quia unius una est forma. . . . qua amans a seipso separatur in amatum tendens."*

14. *In sent.* III 27.1.3: *"omnis motus affectivae procedat ex quietatione et terminatione amoris."*

Each thing acts according to the exigencies of its form, which is the principle of action and the rule of operation. Now the loved good is the end, and in actions the end functions as a principle in the same way that first principles function in cognition.[15]

Just as the intellect through being informed by the essences of things acquires knowledge of principles and then reasons according to these principles to conclusions, so too love generates actions according to the form it has received. The lover, by having his "affect informed by the good itself" becomes inclined to act "according to the exigencies of the beloved." By containing the form of the beloved in his appetites, the lover now acts according to this form. This action "becomes entirely pleasing to him as being in harmony with *(conveniens)* his own form."[16]

In Aquinas' view, the above description of love accurately describes love as it exists both in the passions and in the will. There is this difference, however: love as it exists in the will is the product of a power that acts freely as an internal principle of action, while love in the passions is determined by the action of an external agent.[17] In his subsequent analysis of charity, Aquinas adds that since love in the will "includes choice *(electio)*," the will's love is properly called *"dilectio."*[18] Aquinas also affirms at this point that love in the will entails benevolence, because a lover desires good for his beloved. A little later we learn that love has a twofold tendency. "Love of benevolence" properly terminates in a rational creature with whom we can share a "certain society." Included in this love, however, is the "love of concupiscence" directed toward the good we desire for our friend.[19]

The psychology of love Aquinas develops in his *Commentary on the Sentences* provides a profound and nuanced account of love's role in action. Nevertheless, Aquinas' early psychology of love contains several serious drawbacks. The most fundamental drawback is Aquinas' attempt to define love in terms of form. Already in his *Commentary on the Sentences* Aquinas recognizes that the cognitive power receives the

15. *In sent.* III 27.1.1.

16. Ibid.

17. *In sent.* III 27.1.2.

18. *In sent.* III 27.2.1.

19. For a concise presentation of the history of this distinction and how St. Thomas developed his own explanation of this distinction over the course of his life, see Mansini, *"Duplex amor,"* 137–196.

"species" of things within it, while the appetitive power tends outward toward the objects themselves. He also sees that this difference corresponds to the differences existing between the objects of these two powers. The intellect's object is truth, "which is in the soul," while the will's object is good, "which is in things."[20] Aquinas, however, does not yet grasp what this distinction implies about the role of form in the genesis of love.

According to Aristotle's physics, any change or motion can be described as a transformation. When a thing changes—even when the thing in question is a spiritual power existing in the soul—one form (way of being or actuality) is lost and another form (way of being or actuality) is gained. According to this theory, a "passive potency" is the principle within the subject of the change enabling it to be changed in this way. It is the principle that enables the subject to receive the form imparted by the active principle.[21] In some instances the active principle imparts its own form to the potency, as occurs in natural generation; yet this is not always the case. Often the active principle imparts some lesser form. Elsewhere in his *Commentary on the Sentences,* Aquinas acknowledges this;[22] yet, in his analysis of love he neglects this fact and makes the general claim that active potencies impart their *own* form to the passive potencies they actualize: "every passive potency is perfected by being informed by the form of its active potency."[23] This leads Aquinas to conclude that love is the form of the loved object received into the appetite.

> Hence, love is nothing other than a certain transformation of the affect into the thing loved.[24]

> Love is itself the union or nexus or transformation by which the lover is transformed into the beloved and is in a certain way converted into him.[25]

20. *In sent.* II 39.1.2.

21. *MP* 5.12 (1019a20–23); *In metaphysic.* 5.14.

22. See *In sent.* I 2.1.2 and *In sent.* I 35.1.4 ad 1.

23. *In sent.* III 27.1.1.

24. *In sent.* III 27.1.1: *"unde amor nihil aliud est quam quaedam transformatio affectus in rem amatam."*

25. *In sent.* III 27.1.1 ad 2: *"[amor] est ipsa unio vel nexus vel transformatio qua amans in amatum transformatur, et quodammodo convertitur in ipsum."*

This description becomes problematic when we recognize that it is virtually indistinguishable from Aquinas' description of intellection. As we have seen, in Aquinas' view the intellect receives into itself the intelligible "species" of things. Another word for species, however, is form, as Aquinas himself notes. He speaks of the intellect being "informed by the intelligible form."[26] If, however, the will also receives the form, how do intellect and will differ? Indeed, if the will receives the form, why isn't the will also a cognitive faculty?[27]

A similar question arises from Aquinas' effort to justify how love in the will functions as a principle of activity. Aquinas justifies love's role as the principle of the agent's actions by appealing to the natural connection between forms and inclinations: just as each thing inclines and acts according to the exigencies of its form, so too the lover acts according to the exigencies of his beloved's form existing in his will as love. Love acts as a principle of motion because, as the form of the loved object existing in the will, inclinations and motions flow from love according to the exigencies of this form.[28] Yet, if the form of the beloved acts this way when present in the will, why does it not do so when present in the intellect? In other words, why doesn't the form as existing in the intellect generate inclinations? Aquinas appears to be faced with a dilemma: if he downplays the necessary connection between form and inclination, love's role as the principle of action in the will ceases to be intelligible. Yet, if he emphasizes the relationship between form and inclination, this would imply that the intellect itself could be a principle of action.

The inadequacy of Aquinas' early understanding of knowledge and love is further revealed in his treatment of whether knowledge is higher

26. *In sent.* III 27.1.1.

27. Aquinas faces an even more troubling difficulty from his tendency in the *Commentary on the Sentences* to describe love as causing "the lover himself" (and not merely the lover's appetite) to become the form of the beloved: *"amor transformat amantem in amatum"* (*In sent.* III 27.1.1 ad 4); *"amor facit amatum esse formam amantis"* (*In sent.* III 27.1.1 ad 5); *"amor magis intrat ad rem quam cognitio: quia cognitio est de re secundum id quod recipitur in cognoscente: amor autem de re, inquantum ipse amans in rem ipsam transformatur, ut dictum est prius. In hac autem via, qua perficitur anima in ordine ad res alias, dictum est, quod voluntas cognitionem excedit, ad quam viam pertinet esse magis vel minus intimum rei"* (*In sent.* III 27.1.4 ad 10). If this is the case, how does the lover retain his or her personal identity?

28. *In sent.* III 27.1.1.

than love. In describing how the intellect and will mutually include each other, Aquinas states:

> Just as the cognitive power is ordered to all things, so too is the appetitive power; hence they also mutually include each other, since the intellect knows the will and the will loves and desires those things that pertain to the intellect.[29]

Notice that while Aquinas describes the intellect as knowing the will, he does not say that the will loves and moves the intellect. Instead, he states that the will loves and desires "those things that pertain to the intellect," a phrase which presumably refers to the objects known by the intellect. Likewise, although Aquinas affirms that the "inclination" of the will is free and that love in the will "includes choice," he does not address whether rational love is the product of free choice or whether it is a necessary change that precedes free choice.[30]

Each of these features of Aquinas' treatment of love in the *Commentary on the Sentences* points to what we discovered in our study of agency in the *De veritate.* Aquinas in his early works has not yet fully grasped (or at least has not yet found a way to explain clearly) the nature of the causality exercised by the intellect and will in human action. This fact hinders his ability to express the character of human love and its relationship to knowledge. By the time he writes the *Secunda pars* of the *Summa theologiae,* however, Aquinas has given greater attention to the nature of causality, and this influences his treatment of love.

Love in the *Summa theologiae*

The first thing to notice about St. Thomas' analysis of love in the *Summa theologiae* is the absence of the language of form. While in the *Commentary on the Sentences* he defines love as a "transformation," in the *Summa* he describes it as a pleasant affective affinity *(complacentia).* This affinity is the aptitude, inclination, or proportion existing in the appetite for the loved object.

29. *In sent.* III 27.1.4.
30. *In sent.* III 27.2.1.

The aptitude of the sensitive appetite or of the will to some good, that is to say, its very complacency *(complacentia)* in good, is called sensitive love or intellectual or rational love. So that sensitive love is in the sensitive appetite, while intellectual love is in the intellectual appetite.[31]

The first change caused in the appetite by the appetible object is called love, and is nothing else than complacency *(complacentia)* in that object.[32]

The very aptitude or proportion of the appetite to good is love, which is complacency *(complacentia)* in good.[33]

Good, therefore, first causes in the appetitive power a certain inclination, aptitude or connaturalness toward the good, and this pertains to the passion of love.[34]

The first principle of appetitive motion is love, which is the first inclination of the appetite toward attaining the good.[35]

Aquinas now sees clearly that while the object imparts its form in the cognitive powers, it imparts an affective proportion in the appetitive powers. Cognition receives the form and appetite receives an inclination toward that form as it exists in the thing itself.[36] Moreover, Aquinas now explains unambiguously that although the objects known cause love to arise in the appetite, in the case of the rational appetite or will this love is also the result of the lover's free choice. These insights lead Aquinas to emphasize from the beginning that (a) love depends upon cognition; (b) love is primarily the principle (not the terminus) of the agent's action; and (c) love as it exists in the will is the result of the agent's free choice.

Aquinas introduces these insights in the very first article of his treatment of love. Love, he explains, pertains to appetite. Appetites differ according to their differing relationships to cognition. First, there is an appetite that arises from a cognition existing not in the subject of the appetite but in God as the author of nature. This is the natural appetite, which necessarily and unswervingly inclines toward the good that is fitting to it. Second, there is an appetite that arises from a cognition exist-

31. *ST* I-II 26.1.

32. *ST* I-II 26.2.

33. *ST* I-II 25.2.

34. *ST* I-II 23.4.

35. *ST* I-II 36.2.

36. *ST* I-II 23.4. See also *In divinis nominibus,* 4.11.

ing in the subject of the appetite, "but from necessity and not from free judgment." This is the sense appetite proper to non-rational animals, but which "in the human person has a certain share of freedom in so far as it obeys reason."[37] Lastly, "there is another appetite following an apprehension in the subject of the appetite according to free judgment. This is the rational appetite, which is called the will."[38] Aquinas next affirms that "in each of these appetites, the name love is given to the principle of movement toward the loved end."[39] In the natural appetite there is natural love, which is nothing other than an object's "connaturalness" for its proper perfection. Next, in the sense appetite there is sense love, while in the will there is intellectual or rational love.[40]

Aquinas' method here is significant. By introducing rational love in the context of natural love, he is presenting rational love's relationship to cognition as part of a larger and more general dynamic. All appetitive principles of action presuppose knowledge. This is true even for non-rational creatures.

> Even natural love, which is in all things, is caused by a kind of knowledge, not indeed existing in natural things themselves, but in him who created their nature.[41]

Not only does God's knowledge order each thing to its proper end, but his knowledge is the source of the "formality" that causes each thing to be what it is. The character of each thing's natural love flows from this formality. For Aquinas, the levels of knowledge and love described above represent different levels of participation in divine agency. Inanimate things are not in any way the agents of their own action. Instead, they are moved by an "extrinsic force" to their proper place.[42] Living things, however, in a certain sense move themselves to act from internal principles of action. As we have seen, the highest level of this participated agency belongs to creatures endowed with intellect and will, where love both presupposes knowledge and is the product of the agent's free choice.[43]

37. *ST* I-II 26.1.
38. Ibid.
39. Ibid.
40. Ibid.
41. *ST* I-II 27.2 ad 3.
42. *ST* I 18.1 ad 2; *ST* I-II 1.2.
43. See *ST* I 18.3; *ST* I-II 26.3.

In the context of this general perspective, we can profitably view the rest of Aquinas' analysis in questions 26 and 27 as an attempt to sketch more fully how love is both caused by knowledge and is the freely chosen principle of the agent's actions. For example, in *ST* I-II 26.2 Aquinas considers the extent to which love is a passion. Love, he explains, is a change caused in the appetite by the loved object. In the sense appetite this change entails a "bodily transmutation" and consequently it is a passion properly so called.[44] As existing in the will, however, this change entails no bodily alteration and is thus only analogously called a passion.[45] Nevertheless, in both cases love is caused by the object's action upon the appetite. Specifically, some good, as that which is "connatural and proportionate" to us, causes love for that good to arise in the appetite.[46] Aquinas adds, however, that the fitting good causes love only by first being known.

For this reason the Philosopher (*NE* 9.5, 12) says that bodily sight is the beginning of sensitive love. In like manner the contemplation of spiritual beauty or goodness is the beginning of spiritual love. Accordingly knowledge is the cause of love for the same reason as good is, which can be loved only if known.[47]

As we noted in the introduction, Aquinas is here being faithful to an Augustinian insight: "as Augustine proves, 'no one can love what he does not know.'"[48]

The intellect causes love to arise not merely because it apprehends a good, but because it judges this good to be "fitting" *(conveniens)*.[49] What is fitting implies a certain likeness or oneness with us. Different types of likeness generate different types of love. Potential likeness, where we have potentially and as belonging to our well-being what something else has actually, causes "love of concupiscence" to arise within us. With this love we desire to have actually the fitting goods that we only have poten-

44. *ST* I-II 22.3.

45. Note also that in the midst of describing love as a passion, Aquinas is careful to emphasize that love is a principle of motion (*ST* I-II 26.2).

46. *ST* I-II 27.1.

47. *ST* I-II 27.2.

48. *ST* I-II 27.2 sc. From Augustine's *De trinitate* 10.1 (*PL* 42, 971).

49. *ST* I-II 29.1.

tially. Actual likeness, on the other hand, exists when we share the same form with the beloved. For example, most generally we share our common humanity with other people. We also may participate in the same family of origin or we may share a similarly virtuous character. This actual likeness causes "love of friendship" to arise within us.[50] With this love we respond to the other and to his or her good as to ourselves and our own good. In both cases, our love depends on reason's judgment about the type of likeness or union existing between us and the beloved.

This union must be considered in relation to the preceding apprehension, because movement of the appetite follows apprehension. Now, since love is twofold (namely, love of concupiscence and love of friendship) each of these arises from some apprehension of the oneness of the thing loved with the lover. For when we love a thing with the love of concupiscence we apprehend it as belonging to our well-being. Similarly, when we love another with the love of friendship we will good to our friend as to ourselves, which occurs because we apprehend our friend as being another self in so far as we will good to him as to ourselves.[51]

Yet, in his initial analysis of love, immediately after describing the will's love as the result of the object's action on the will (i.e., *ST* I-II 26.2), Aquinas balances this statement by affirming that love in the will is the result of the agent's free choice: "because *dilectio* implies, in addition to love, a preceding choice *(electionem praecedentem),* as the word itself denotes."[52] In his earlier work *Commentary on the Sentences,* Aquinas considers love's relationship to choice only in passing and only outside of his general treatment of love, addressing it in his analysis of charity. Moreover, in this earlier analysis, he merely affirms that rational love "includes choice." Now, however, he places the issue of choice at the heart of his general treatment of love—immediately after his consideration of passion—and he makes it clear that choice precedes rational love: even though objects present themselves to us and in a certain way specify our love through the action of the intellect, our love is the product of our own choices.[53]

50. *ST* I-II 27.3.

51. *ST* I-II 28.1.

52. *ST* I-II 26.3.

53. See Josef Pieper, *About Love,* translated by Richard and Clara Winston (Chicago:

Aquinas also explains more clearly the nature of this freely chosen act. Drawing on Aristotle, Aquinas affirms that "to love is to will good to someone."[54] As such, "love has a twofold tendency: towards the good that a person wishes to someone (to himself or to another) and towards the one to whom he wishes some good."[55] Love is essentially love for someone.[56] This is the essence of the love of friendship. Yet, when we love a person we are always affirming some good for that person. This is the essence of the love of concupiscence. Aquinas is clear that these are not two separate loves. Rather, human love always has two components, one of which is subordinated to the other.[57] Love of concupiscence is contained within the dynamism of our love of friendship for ourselves or for someone else.[58] Aquinas concludes his analysis of love by underlining that love is the principle of all that the agent subsequently does.

> Every agent acts for an end, as stated above. Now the end is the good desired and loved by each one. Thus, it is evident that every agent, whatever it be, does every action from some kind of love.[59]

Our actions, therefore, flow from our freely chosen love: from our love for the goods we affirm and from our love for those for whom we affirm them.

When we study Aquinas' mature treatment of love in the context of his earlier analysis we see clearly that not only does he reserve formal language to the intellect, he has integrated knowledge more closely into the dynamism of love. This especially becomes apparent when we compare his earlier and later descriptions of how love causes mutual in-

---

Franciscan Herald Press, 1972), 10; reprinted in *Faith, Hope, Love* (San Francisco: Ignatius Press, 1997), 152–153.

54. *ST* I-II 26.4: *"amare est velle alicui bonum."*

55. *ST* I-II 26.4.

56. In other words, for God and for spiritual creatures of an intellectual or rational nature (angels and humans): *ST* I 20.2 ad 3; *ST* II-II 25.3; *ST* II-II 25.2 ad 1.

57. *ST* I-II 26.4; *ST* II-II 25.2 and 3.

58. Since friendship is founded on union, not unity, we do not have friendship *(amicitia)* for ourselves, but something more than friendship (*ST* II-II 25.4). Nevertheless, the love we have for ourselves is the type of love that is proper to friendship (*ST* I-II 28.1 ad 2). It is an *amor amicitiae.* Indeed, the love we have for ourselves, whereby we will good for ourselves, is the model for love of neighbor (*ST* II-II 25.4).

59. *ST* I-II 28.6. See also *ST* II-II 47.1 ad 1.

dwelling, and ecstasy. In the *Commentary on the Sentences,* Aquinas describes these features of love solely in terms of form and solely in relation to the appetite. In the *Summa theologiae,* however, he explains these features in relation to cognition and appetite, and the language of form is removed from his description of appetite. What before arose only in the appetite now also arises in cognition: "The effect of mutual indwelling may be understood as referring both to the apprehensive and to the appetitive power."[60] "To suffer ecstasy means to be placed outside oneself. This happens according to the apprehensive power and according to the appetitive power."[61]

The lover's cognitive "apprehension" causes mutual indwelling because, while the beloved abides in the thoughts of the lover, the lover's mind also goes out to the beloved seeking ever deeper knowledge of the inner life of the beloved. Thus, while the beloved cognitively dwells in the lover, the lover also cognitively dwells in the beloved. Similarly, the appetite generates a mutual indwelling. Previously Aquinas described this indwelling as the result of the oneness in form between lover and beloved. Now, however, he explains it in relation to the lover's *complacentia* for the beloved.

With respect to the appetitive power, the beloved is said to be in the lover by being in his affections through a certain *complacentia:* with the result that the lover either takes pleasure in the beloved or in the beloved's good, if they are present; or if they are absent, by desire he tends toward the beloved, loving him with the love of concupiscence; or he tends toward the good that he wills for his beloved, loving him with the love of friendship. The lover acts this way not because of some extrinsic reason (as if he were desiring the beloved for the sake of another, or as if he were willing good for the beloved for the sake of something else) but because *complacentia* for the beloved is deeply rooted within him. . . . On the other hand, the lover is said to be in the beloved in one way through the love of concupiscence and in another way through the love of friendship. The love of concupiscence does not rest in any external or superficial attainment or enjoyment of the beloved, but desires to have the beloved perfectly, entering into the beloved's inner recesses, as it were. In the love of friendship, the lover is in the beloved to the extent that he considers

60. *ST* I-II 28.2.
61. *ST* I-II 28.3.

what is good or evil for his friend as being so for himself, and his friend's will as his own, so that he seems to experience and be affected by the goods or evils experienced by his friend.[62]

We should note two features of this description. First, by replacing the language of form with the language of *complacentia,* Aquinas has now shifted the focus from love as the *appetite's rest* to love as the *principle of action.* Love is a *complacentia* that causes the lover to enjoy his beloved or his beloved's good, when they are present, or to desire his beloved or the beloved's good, when they are absent. This affective affinity causes the lover to seek deeper union with the beloved and to act for the beloved's good as if it were his own good.

In this description, Aquinas now seems to recognize more clearly that the "rest" proper to love is not inactivity, but full actuality.[63] According to Aristotle's theory of motion, motion implies imperfection.[64] A thing is perfect only when it rests in the goal of its motion. The primary example of this is local motion. The projectile has attained its goal when it comes to rest in the target. The spiritual powers of intellect and will, however, are not like this.[65] Their goal is to be fully in act. The will is said to rest in the beloved when it engages in the activity of delighting in the beloved. This enjoyment *(fruitio)* is perfect when the lover has attained real union with the beloved. Yet, even before the lover attains this full union, the lover can still be said to enjoy the beloved if the beloved is

62. *ST* I-II 28.2.

63. St. Thomas' mature understanding of rest as full actuality also has implications for his theology of the beatific vision. The vision of God in heaven will bring our powers to rest in him, but this rest is a full actuality. We will be intellectually and affectively fully alive, delighting in the infinite goodness of God who is our constant thought and the eternal object of our love. Thus, St. Thomas describes the loving contemplation of God as an activity where "one delights in the vision of the loved object, and the very delight in the object seen incites greater love" (*ST* II-II 180.7 ad 1) He even joins Gregory the Great in describing the vision of the beloved as something that "inflames greater love for him" (ibid.). Consequently, Thomas states that although "it is true that contemplation enjoys rest from external movements, nevertheless to contemplate is itself a movement of the intellect, in so far as every operation is described as a movement" (*ST* II-II 179.1 ad 3). See also his treatment of the effects of love (*ST* I-II 28) and his description of delight (*ST* I-II 34.3).

64. *PS* 3.1 (201a10–201b15).

65. *ST* I 18.1; *ST* I-II 3.2 ad 3.

present in thought.[66] The thought of the beloved causes love to arise in the will. The lover enjoys the beloved as cognitively present, but also desires the beloved as substantially absent.

Aquinas seems to choose the term *complacentia* to express this feature of love. As a word that literally signifies "with pleasing assent" *(cum + placentia),* it can convey incipient enjoyment, without excluding full enjoyment.[67] In other words, it can signify love as the principle of both desire and enjoyment. Aquinas' other terms—*coaptatio, aptitudo, convenientia, proportio, connaturalitas*—all convey an aspect of this dual character of love. Aquinas had employed some of these terms in his earlier account.[68] Now, however, he uses them more clearly to underline love's

66. *ST* I-II 11.4.

67. In a series of three articles in *Theological Studies,* Frederick Crowe offers an extended analysis of Aquinas' description of love as *complacentia.* In response to the work of H.-D. Simonin, Crowe concedes that Aquinas in his mature work often describes love as a motion, tendency, or "spontaneous impulse" toward the loved object. This is love as an *inclinatio boni.* Crowe counters, however, that this is only one aspect of Aquinas' description of love. Aquinas also describes love as a harmonious and quiet resting in the beloved antecedent to one's motion toward the beloved. This is love as *complacentia.* In Crowe's view, Aquinas never integrated these two conflicting descriptions of love into a unified account. Drawing on the work of Bernard Lonergan, Crowe offers a first sketch of a unified account that seeks to be faithful to Aquinas' insights. Crowe is to be lauded for drawing attention toward the centrality of *complacentia* in Aquinas' mature theory of love. Yet, his interpretation of Aquinas is marred by a failure to recognize the primary meaning of *inclinatio* in Aquinas. Like H.-D. Simonin and Pierre Rousselot, Crowe reads *inclinatio* as primarily signifying a motion or impulse. For Aquinas, however, *inclinatio* primarily signifies a *principle* of motion. It is the appetitive orientation of the appetite toward its object. Consequently, the synthesis Crowe seeks between receptive and active elements of love (between "complacency" and "concern") are already present in Aquinas. Indeed, I would argue that Aquinas' description of rational love *(dilectio)* as a freely chosen receptivity to and orientation toward the beloved offers a more successful synthesis of the active and receptive elements of love than the one advanced by Crow. See Frederick E. Crowe, "Complacency and Concern in the Thought of St. Thomas," *Theological Studies* 20 (1959): 1–39; 198–230; 343–382. For recent reappraisals of Crowe's analysis from within the perspective of Bernard Lonergan's thought, see Mark J. Doorley, "Resting in Reality: Reflections on Crowe's 'Complacency and Concern,'" *Lonergan Workshop* 13 (1997): 33–55; Robert M. Doran, "'Complacency and Concern' and a Basic Thesis on Grace," *Lonergan Workshop* 13 (1997): 57–78.

68. In the *Commentary on the Sentences,* St. Thomas describes love as making the lover *connaturale* and *conveniens* with the beloved. (*In sent.* III 27.1.3 ad 2; *In sent.* III 27.1.1 ad 2). He also employs the verbal form of *complacentia (complacere)* to describe the lover's attitude toward the loved object. Even here, however, Thomas still describes love as the

role as a principle. Love is the principle of the agent's action, whether this action be love itself, desire or enjoyment.

The second feature to notice is the interdependence of knowledge and love in the mutual indwelling between lover and beloved described by Aquinas. For example, the intellect can "strive to gain intimate knowledge of everything pertaining to the beloved" only if it is moved to do so by a will that loves this beloved. Likewise, the will can desire this deeper knowledge only if the intellect has already come to know something of the beloved. Indeed, the interdependence of knowledge and love is implied in the description of mutual indwelling as an "effect of love."[69]

In his treatment of mutual indwelling, Aquinas only explicitly addresses love's dependence on knowledge.[70] Nevertheless, Aquinas refers to cognition's dependence on love in his description of ecstasy. There we learn that cognitive ecstasy—which occurs when a person acquires knowledge beyond the knowledge normally proper to him—is caused by love dispositively, because "love makes the lover meditate on the beloved, and intense meditation on one thing draws the mind away from other things."[71] Love, therefore, directs our thoughts and can focus the mind's attention on one thing and away from others. This insight is in line with Aquinas' description of the will's priority on the level of exercise. It is also implied in his affirmation that love is the cause of whatever the agent does.[72] Aquinas, therefore, is true to his insight concerning the different lines of causality. Knowledge has priority over love on the level of specification, while love has priority over knowledge on the level of exercise. As we shall see in greater detail below, by employing the notion of "natural love," Aquinas again locates the ultimate foundation of the mutual interaction between knowledge and love (intellect and will) in the natural principles of action instilled within us by God.

---

form of the beloved existing in the appetite: *In sent.* III 27.1.1: "*quando affectus vel appetitus omnino imbuitur forma boni quod est sibi obiectum, complacet sibi in illo, et adhaeret ei quasi fixus in ipso; et tunc dicitur amare ipsum. Unde amor nihil aliud est quam quaedam transformatio affectus in rem amatam.*" See also *In sent.* III 27.1.1 ad 3.

69. See *ST* I-II 28.2.

70. *ST* I-II 28.2 ad 2.

71. *ST* I-II 28.3.

72. *ST* I-II 28.6.

Development in St. Thomas' Theory of Love: Evaluation

There is an evident continuity between St. Thomas' earlier and later theories of love. In both the *Commentary on the Sentences* and the *Summa theologiae,* Thomas presents love as a change arising in the appetite as the result of its contact with some good. Furthermore, Aquinas recognizes throughout his career that the appetite encounters the good through cognition. It is the good as judged to be fitting by the intellect that moves the will and causes love to arise. Moreover, in both the *Sentences* and the *Summa,* Aquinas describes the will as a principle of action. As a connatural appetitive harmony or agreement *(convenientia),* love is the principle that underlies all that the agent does. In addition, in his early and later works Aquinas recognizes love's relationship to union. Love both presupposes union and likeness between lover and beloved, and causes deeper union. It causes mutual indwelling between lover and beloved, and even an ecstasy that draws the lover out of himself and toward the beloved. Lastly, in both his early and later works Aquinas discerns a twofold tendency in love: the action of love is directed toward a person (in the love of friendship) and toward the good we affirm for that person (in the love of concupiscence).

As we have just seen, however, Aquinas in his later works introduces a series of changes that delineate more clearly the interaction and mutual dependence existing between knowledge and love. While in the *Commentary on the Sentences* Aquinas defined love in terms of form, in the *Summa theologiae* he now reserves form to the intellect and describes love as an aptitude, proportion, or *complacentia* of the appetite for the loved object that arises in conjunction with the cognitive form. Viewed in this way, love ceases to be primarily the terminus of an action, as it had been in his earlier presentation, and becomes a principle of action. It becomes the principle underlying both desire and enjoyment. In developing this theme Aquinas outlines how each key feature of love involves not only appetite but also cognition. Love both depends on the form of the beloved existing in the intellect and directs the intellect in the specification of that form. Aquinas makes it clear that as the principle of action, love in the will is also the principle of the intellect's action on the level of exercise. This recognition enables Aquinas to integrate knowledge and love more closely. Knowledge specifies our loves, while love directs our knowledge. As we shall see, this closer integration of knowledge and love has implications for Aquinas' theory of love's role in the pursuit of happiness, in practical reasoning, and in living the virtues.

Knowledge and Love in Human Happiness

Before turning our attention to love's relationship to knowledge in practical reasoning, it will be helpful to acknowledge briefly the influence St. Thomas' theory of love has on his description of happiness. Thomas describes happiness as both an operation and that which we attain through this operation.[73] Ultimately, God is our happiness. Secondarily, happiness is an operation of the spiritual soul. Our happiness is to know and love God. Indeed, we attain our ultimate end "by knowing and by loving God."[74] We are naturally ordered to this twofold activity by the natural principles in the intellect and the natural love in the will.[75] Aquinas, however, is very clear that although happiness involves acts of the will, the act of happiness is essentially an operation of the intellect.[76] The intellect is the power that conforms to the essences of things. The operation that constitutes our happiness is the intellectual act of attaining God in the vision of the divine essence.[77] The will, for its part, is the power that moves us toward our happiness and delights in that happiness once it is attained.

St. Augustine had described happiness as "joy in the truth."[78] Since joy is an act of the will,[79] it would seem that the operation that constitutes our happiness is an act of the will. Aquinas, however, is emphatic that happiness is the will's object, not its act. The distinction is subtle and disarmingly simple. As we have seen, love is the will's fundamental

73. *ST* I-II 3.1; *ST* I-II 5.2. See also *ST* I 26.3; *ST* I 26.3 ad 2.

74. *ST* I-II 1.8: *"cognoscendo et amando deum."*

75. *ST* I-II 4.3.

76. *ST* I-II 3.4.

77. *ST* I 12.9 ad 1.

78. Augustine, *Confessiones* 10.23 (*PL* 32, 793). See *ST* I-II 3.4.

79. See *ST* I-II 31.4.

act. Love underlies desire (when the loved object is absent) and delight (when the loved object is present). If the act of love itself were the operation that constituted human happiness, this would mean that we would be happy, whether or not we had what we desired. In other words, we would be happy merely by loving, whether or not our love underlay desire or delight. The only other alternative would be to affirm that we attain our ultimate end merely in and through an act of the will, such that desire becomes delight in the very act of loving something. This amounts to saying that desire of itself causes the ultimate end to be present. Aquinas reveals the absurdity of this view by drawing a comparison with money.

> If money were attained by an act of will, then the covetous person would have it from the first instant that he wished for it. But at that moment it is absent. He attains it by grasping it in his hand, or in some like manner; and then he delights in the money got.[80]

Consequently, since it is by our intellects that we grasp *(apprehendere)* the spiritual good we desire, the essence of happiness is an act of the intellect. The will moves us toward this act and delights in this act once attained.

Aquinas is here again developing the implications of his theory of love's relationship to knowledge. "The intellect apprehends the end before the will does, yet motion towards the end begins in the will."[81]

> Accordingly, the vision of God: as a vision, it is an act of the intellect, but as a good and an end, it is the object of the will, and in this way it is the enjoyment of it. Thus, the intellect attains this end as the acting power, but the will as the power moving toward the end and enjoying the end once attained.[82]

The will's object is the universal good which it attains through the intellect. As long as anything less than universal good is present in the intellect, the will moves the intellect—and the soul's other powers—to seek that object which is universally good, that object which is perfect and will bring the human person to perfection.[83] The will is here acting as an

80. *ST* I-II 3.4.
81. *ST* I-II 3.4 ad 3. See also *ST* I-II 4.4 ad 2.
82. *ST* I-II 11.1 ad 1.
83. See *ST* I-II 5.8 corpus, ad 2 and ad 3.

efficient cause. More accurately, the human agent moves himself toward happiness through the action of his will. Hence, the attainment of happiness requires the rectitude of the will: that the will be rightly ordered to those things that lead to ultimate happiness.[84] The intellect, for its part, functions as a specifying or formal cause, uniting the agent in a certain way with the divine essence or form.[85]

The different types of causality exercised by the intellect and will in knowing and loving establish two distinct relationships between them. "Love ranks above knowledge in moving, but knowledge precedes love in attaining: for 'nothing is loved unless it be known.'"[86] The will always acts as informed by the intellect.[87] Hence, the vision of God is a higher good *(principalius bonum)* than the will's act of delighting in God.[88] Yet, since the love of charity moves us to penetrate the very depths of God and brings our knowledge of God to its perfection, "to love God is something greater than to know him, especially while one is in this life."[89] The insights that shape his treatment of happiness, therefore, are rooted in his psychology of love and his understanding of love's relationship to knowledge. Love has priority in one way, knowledge has priority in another. Consequently, happiness is an activity involving and perfecting both one's intellect and will. The search for happiness begins and ends in one's knowledge and love of God, inchoate in the beginning, perfect when one attains the end. The motion from beginning to end is through practical reasoning and the virtues. It is to a consideration of love's relationship to knowledge in these facets of human action that we now turn.

84. *ST* I-II 4.4.

85. *ST* I 12.2 ad 3; *ST* I 12.5 ad 3.

86. *ST* I-II 3.4 ad 4: *"dilectio praeeminet cognitioni in movendo, sed cognitio praevia est dilectioni in attingendo, 'non enim diligitur nisi cognitum.'"*

87. *ST* I-II 5.8 ad 2.

88. *ST* I-II 4.2.

89. *ST* II-II 27.4 ad 2.

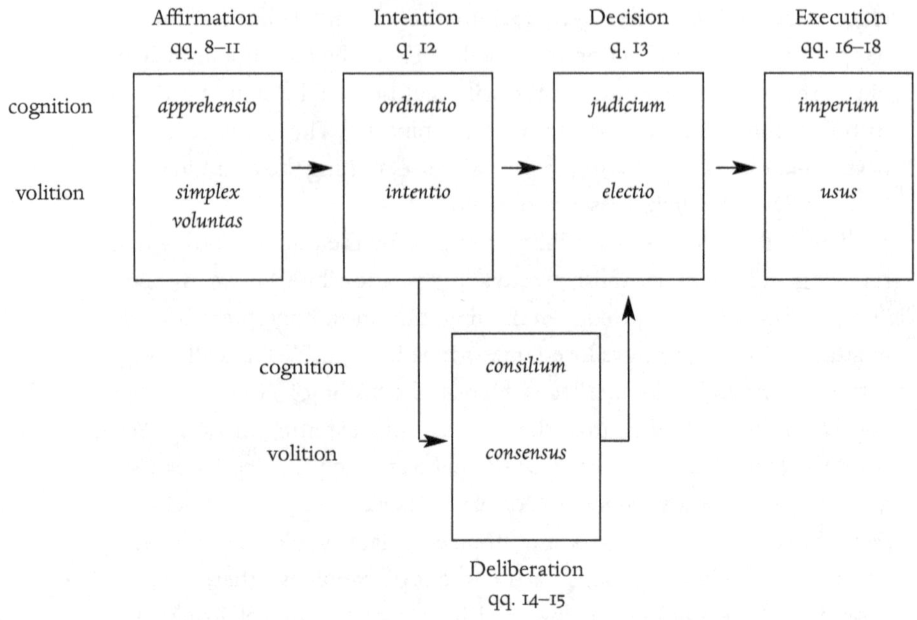

FIGURE 1. Stages of Action

Knowledge and Love in Practical Reasoning

Love and the Stages of Action

St. Thomas begins the *Prima secundae* by affirming that properly human acts, acts for which we are morally responsible, are those that flow from intellect and will. They are what Thomas calls acts of a "deliberated will."[90] After demonstrating that the human person acts for an end, and after investigating the nature of the happiness that is the human person's ultimate end (*ST* I-II 1–5), Thomas traces the stages of deliberation that underlie the properly human act (*ST* I-II 6–17). In other words, he analyzes the intellectual and voluntary components underlying a deliberated will.

A fully human act is the product of a four stage (sometimes five

90. *ST* I-II 1.1; *ST* I-II 1.3.

stage) process, each stage of which contains a cognitive and a voluntary component (see figure 1).[91] First, there is the apprehension of some good and a corresponding simple act of the will *(simplex voluntas* or *velle)*. This is to know and will some good. This twofold act, however, only becomes a principle of action when we intend to attain the known good through some means. This occurs at the second stage: intention. In an act that Aquinas describes as an *"ordinatio,"* practical reason apprehends the good as an end attainable by us (although we may not yet specifically know or have chosen the means to this end) and the will intends the good as an attainable end. Next, reason then specifies something as the appropriate means and the will chooses it. This stage of the process can occur with or without deliberation. If there is uncertainty about what means are possible, reason and will deliberate—through reason's counsel and the will's consent—about which means are desirable. Whether or not reason and will pass through the stage of deliberation, reason must judge that some act is an appropriate means and the will must choose it.[92] Lastly, reason commands the powers of the soul to undertake the chosen act and the will moves these powers to act. It "uses" them.[93]

When we analyze the stages of action in the context of Aquinas' theory of love, the question of love's relationship to these stages begins to

91. This figure is a modified version of a schematic developed by Daniel Westberg in *Right Practical Reason*, 131. I have revised Westberg's schematic by adding a preliminary stage neglected by Westberg, which I have labeled "affirmation." My views on this preliminary stage have been influenced by Servais Pinckaers' analysis. See Pinckaers, "La structure de l'acte humain," 393–412.

92. It would no doubt be at this point in the process that the drama of conscience would unfold. As we noted earlier, Aquinas in his later works never explicitly explains the relationship between conscience and the particular judgment of choice that leads to action. If Ralph McInerny is correct—that Aquinas' mature description of the incontinent person demonstrates that Aquinas still distinguishes between conscience, as a judgment of particulars that does not necessarily lead to action, and the judgment of choice that results in action—then the judgment of conscience would take place at the threshold of decision (see figure 1). In the incontinent person, between the judgment of conscience and decision a major premise (such as all pleasure is to be pursued) intervenes and becomes the major in the act of decision. Yet, as McInerny notes, in the virtuous person the judgment of conscience flows into the judgment of choice. See McInerny, *Aquinas on Human Action*, 225–231.

93. *ST* I-II 17.3 ad 1.

emerge. The first thing to recognize is that Aquinas is not as clear as we would like concerning love's place in the stages of action. Nevertheless, there are elements in his account of action that enable us to see that Aquinas does intend to integrate his theory of love into these stages. This intention becomes apparent when we recognize that Aquinas integrates the two terms most central to Augustine's theory of love *(frui* and *uti)* into his description of the stages of action. In Augustine's view, charity is the love whereby we enjoy *(frui)* God for his own sake and "use" *(uti)* other things by referring them toward our enjoyment of God.[94] This distinction became the starting point of subsequent analyses

94. Augustine in the *De doctrina christiana* defines charity in the following way: "I call 'charity' the motion of the soul toward the enjoyment of God for his own sake, and the enjoyment of one's self and of one's neighbor for the sake of God" (3.10 [16]). Elsewhere Augustine explains that to enjoy *(frui)* is to "cling to something with love for its own sake" (*De doctrina christiana* 1.4 [4]). Strictly speaking, we should only enjoy God. God alone is one to whom we should cling with love for his own sake. On the other hand, Augustine affirms that when we speak of enjoying our neighbor for the sake of God, it would be more accurate to say that we are "using" *(uti)* our neighbor. Augustine does not mean to imply that we should treat others in a purely utilitarian or exploitative fashion. The Latin term *"uti"* has a richer meaning than this. For example, Lewis and Short tell us that *uti* can mean *"to enjoy the friendship of* any one; *to be familiar* or *intimate with, to associate with* a person" (*A Latin Dictionary Founded on Andrews' Edition of Freund's Latin Dictionary,* revised, enlarged, and in great part rewritten by Charlton Lewis [and Charles Short] [Oxford: Clarendon Press, 1991], 1947). Hence, Cicero can describe the man he introduces to the Proconsul of Cilicia as *"quo multos annos utor valde familiariter,"* which the Loeb translation renders, "who has for many years been a very intimate friend of mine" (Marcus Tullius Cicero, *Letters to his Friends,* volume 1, translated by W. Glynn Williams, Loeb Classical Library [Cambridge, Mass.: Harvard University Press, 1979], book 1, letter 3, n. 1, pages 12–13). Augustine employs the term *uti* to underline that we should refer the joy we have in our love for others toward God, toward the one from whom all true joy springs and in whom all true joy finds lasting fulfillment. Thus, Augustine defines *uti* as "to refer that which comes into use toward obtaining that which you love" (*De doctrina christiana* 1.4 [4]. See also *De trinitate* 10.13.). He recognizes that *uti* can signify more generally the act of "drawing something *(assumere aliquid)* into the faculty of the will," and thus even enjoyment can be viewed as a type of using (*De trinitate* 10.17. See *ST* I 39.8). Nonetheless, the proper note that Augustine wishes to convey with the term *uti* is the note of reference: to use something is to refer it to another. Aquinas follows Augustine on this point: *"uti, sicut dictum est, importat applicationem alicuius ad aliquid"* (*ST* I-II 16.3). For a fuller analysis of Augustine's distinction between *frui* and *uti,* see Oliver O'Donovan, *"Usus* and *Fruitio* in Augustine, *De doctrina christiana I,"* *Journal of Theological Studies* 33 (1982): 361–397; William Riordan O'Connor, "The *Uti/Frui* Distinction in Augustine's Ethics," *Augustinian Studies* 14 (1983): 45–62.

of charity in the Latin West.[95] Peter Lombard, for example, gives it a prominent place in the *Sentences.*[96] Even authors such as William of Auxerre and Philip the Chancellor, who attempt in their *Summae* to go beyond Augustine's formulation, continue to employ the distinction between enjoyment and use in their own treatments of charity.[97] When, therefore, Aquinas inserts questions on "enjoyment" and "use" into his analysis of the stages of action, the significance of this placement would not have been lost on his contemporaries. Anyone familiar with Augustine's treatment of love would have seen that Aquinas was placing love at the heart of his theory of action.

The significance of Aquinas' placement of the questions on enjoyment and use becomes clearer when we consider Aquinas' theory that the will has a twofold relationship to its object. In his analysis of *usus* and its relationship to *electio,* Aquinas offers the following distinction.

> The will has a twofold relation to the thing willed. One according as the thing willed is in a certain way in the willer, through a kind of proportion or order to the thing willed. Hence even those things that are naturally proportionate to a certain end are said to desire that end naturally.—Yet to have an end in this way is to have it imperfectly. Now every imperfect thing tends to perfection. Thus, both the natural and the voluntary appetite tend toward having the end itself in reality, which is to have it perfectly. This is the second relation of the will to the thing willed.[98]

95. This is not to say that all later authors agreed with Augustine or employed his distinction. In fact, disputes arose in the 1130's precisely over the adequacy of Augustine's definition of charity (See Robert Wielockx, "La discussion scolastique sur l'amour d'Anselme de Laon à Pierre Lombard d'après les imprimés et les inédits" [Ph.D. diss., Catholic University of Louvain, 1981], 300–306). Nevertheless, even those who disagreed with Augustine were forced to grapple with his categories.

96. Peter Lombard, *Libri iv sententiarum, liber* i, *distinctio* 1, *capitula* 2–3. For more on the centrality of the *uti/frui* distinction in Peter Lombard's *Sentences,* see Romanus Cessario, "Toward Understanding Aquinas' Theological Method: the Early Twelfth-Century Experience," in *Studies in Thomistic Theology,* edited by Paul Lockey (Houston: Center for Thomistic Studies, 1995), 52–57; Marie-Dominique Chenu, *Toward Understanding Saint Thomas,* translated by A.-M. Landry and D. Hughes (Chicago: Regnery, 1964), 309–310.

97. See Philip the Chancellor, *Summa de bono, liber* 3, *capitulum* 3 *(De caritate), questiones* 4–5; William of Auxerre, *Summa aurea, liber* 2, *tractatus* 2, *capitula* 1–3; *liber* 3, *tractatus* 36, *capitula* 1–2.

98. *ST* I-II 16.4.

In this passage Aquinas first offers a general statement—"the will has a twofold relation to the thing willed"—and then provides the specific example of the will's relationship to the end: the first relation of the will to the end is by having a proportion or order to that end. The second relation of the will toward the end is by the will having the end perfectly and in reality.

Aquinas next explains that the will has this twofold relationship not only with the end, but also with the means, with "those things that are ordered to the end."[99] He then identifies which acts generate the will's first and second relations to the means.

> The last thing that pertains to the first relation *(habitudo)* of the will toward the means is choice, for there the will becomes fully proportionate by willing the means fully. Use, however, pertains to the second relation of the will, by which it tends toward attaining the thing willed.[100]

We might be tempted to think that the "thing willed" mentioned at the end of the second sentence refers to the means. This would imply that the will's second relation to the willed object is not perfect attainment but the tendency toward perfect attainment.[101] Yet, just as the second relation of the will to the end is not tendency to the end, but perfect attainment of the end,[102] so too, the will's second relation to the means is not tendency to the means but union with the means. (Hence, "the thing willed" referred to here is the end.) Aquinas makes this clear in a later article, when he states that "use in the user is united to the thing used."[103] Aquinas defines use as "the application of one thing to another," and explains that the "thing used" is the means.[104] When the will applies the means to the end, the will is united to the means.[105] Hence, two

99. Ibid.

100. Ibid.

101. Cf. Stephen Brock, "What is the Use of *Usus* in Aquinas's Psychology of Action," in *Moral and Political Philosophies in the Middle Ages,* edited by B. Carlos Bazán, Eduardo Andújar, Leonard G. Sbrocchi (Ottowa: Legas, 1995), vol. 2, 658.

102. *ST* I-II 16.4; *ST* I-II 11.4.

103. *ST* I-II 17.3.

104. *ST* I-II 16.3.

105. Indeed, it is precisely because the second relation of the will to the means unites the will to the means that the second relation can be that "by which [the will] tends toward attaining" the end.

distinct acts of the will generate two distinct relations to the means willed. First, the act of *electio* causes a *proportio* toward the means, toward that which is *ad finem,* to exist in the will. Second, the act of *usus* causes the will to be united to the means in the way a cause is united to its effect: they are simultaneously in act and are in motion together toward the desired end.[106]

Although in question sixteen Aquinas describes the first and second relations of the will toward the end, he does not name the acts of will that generate these two relations. This is not surprising since the issue under consideration is the relationship between choice and use, both of which are acts directed toward the means. If Aquinas were going to name the acts that generate relations toward the end, we would expect him to do so in the questions that consider the acts of will directed toward the end. This is exactly what he does. In his analysis of enjoyment *(fruitio)* he makes the following distinction.

> To enjoy implies a certain comparison of the will to the ultimate end, according as the will has something with respect to the ultimate end. Now an end is had in two ways, perfectly and imperfectly. Perfectly, when it is had not only in intention but also in reality; imperfectly, when it is had in intention only. Perfect enjoyment, therefore, is of the end already had in reality; while imperfect enjoyment is also of the end had, yet not in reality, but only in intention.[107]

As in the earlier cited passage, Aquinas distinguishes between perfect and imperfect attainment of the end. Here, however, he also names the acts. Intention attains the end imperfectly, while perfect enjoyment (enjoyment properly so called) attains the end perfectly. Placed in the language of the earlier cited passage, Aquinas seems to be saying that *intention* is the act that establishes the will's first relation to the end, while *enjoyment* is the act that establishes the will's second relation to the end.

The parallel between Aquinas' two descriptions is almost exact. He describes both "enjoyment" (11.4) and the unnamed act proper to the "second relation" (16.4) as having the end in reality *(realiter* or *in re).*[108]

106. Brock, "What is the Use of *Usus,*" 654–664.

107. *ST* I-II 11.4.

108. Ibid. and *ST* I-I 16.4.

Moreover, both "intention" and the unnamed act proper to the "first relation" attain the end imperfectly. The one discontinuity between the two accounts is that while in 16.4 Aquinas describes the act of the first relation as establishing a "proportion or order" between the will and the end, in 11.4 he does not explicitly describe intention in this way. Nonetheless, in the very next question Aquinas portrays intention as the act whereby the will is "ordered" by reason toward a specific end.[109] Thus, like choice, intention is also an order or proportion: it is the will's ordered proportion to the end. Consequently, when we read these two passages together, we can discern the following parallel progressions (see figure 2). The process moves from the will's first relation to the end to the will's second relation to the end, through the will's first and second relations to the means. Specifically, there is intention, which entails a proportion to the end, followed by choice, which causes a proportion to the means. Then there is use, which unites the will to the means, followed by enjoyment resulting from union with the end.

Aquinas' distinction between the will's first and second relations to its object becomes significant when we recognize that Aquinas reserves Augustine's terms for love to the second relations. *Use* pertains to the will's second relation to the means, while *enjoyment* pertains to the will's second relation to the end. Aquinas' insight is that Augustine's analysis of love primarily focuses on union and attainment. Enjoyment is union with the end, while use is union with that which is ordered to the end.[110] As we have seen, however, Aquinas affirms that love has an even more fundamental meaning. In Aquinas' view, love properly so called is more fundamentally a principle of action. It is the principle that underlies all action. From this perspective, enjoyment and use are love's activities. They are what love is when the will is united to the end and to the things that are ordered to the end.[111] Underlying both these activities, however, is love as the primary appetitive principle of action. This fact gives added meaning to Aquinas' description of the will's first relation to its object. As we have seen, he describes it as a proportion.

109. *ST* I-II 12.1 ad 3; *ST* I-II 12.3 ad 2.

110. *ST* I 43.3.

111. *ST* II-II 28.4. St. Thomas describes *gaudium* as the proper act of charity (*ST* II-II 28.4 ad 1).

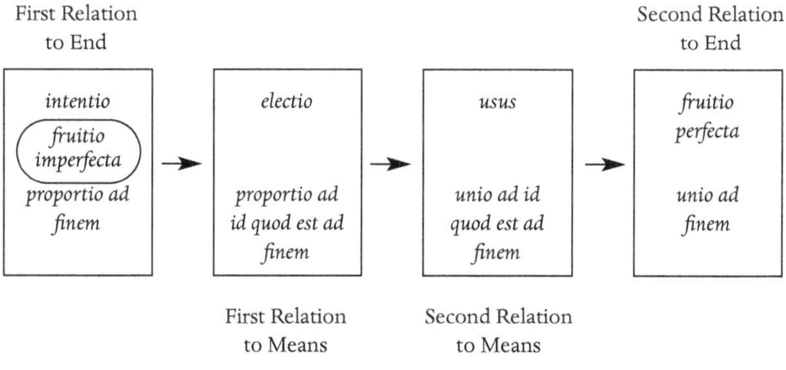

FIGURE 2. Will's Relations to the End

In the *Summa theologiae,* Aquinas refers to a "proportion" in the will in only one other context: in his analysis of love.

> Whatever tends to an end first has an aptitude or proportion to that end; second, it is moved to that end; third, it rests in the end after having attained it. Now, the very aptitude or proportion of the appetite to good is love, which is complacency in good.[112]

After introducing in his analysis of action the notion of a proportion in the will, he now reveals in his treatment of love that this proportion is nothing other than love itself. The proportion proper to the will's first relation to its object is love. Love establishes the will's relation to both the end and those things that are ordered to the end.[113] More precisely, intention, by producing in the will a proportion for the end, generates love for the end; choice, by producing in the will a proportion for the means, generates love for the means. Consequently, we can describe Aquinas' portrayal of the will's relationship to its object as follows (see figure 3). The will's first relation to the end is love of the end, while its second relation to the end is love's perfect act, enjoyment of the end. The will's first relation to the means is love of the means, while its second relation to the means is use of the means.

112. *ST* I-II 25.2. See also *ST* I-II 25.
113. *ST* I-II 26.4.

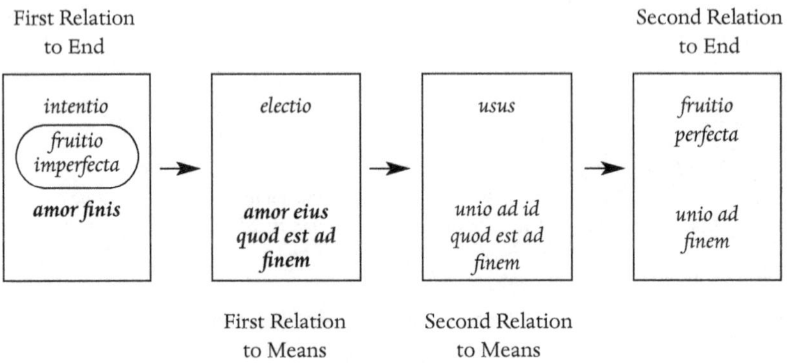

FIGURE 3. Love and Will's Relations to the End

One way of understanding love's role in action is to view the distinction between love of friendship and love of concupiscence as corresponding to the distinction between the end and that which is ordered to the end. From this perspective, love of friendship is the will's proportion to the end, while love of concupiscence is the will's proportion to that which is ordered to the end.[114] On one level, this way of portraying love's place in the stages of action is too simplistic, because the love of friendship is always directed toward a person, while the particular end of an act is an operation and thus is loved with the love of concupiscence. On a deeper level, however, the portrayal is accurate because love of some person always underlies the ends we pursue in action. (The operation that is the end of our act is always simultaneously union with and enjoyment of our beloved.) Ultimately, some person (oneself or another) is always the final goal of all our actions. We always do what we do for love of someone.[115]

Integral to Aquinas' account is the recognition that this personal love

114. See, for example, *ST* I-II 26.4.

115. Aquinas explains that even when we act for love of some person or thing, an operation stands between us and the person or thing that is the end of our action. Thus, for example, although on one level the goal of a miser's action is money, on another level the miser's goal is the act of enjoying the money. Consequently, as we have seen, the ultimate end of all our actions, happiness, is both a thing and an operation whereby we are united to that thing (See *ST* I-II 3.1).

exists prior to and is more fundamental than love's role as a principle of action. Before becoming the principle of our subsequent actions, love already exists as a response to the goodness and value of a person. This is love at the level of the will's *simplex voluntas* arising in response to reason's recognition of a person's goodness.[116] At this level, love already contains both its personal *(amor amicitiae)* and concupiscible *(amor concupiscentiae)* components, but at this point the good that we will for the beloved is simply the good of existence. "The first thing that one wills for a friend is that he be and live."[117] Love at this level is the affirmation, "It's good that you exist."[118] Only subsequently do we then will particular good things for our beloved and direct our actions accordingly.[119] In other words, before love is a principle of action, love is a response to value. It is a response to God's goodness, to rational creatures' fellowship in this goodness, and to the goodness proper to non-rational creatures in their ordered relationship to God and our fellowship with him.[120]

Love becomes a principle of action only when we recognize that (a) fuller union with our beloved is possible through some means, or (b) we can attain some good for our beloved (for ourselves or for another) through some means. In other words, love becomes a principle of action when we recognize our beloved as an end toward which we can order our actions. From the perspective of Aquinas' description of the stages of action, love functions as a principle of action by underlying these stages. First, there is the primal stage of love where in a simple act of *vol-*

116. *Super librum dionysii de divinis nominibus* (henceforth cited as *In divinis nominibus*) 4.11: *"primum enim in quolibet genere oportet esse simplex, unde cum primus motus appetitus sit amor, oportet quod simplex sit."*

117. *ST* II-II 25.7.

118. Pieper, *About Love,* 22; reprinted in *Faith, Hope, Love,* 167. The entire second chapter of this work offers refreshing insights into this aspect of Aquinas' thought (*About Love,* 18–25; *Faith, Hope, Love,* 163–172).

119. We see this progression described when we read the above cited sentence from *ST* II-II 25.7 in its larger context: "every friend first wills for his friend to be and to live; second, he wills good things for him; third, he does good things for him; forth, he lives with him joyfully; fifth, he agrees with him, as rejoicing and sorrowing in the same things." See also *ST* I 20.2.

120. *ST* I 20.2. See also *ST* I 20.2 ad 3. From Aquinas' perspective, the difference between God's love and our love can be expressed as follows. God's love essentially proclaims, "Let there be," while our love is an "Amen" to the objects of that creative love.

untas the will affirms the goodness of some person known through cognition. The intellect beholds and recognizes someone's goodness and the will affirms it in the primal act of love. This act can be complete in itself as an act of loving contemplation. (In such a case it is an "action" and is thus itself the product of the very process we seek to describe: i.e., it is an act we freely choose to do in a choice that is the product of the four stages described above.) More often this primal stage is embedded in the recognition of some more mediate good: in the recognition and affirmation of some action or thing as good for us or for our beloved. Love of this action becomes the principle of our own action when we recognize it as attainable by us through some means. Only then does the will move from *simplex voluntas* to *intentio;* only then does the will's *proportio* for a good become a *proportio* for an end.[121]

At this point in the process love is still not complete as a principle of action. In the act of intention, the will desires the existence of the end, but does not yet desire any specific means to that end. Only after the intellect has judged and the will has chosen specific means to the desired end is the will "proportioned" to the means; only then does the will begin to love *(amor concupiscentiae)* those means. The transition to action properly so called can now occur, as the agent moves him or herself to act in the will's act of use.

Love's Receptivity and Free Choice

In the context of the goals of our current study, two aspects of love's role in the structure of practical reasoning merit closer attention: love's dependence on knowledge and its relationship to free choice.

At each stage of the process love acts as a principle in and through knowledge. Enjoyment of the end occurs through knowledge of the end. Use of the means occurs through reason's command concerning the means. The proportion for the means (love of the means) arising

121. The distinction between good and end should not be exaggerated. The good is always simultaneously an end, but in *simplex voluntas* the good in question is an end by being that in which the will already rests, even if the will is resting in it as something present only in thought. This good becomes the end of a further action only when reason estimates that we can be more fully united to it by some further action.

from choice presupposes reason's judgment about the means, while the will's proportion for the end (love of the end) arising from intention presupposes reason's ordering apprehension of the end. Underlying each of these stages is the will's loving affirmation *(simplex voluntas)* of some good resulting from the intellect's knowledge of that good.

Notice that Aquinas does not define love's primary act apart from its object. Love is not merely *complacentia,* it is *complacentia boni:* it is an affective enjoyment and affirmation of some good thing made known to us by reason. In other words, love's object is the *bonum rationis.*[122] Love's dependence on knowledge at this most basic level (the stage that I have called affirmation) has profound implications for Aquinas' entire theory of action. It means that for Aquinas love, and thus also human action, presupposes a voluntary receptivity to reality. At its most basic level, love is a response to the goodness of reality, a response to the real as it is or as it could be. Before reason assesses whether a particular good is fully attainable by us, reason first recognizes it as a good that is somehow already in harmony with us. It is a part of the same creation in which we participate and as such is something we can already celebrate and enjoy. Love as *complacentia boni* in the act of *simplex voluntas* is this affective response to the goodness of created being, and ultimately to the goodness of God.

This leads us to the threshold between theoretical and practical reason, between contemplation and action. "Contemplation of spiritual beauty or goodness is the beginning of spiritual love. Hence knowledge is the cause of love for the same reason as good is, which cannot be loved unless it be known."[123] Thomas recognizes that "from the very fact that truth is the end of contemplation [i.e., the end of a human operation], it has the aspect of a good that is desirable, lovable and delightful."[124] All creation can be regarded as the goal of our action from the very fact that it can be known and loved by us. Before any particular

122. *Quaestio disputata de caritate* (henceforth cited as *De caritate*) 2: *"voluntati eius naturaliter inest huius boni amor, quod est bonum rationis." ST* I-II 50.5 ad 3: *"voluntas ex ipsa natura potentiae inclinatur in bonum rationis."*

123. *ST* I-II 27.2.

124. *ST* II-II 180.1 ad 1.

thing becomes the goal of a more specific action on our part (in the act of intention), it is already the goal of our knowledge and loving delight (in the act of *simplex voluntas*). In other words, underlying the will's character as a principle of action is a receptivity to created goodness. At the heart of human agency there is a certain receptive passivity.

The moment we recognize passivity in the will we are confronted with the question of freedom. Many of Aquinas' contemporaries feared that to acknowledge receptivity in the will was to endanger or deny human freedom.[125] This concern was present in the condemnations of 1270.[126] Recent commentators also share this same concern.[127] The con-

125. See, for example, William de la Mare's concerns expressed in his *Correctorium fratris thomae,* and a reaction to them in a document known as *"Quare"* (P Glorieux, *Les premières polémiques thomistes: I.—Le* Correctorium corruptorii "quare," *Bibliothèque thomiste* 9 (Kain, Belgium: Le Saulchoir, 1927), 230–240. For more on reactions to theories that recognized a passive element in the will, see Bonnie Kent, *Virtues of the Will: the Transformation of Ethics in the Late Thirteenth Century* (Washington, D.C.: The Catholic University of America Press, 1995), 117–149. See also Odon Lottin, *Psychologie et morale aux xiie et xiiie siècles* (Louvain: Abbaye du Mont César, 1942), volume 1, 226–389; A. San Cristobal-Sebastian, *Controversias acerca de la Voluntad desde 1270–1300* (Madrid: Editorial y Libreria Co. Cul., 1958); Vernon J. Bourke, *Will in Western Thought: an Historico-Critical Survey* (New York: Sheed and Ward, 1964), 84–88.

126. For example, the ninth thesis condemned by the Bishop of Paris, Étienne Tempier, in 1270 reads: *"Quod liberum arbitrium est potentia passiva, non activa; et quod necessitate movetur ab appetibili."* At first glance this thesis seems close to St. Thomas' view. Notice, however, that while Thomas affirms that the will is a passive potency, the condemned thesis affirms that *liberum arbitrium* is a passive potency, something that Thomas never held. See H. Denifle and A. Chatelain, *Chartularium universitatis parisiensis* (Paris: Frairs Delalain, 1889), vol. I, 486–487. For an English translation of the thirteen theses, see James Weisheipl, *Friar Thomas d'Aquino. His Life, Thought and Works,* 2nd edition (Washington, D.C.: The Catholic University of America Press, 1983), 276, or J. Wippel and A. Wolter, *Medieval Philosophy from St. Augustine to Nicholas of Cusa* (New York: Free Press, 1969), 366. For the historical context of the condemnations of 1270, see John F. Wippel, "The Condemnations of 1270 and 1277 at Paris," *Journal of Medieval and Renaissance Studies* 7 (1977): 169–201.

127. Odon Lottin, "Liberté humaine et motion divine de s. Thomas d'Aquin à la condamnation de 1277," *Recherches de théologie ancienne et médiévale* 7 (1935): 52–69, 156–173; Bernard Lonergan, "St. Thomas's Thought on *Gratia operans,*" *Theological Studies* 3 (1942): 69–88; Klaus Riesenhuber, "The Bases and Meaning of Freedom in Thomas Aquinas," *Proceedings of the American Catholic Philosophical Association* 48 (1974): 99–111; Otto Pesch, "Philosophie und Theologie der Freiheit bei Thomas von Aquin in *Quaest. disp. VI De malo:* ein Diskussionsbeitung," *Münchener Theologische Zeitung* 13 (1962): 1–25; H. M. Manteau-Bonamy, "La liberté de l'homme selon Thomas d'Aquin: la datation de la question

demnations of 1270 probably influenced Aquinas in his later work: for example, in the works composed after 1270 Aquinas avoids referring to the will as a "passive power." Nevertheless, the change in terminology should not blind us to the fact that Aquinas even in his later works continues to affirm a fundamental receptivity in the will.[128] Aquinas wrote the questions on love after the condemnations of 1270 and in them he presents love belonging to a passive power *(vis passiva)* and as caused by the goodness of things made know to us through cognition.[129]

As we saw in the previous chapter, what saves Aquinas' theory from determinism is his recognition that the will's receptivity toward any particular good is freely chosen. Love's primary act is rooted in a receptivity before the real, but this receptivity is not deterministic. We love the goods we perceive, but we can choose not to see them, or we can choose to consider them under the aspect of their limited goodness and thus as not good here and now.[130] In the language of *ST* I-II 9.1 and 10.2, although knowledge has priority on the level of specification, love has priority on the level of exercise. This implies that although an act of *simplex voluntas* underlies our acts and the process of choosing those acts, this *simplex voluntas* is itself an act we freely choose. In other words, although a primal act of love underlies our future acts and the cognitive

disputée *De malo," Archives d'histoire doctrinale et littéraire du moyen âge* 46 (1979): 7–34. Keenan, *Goodness and Rightness,* 26–34.

128. Even in later works Aquinas is willing to describe the will as a passive potency or principle (*ST* I-II 51.2; *ST* I-II 18.2 ad 3; *ST* I-II 51.3). Aquinas remained true to the insight that any power that receives a *habitus* (i.e., an acquired or infused operative virtue) must be something that is acted upon. Even those powers that are active principles of action, if they receive habits, must also be acted upon or moved; thus, they must contain some passivity. They are both an *"agens"* and an *"acta"* or *"mota."* (See *De virtutibus in commune* 1). Even in his later works he explicitly describes these powers as passive potencies: *"subiectum habitus est potentia passiva"* (*ST* I-II 54.1). He explicitly recognizes that the will is this type of *agens et acta* power, describing it as *"susceptiva habitualis inclinationis"* (*De virtutibus in communi* 8). See also objections where Aquinas responds to the problems inherent in calling the will a passive power: *ST* I-II 6.4 obj. 2; *ST* I-II 77.1 obj. 1; *De malo* 6 obj. 7. In responding to these objections he qualifies but does not deny the will's passivity. See especially *De malo* 6 ad 7, where Aquinas describes the will as *"in potentia."*

129. *ST* I-II 27.1.

130. Aquinas notes that before reason's act of *imperium*—and presupposed in the act—is an act of usus in the will (*ST* I-II 17.3; *ST* I-II 16.4). On love's ability to reflect on itself, see *ST* II-II 25.2.

and affective stages that lead us to choose those acts, this primal act of love is itself a human act, and as such it is something we have freely chosen.

Yet, to affirm that the will's primary act of love is something we freely choose confronts Aquinas' theory of love with the same problem we addressed in our analysis of action in the previous chapter. It confronts it with an apparently infinite regression: the principle underlying our freely chosen love seems to imply a previously freely chosen act of love, and so on to infinity. If this is the case, how do we ever choose to love something? In the previous chapter we saw that Aquinas resolves the question of the ground of human agency by appealing to the natural principles that underlie the intellect and will. Reason commands all of the will's acts except the will's first act, which is instilled in it by nature, while the will moves the intellect to engage in all its acts except the intellect's first act, which is instilled in it by nature.

As we have seen, the ultimate source of these natural principles is God himself: "What first moves the will and the intellect is something above the will and the intellect, namely God."[131] On the level of specification the will necessarily wills certain things. It wills God and those things that are ordered to God. Yet, on the level of exercise (on the level of willing or not willing), this is not the case. Since God moves all things according to their nature, on the level of exercise "he also moves the will according to its condition, not from necessity, but as relating indeterminately to many."[132] Consequently, the will is even able to direct the agent to not think of happiness and thus not to will it.[133]

Once we learn that love is the principle of the will's actions,[134] we discover that Aquinas' description of the will's relationship to its natural principles also describes intellectual love's relationship to natural love. Aquinas makes this clear in his analysis of love in the angels. "There exists in angels a natural love *(dilectio naturalis)* and an elective love *(dilectio*

131. *De malo* 6: *"id quod primo movet voluntatem et intellectum, sit aliquid supra voluntatem et intellectum, scilicet deus."* See also *ST* I-II 109.2 ad 1.

132. *De malo* 6: *"[is] etiam voluntatem movet secundum eius conditionem, non ut ex necessitate, sed ut indeterminate se habentem ad multa."*

133. *De malo* 6.

134. *ST* I 20.1.

electiva). Their natural love is the principle of their elective love."[135] To explain this Aquinas turns to the example of human love.

This is clear in humans concerning both intellect and will. For the intellect knows principles naturally, and from such knowledge there is caused in us knowledge of conclusions, which are known by us not naturally, but by discovery or by teaching. Similarly, the end functions in the will in the same way that a principle functions in the intellect, as is said in book two of the *Physics.* Consequently, the will tends naturally to its last end, for everyone naturally wills happiness. All other acts of the will are caused by this natural act of the will, since whatever humans will they will on account of an end. Therefore, the love of the good that we naturally will as an end, is natural love *(dilectio naturalis),* while the love derived from this, whereby we love a good for the sake of the end, is elective love *(dilectio electiva).*[136]

The will's natural love is the internal foundation of its elective love. As a principle instilled in us by God, natural love is always well ordered and is not a matter of choice.[137] Natural love, however, inclines us toward good in general: it inclines us toward God as the universal common good and toward those goods that constitute our participation in the common good. To be a principle of human action, these general principles must be rendered more specific in a love we freely choose. This is what Aquinas here calls "elective love" *(dilectio electiva),* which he elsewhere simply calls *"dilectio."*[138] Practical reasoning determines the particular good act to be done here and now. In the process of practical reasoning, our general natural love becomes specified in the act of choice, being embodied in our elective love *(dilectio).* As such, it becomes the principle of our chosen action.

Aquinas' description of human freedom as rooted in a habitually well ordered natural love points to how profoundly Aquinas' theory of freedom differs from notions of freedom that regard freedom as a spontaneous act of the will unconditioned by reason, nature or our social environment.[139] Instead, Aquinas portrays human freedom as rooted in a

135. *ST* I 60.2.
136. Ibid.
137. *ST* I 60.1 ad 3.
138. *ST* I-II 26.3.
139. For a brief but probing analysis of freedom as spontaneity, see Yves Simon, *Freedom of Choice,* edited by Peter Wolff (New York: Fordham University Press, 1969), 1–4.

cognitive and affective orientation toward a specific end. Aquinas' insight is that just as absolute determinism would destroy human freedom, so too would absolute indeterminism. Freedom is always freedom for something. A free act always entails choosing a means to some end. Without an end, there are no means and consequently no choice of them.[140] In Aquinas' view, a freedom without some fixed end would not be a human act. It would instead be a form of insanity and would render the act involuntary by definition.[141] Aquinas' guiding insight is that although *dilectio* is a love we freely choose, this choice presupposes cognitive principles (the principles of practical reason) that reveal the generically fitting objects of our love, and an appetitive principle (natural love) that inclines us toward these generically fitting objects. We knowingly choose our loves in a freedom rooted in a natural knowledge and love we do not choose.

Knowledge, Love, and the Moral Act

Once we recognize the relationship between the will's acts and its natural principles, it becomes easier to grasp St. Thomas' explanation of the moral goodness or badness of a human act. The task of the moral life is to choose and to do those acts that are truly ordered to the end of knowing and loving God. The challenge is to apply the general princi-

140. A given end can itself be a means to some greater end, but the process must begin somewhere. The choice of this intermediate end presupposes some most basic end in view of which we choose the intermediate end.

141. *ST* I-II 1.1. Responding to the objection that humans do many actions without deliberation, Aquinas states, "such actions are not properly human, because they do not proceed from the deliberation of reason, which is the proper principle of human acts. Such acts, therefore, have some imagined end, which however is not established by reason" (*ST* I-II 1.1 ad 3). For Aquinas' description of actions not directed by reason and will to a determined end as actions of an "insane" person *(amens)*, see *ST* I-II 10.3. Yves Simon notes that some theorists unflinchingly embrace the paradox that freedom is most fully exhibited by the insane. He gives the example of Philip Frank who holds that the best approximation of complete freedom is found in the person who "while deeply engaged in the course of his ideas, suddenly elicits an act . . . suggested by an association, or by an image springing from his unconscious." Frank adds that "something of the same kind occurs in certain cases of insanity, in which acts are very little influenced by external circumstances" (Das Kausalgesetz und seine Grenzen [Vienna: Springer, 1932], 150; cited by Simon in *Freedom of Choice,* 17–18).

ples of action—the natural love in the will and the principles of practical reason in the intellect—to particular situations. What acts in a given situation are truly particular embodiments of our general knowledge and love of the good? Thomas regards the challenge this question poses as analogous to the challenge faced by an artist or craftsman in practicing his or her art.[142]

An apprentice may know the general principles of an art and have a deep love for that art, but he or she will only be a true artist or craftsman when he or she knows how to apply these principles to produce a quality work of art. In Aquinas' view, the principles of practical reason, which he also describes as the natural law, are analogous to the rules or guiding measure of a practical art.[143] The human act is like a work of art. Just as a work of art must conform to the measure of that art *(regula artis)* if it is to be a good work of art, so too a human act must conform to the measure of the moral life *(regula prudentiae)* if it is to be a morally good act *(opus justum)*.[144]

The moral life, however, differs from the life of an artist, *as an artist,* in this respect. One can know one's trade and produce quality works of art even if one's loves are disordered. This is not the case with the morally good act. To do a morally good act in the way a morally good person would do it (i.e., to do a morally good act in a way that makes

142. Artistic action differs from moral action because the arts are about making while morality is about doing (*ST* I-II 57.5 ad 1; *ST* II-II Prol. See also *ST* I-II 68.4 ad 1 and ad 3). Nevertheless, throughout the *Summa theologiae* Aquinas treats goodness in the moral life as analogous in some ways to goodness in the arts (see Jordan, "*Pars moralis* of the *Summa*," 468–481). We should also note that an artistic act to the extent that it is a human act is also a moral act. Whenever an artist engages in artistic activity, his action presupposes a choice on his part to do that activity instead of something else. This choice has moral value. Thus, although to do a good piece of art only requires that the agent be a good artist, to do art when and how one should in order to be a morally good person requires more than the virtue of art: it requires that the person have prudence and the moral virtues (*In ethic.* VI 4.12; see also *ST* I-II 21.2 ad 2; *ST* I-II 57.5; *De virtutibus in communi* 7.).

143. *ST* II-II 57.1 ad 2; *ST* I-II 104.4; Jordan, "*Pars moralis* of the *Summa*," 468–481. For an analysis of Aquinas' description of the principles of practical reason as the natural law, see Westberg, "Relation of Law and Practical Reason in Aquinas," 279–290, and Porter, "What the Wise Person Knows," 57–69.

144. *ST* I 21.2; *De virtutibus in communi* 13. For Thomas' description of the natural law as the *regula prudentiae,* see *ST* II-II 57.1 ad 2.

the agent morally good), one must have a well ordered love. In part this is so because, unlike artistic knowledge, moral knowledge depends on rightly ordered love in the will. As we have seen, what we love has a role in shaping our moral judgments. It moves the intellect to engage in the process of practical reasoning, and can focus the intellect's attention upon certain objects instead of others because of the intensity of the love it has for those objects. Thus, in order for reason to discover the right act to be done here and now, love in the will must be rightly ordered toward the practical good.

The recognition that human action depends on both the intellect and will leads Aquinas to discern two proximate internal causes of error in human action. Error can be caused by the intellect or by the will. Moreover, recognizing that our intellect and will function through sense cognition and the sense appetites, Aquinas sketches the proximate causes of error in relation to these corporeal powers, which he describes as the remote internal causes of error.[145] A full account of Aquinas' theory of moral goodness and sin is beyond the scope of this current study.[146] Our present goal is merely to show that in analyzing the moral goodness or badness of acts, Aquinas remains true to his distinction between specification and exercise in action. The intellect informs (specifies) every act, but we choose and do an action through the executive power (the exercise) of the will. This means that the threshold of the human act is reached in the will's act of choice.[147] When through an act of the will we choose the act, this act becomes a human act properly so called, and is thus something for which we are morally responsible. Yet, in order for

145. *ST* I-II 75.2.

146. See David Gallagher, "Aquinas on Goodness and Moral Goodness," in *Thomas Aquinas and His Legacy,* edited by David Gallagher (Washington, D.C.: The Catholic University of America Press, 1994), 37–60; Bonnie Kent, "Transitory Vice: Thomas Aquinas on Incontinence," *Journal of the History of Philosophy* 27 (1989): 199–223; Lawrence Dewan, "St. Thomas and the First Cause of Moral Evil," in *Moral and Political Philosophies in the Middle Ages,* edited by B. Carlos Bazán, Eduardo Andújar, Leonard G. Sbrocchi (Ottawa: Legas, 1995), vol. 3, 1223–1230.

147. From one perspective, the moral act begins with the will's intention of the end; thus, Aquinas affirms that the goodness of the will depends on the intention of the end (*ST* I-II 19.7); Yet, the intention of this end is also a choice: one end was intended instead of another. This is so because, as Thomas reminds us, every intermediate end can be viewed as the means to some further end (*ST* I-II 14.2).

this act to be a human act (in order for it truly to be something we choose) the will's act must be informed by reason. In other words, as we have seen, the human act is not just an act of the will, it is the act of a "deliberated will."[148]

This perspective on action shapes Aquinas' analysis of human error. It underlies his hierarchical distinction between evil *(malum),* fault *(peccatum),* and what we can translate as moral fault *(culpa).*[149] Evil is the most general of the terms. Evil is any privation of a due good, whether in things or in actions. Fault is less general and specifically refers to evil in actions. Fault applies to any action, whether natural, technical or moral, lacking a good that is proper to it. Lastly, there is the special class of fault (moral fault), which refers solely to human actions. Faults are moral faults only if they are voluntary. They are freely chosen human actions that lack the form, measure, or proportion that are proper to them. These acts are faults because they are disordered actions; they are moral faults because they are freely chosen, and hence we are morally responsible for them.

This distinction enables Aquinas to affirm that (a) every fault in human action presupposes ignorance in the intellect. Yet, (b) in order for this fault to be a moral fault (an action for which we are morally culpable), we must in some way choose this ignorance through an act of the will. (Otherwise, the will's act would be informed by an ignorance we have not chosen, a state of affairs that either reduces culpability or removes it entirely.)[150] These affirmations pose once again the question of the principles of action. What is the first principle of sin? Does it reside in the intellect or in the will?

Aquinas resolves this question in the way we have come to expect. As the efficient cause of all our acts and as the power that moves the other powers to their acts, the will is the first principle and internal subject of sin.[151] Yet, since every free act of the will is informed by reason, every

148. *ST* I-II 1.3.

149. *De malo* 2.2. See Gallagher, "Aquinas on Goodness," 50–53.

150. *ST* I-II 76.3 ad 3.

151. *ST* I-II 74.1. For the sense in which the will's action is an "accidental" or "indirect" efficient causality, see *ST* I-II 75.1.

sinful act presupposes some deficient action in the intellect.[152] Of itself, this deficient act in the intellect is not sinful. Ignorance in the intellect—not to consider something—is not of itself a sinful action. This ignorance becomes a component of sin only when we choose, through an act of the will, to act from this ignorance.[153] (At that point, an ignorance that was a mere negation becomes a privation: it is the privation of a knowledge that should be informing the action.)[154] Aquinas' point seems to be something like this. A person might be in a market considering the utility of a well-made hammer or the refreshing juiciness of a ripe peach, without at that moment considering that the hammer and the peach belong to the merchant and that the only just way to attain these goods would be through some exchange agreeable to the merchant. At that moment the failure to consider the "rule of reason" in this situation (that these goods belong to the merchant and that one must pay for them) is not a sinful ignorance. It only becomes a morally culpable ignorance if the person chooses to act from this ignorance: only if he chooses, from this chosen ignorance, to take the hammer and the peach without paying for them.[155] The thief retains habitual knowledge of the whole picture (that taking these things would be sinful), but in the moment of stealing he or she chooses to focus only on one aspect of the object (its goodness for me here and now). In Aquinas' view, in the act of choice—in choosing to steal—only this knowledge is actual in the intellect. Hence, Aquinas states that "the will in failing to apply the rule of reason or of the divine law, is the cause of sin."[156] Once again, therefore, we find Aquinas affirming that in every human act the will is specified by reason, but the will, through its power of exercise, has a role in shaping this specification. The will can only act as informed by reason, but the will can move reason to focus on one aspect of an object instead of another. Stated more accurately, because of the interrelationship existing between intellect and will, the agent is able to focus freely on one as-

152. *ST* I-II 77.2.
153. *ST* I-II 75.1 ad 3.
154. See Dewan, "St. Thomas and the First Cause of Moral Evil," 1223–1230.
155. *ST* I-II 74.1 ad 2.
156. *ST* I-II 75.1 ad 3.

pect of an object, and thus act according to his freely chosen myopic perspective.

Aquinas is also attentive to the role of sense cognition and of the sense appetites (passions) in human action and sin. The passions cannot directly cause a person to sin, but they can indirectly incline a person to sin by influencing the reasoning process.[157] They can dispose us to act contrary to the universal and even the particular truths that we habitually know by inclining us to focus our attention on a sense good that is a particular aspect of the action.[158] Yet, although intense passion can suspend the reasoning process (and thus remove moral responsibility), the passions cannot directly and necessarily cause us to sin.[159] If the will is well ordered in relation to the passions, it need not surrender to their disordered inclinations, although the agent may nonetheless surrender to them from a negligent lack of resolve.[160] For this reason, Aquinas maintains that sins committed from the chosen *habitus* of the will, which he describes as sins of certain malice, are far more serious than sins committed under the influence of the passions.[161] The passions can incline us to sin, but we sin through acts of the will.

Since love is the principle of the will's action, it is not surprising that Aquinas describes love as the principle of both virtue and sin. "Ordered love is included in every virtue, since every virtuous person loves the good proper to virtue, while inordinate love is included in every sin, because inordinate love gives rise to inordinate desire."[162] Aquinas follows Augustine in affirming that two loves build two cities: well ordered love builds up the city of God, while disordered love builds the city of Babylon.[163] Well ordered love is love rightly directed toward God as its end. One who loves God rightly loves him in and through actions that can be ordered to him, actions that are *"ad finem."* Disordered love, on the oth-

157. *ST* I-II 77.1.

158. *ST* I-II 77.2.

159. *ST* I-II 10.3; *ST* I-II 10.3 ad 1.

160. This becomes clear in Aquinas' assertion that the passions are equally disordered in the continent person and the incontinent person; the actions of these two types of people differ because of the differing statuses of their wills (*ST* II-II 155.3; *ST* II-II 156.2 ad 2).

161. *ST* I-II 78.4.

162. *ST* II-II 125.2.

163. *ST* I-II 77.4 sc.

er hand, is love directed to the self as its end. Thus, Aquinas presents disordered self-love as the root of all sin.[164]

Aquinas' conception of sin rests on his previously expressed insight that the act of love always comes to rest in a personal being, in a *suppositum*. Love either comes to rest in God or in oneself. Since love is the principle of all human action, we are always either ordering our acts toward God or toward ourselves. Love that is rightly directed to God makes the agent good and promotes the common good of the community. Disordered self-love, on the other hand, destroys community and fragments the human person, rendering him more like a beast than a human being.[165]

Shortly after describing disordered self-love as the root of sin, Aquinas reminds the reader that sin is an act of *liberum arbitrium,* and, as such, is the product of both reason and will.[166] Aquinas is reminding us that disordered love is not the sole cause of sin. Disordered knowledge (disordered because partial) is also a principle of sin. Fragmentary knowledge and disordered love form the co-principles of sinful action. This implies that in order to overcome our sins, we need both integral knowledge and ordered affection. We need to acquire wisdom and love. In the context of the "personal" character of love's goal, Aquinas' teaching implies that in order to perform morally good acts we must discover the truth about God and ourselves, and love this truth in our actions. On the natural level, wisdom and love are attained through the dispositions that the tradition calls the cardinal virtues.

Knowledge, Love, and Virtue

St. Thomas describes virtue as the perfection of a power that disposes the agent to do some good action.[167] Thomas distinguishes those dispositions *(habitus)* that are virtues "in a certain respect" from those that are virtues properly so called *(simpliciter)*. Any disposition that imparts

164. *ST* I-II 77.4 and 5.
165. *ST* I-II 28.5; *ST* I-II 73.1 ad 3; *ST* I-II 73.5 ad 3.
166. *ST* I-II 77.6.
167. *ST* I-II 55.3.

an aptitude for good action can be called a virtue. Strictly speaking, however, virtue refers to dispositions that not only impart an aptitude for good action, but also incline the agent to employ this aptitude rightly. For example, the theoretical sciences or the technical arts (all of which are in a certain sense virtues that perfect the intellect) do not dispose the agent to use these dispositions in a morally good way. One can use science or technical skill to murder one's neighbor or defraud him of his property. By contrast, virtue properly so called disposes the agent to do good in a good way. These full virtues dispose a person to do morally good acts in a way that makes him or her morally good as well.[168] These are the four virtues the tradition commonly describes as the "cardinal virtues," because upon them the moral life depends.[169] Prudence perfects the practical intellect, while the other three—which the tradition describes as the moral virtues—perfect the appetitive powers: justice perfects the will, courage perfects the irascible appetite, and temperance perfects the concupiscible appetite.[170] A full presentation of Aquinas' theory of the cardinal virtues is beyond the scope of this project.[171] As we noted in the introduction, the focus of our analysis will be Aquinas' portrayal of the relationship between knowledge and love in the virtues.

Early in his treatment of the virtues, Aquinas considers the Socratic theory of virtue. Some maintained that the appetitive powers were subject to reason in the same way that our body's limbs are subject to reason: "subserviently and without any contradiction whatsoever."[172] Aquinas notes that if this were true, in order to be morally good we would only need to have intellectual virtue.[173] This, in fact, was the opinion of Socrates who asserted that "every virtue is a kind of prudence."[174]

168. *ST* I-II 56.3.

169. See *ST* I-II 61.3.

170. *ST* I-II 61.2. Prudence is described as a moral virtue by participation (*ST* I-II 58.2 ad 4).

171. For a fuller treatment of St. Thomas' understanding of the cardinal virtues, see Romanus Cessario, *The Moral Virtues and Theological Ethics* (Notre Dame: University of Notre Dame Press, 1991).

172. *ST* I-II 58.2.

173. Ibid.

174. Ibid. St. Thomas is quoting Aristotle's description of Socrates' view (See Aristotle, *Nicomachean Ethics* [henceforth cited as *NE*] 6.13 [1144b19).

Consequently, Socrates argued that "as long as one possesses knowledge, he or she cannot sin, and everyone who sins does so through ignorance."[175]

Aquinas holds that the Socratic view rests on a false premise. Reason is unable to exercise absolute control over the appetitive powers because "the appetitive faculty obeys reason not subserviently, but with a certain power of opposition."[176] Consequently, as Aristotle notes, although reason "dominates the body like a despot," it is only able to exercise something akin to "political power" over the appetites. It relates to them the way a sovereign "rules over free subjects who have a certain right of opposition."[177] Aquinas interprets this to mean that the dispositions and passions of the appetitive faculty can impede practical reason in its consideration of particular actions. At this point Aquinas recognizes a crucial truth underlying the Socratic view. "There is some truth in the saying of Socrates that as long as one possesses knowledge one does not sin: only, however, if we make this saying refer to the use of reason in a particular act of choice."[178] On the one hand, the Socratic view is wrong on the level of universal knowledge, for many people act contrary to the knowledge they possess of universal moral truth, as the example of an incontinent person readily reveals. On the other hand, Socrates is correct concerning our particular moral judgments. No one ever acts contrary to what he or she knows in the particular act of choice. Thus, every sin implies some ignorance of the true good on the level of the agent's particular judgment.

Yet, even on the level of particular judgment, the Socratic view is incomplete. Socrates fails to recognize that the agent's particular ignorance is the result of his or her disordered appetites: it is either a fully chosen ignorance generated by the will in the sin of certain malice, or it is a reluctantly chosen ignorance motivated by the sense appetites in the sins of passion. "Accordingly, for one to do a good deed, not only must reason be well disposed by means of a *habitus* of intellectual virtue, but also the appetitive power must be well disposed by means of a *habitus* of

175. *ST* I-II 58.2.

176. Ibid.

177. Ibid.

178. Ibid.

moral virtue."[179] This implies that there exists between prudence and the moral virtues a mutual relationship exactly parallel to the relationship between knowledge and love (specification and exercise) traced by Aquinas in the earlier sections of the *Prima secundae.*

St. Thomas defines prudence as "right reason applied to action."[180] The virtue of prudence disposes the agent to apply well and with alacrity universal practical principles to particular situations.[181] Practical reasoning is an ordering process. It orders actions to a given end, establishing those actions as the means to that end.[182] Prudence, therefore, as the virtue that perfects practical reason, disposes us to determine and command the right means to a desired end.

As we have seen, St. Thomas holds that reason's judgment in practical matters depends on the appetites. It depends on the rightly ordered inclination of the will and of the passions. Since prudence perfects practical reason, the virtue of prudence also depends on the rightly ordered affections of the will and of the passions. "Prudence actually has reason as its subject, but it presupposes as its principle the rectitude of the will."[183] Aquinas describes the dependence of prudence on the will in terms of reason's relation to the end. Prudence disposes the agent to order his actions well toward his desired end. That he desire the right ends, however, depends on the appetites, especially the will.

> Since prudence is right reason about things to be done, in order for prudence to exist the agent must be well ordered toward the principles of this reasoning about things to be done, which principles are the ends. The human person is well ordered toward the ends by the rectitude of the will, just as he or she is well ordered toward the principles of theoretical reason by the natural light of the active intellect. Thus, just as the subject of science, which is right reason about theoretical matters, is the theoretical intellect in its relation to the active intellect, so too the subject of prudence is the practical intellect in its relation to the will as rightly ordered.[184]

179. Ibid.
180. *ST* II-II 47.8: *"prudentia est recta ratio agibilium."*
181. *ST* II-II 47.3.
182. *ST* I-II 47.6.
183. *ST* I-II 56.2 ad 3. See also *ST* II-II 47.4.
184. *ST* I-II 56.3.

Desire for an end moves us to reason about the means to that end. Consequently, for the means to be correct we must first desire the proper end.[185] This we do by having rightly ordered appetites.

Since love is the principle of the will's motion, to assert that prudence depends on a rightly ordered will implies that prudence depends on rightly ordered love. As we would expect, this is exactly what Aquinas affirms. While he denies that prudence is essentially love, he nonetheless affirms that prudence depends on rightly ordered love, because "love moves to the act of prudence."[186] It is for this reason, as we noted earlier, that Aquinas can follow Augustine in affirming that the virtues depend on our rightly ordered love. Aquinas can join Augustine in describing prudence as "love discerning well," because love "moves reason to discern."[187]

Love's role in shaping prudence touches on Aquinas' theory of connaturality. To say that something is connatural implies that it is according to or in harmony with one's nature. Aquinas holds that love makes the loved object be in a certain sense connatural to the lover. Since, as Aristotle holds, "as a person is, so does the end appear to him,"[188] to be connatural with something shapes our judgments concerning that thing. Those who love rightly become connatural with the true human good, the good of reason, and consequently judge correctly concerning this good; those who love wrongly, become connatural to a false or apparent good, and this, in turn, warps their judgments.[189]

Lastly, since the moral virtues perfect the appetites and rightly order their loves, prudence depends on the moral virtues.

185. *ST* I-II 19.3 ad 2.

186. *ST* II-II 47.1 ad 1. See also *ST* I-II 56.3 ad 1.

187. *ST* II-II 47.1 ad 1. See Charles J. O'Neil, "Is Prudence Love?" *Monist* 58 (1974): 124, and *Imprudence in St. Thomas Aquinas*, Aquinas Lecture Series (Milwaukee, Wis.: Marquette University Press, 1955), 103–107.

188. *NE* 3.5 (1114a32–b1); *De malo* 6: *"quia, secundum philosophum, qualis unusquisque est, talis finis videtur ei."*

189. For more on Aquinas' theory of *connaturalitas* and its relationship to virtue, see Craig Steven Titus, "The Development of Virtue and 'Connaturality' in Thomas Aquinas' Works" (Licentiate thesis, University of Fribourg, Switzerland, 1990); Marco D'Avenia, *La conoscenza per connaturalità in s. Tommaso d'Aquino* (Bologna: Edizioni Studio Domenicano, 1992); Antonio Moreno, "The Nature of St. Thomas' Knowledge *'Per connaturalitatem,'" Angelicum* 47 (1970): 44–62.

Perfection and rectitude of reason in theoretical matters depend on the principles from which reason argues, just as we said above that science depends on and presupposes understanding, which is the habit of principles. Now in human acts the end is what the principles are in theoretical matters, as stated in the *Ethics* (7.8). Consequently, in order for prudence (which is right reason about things to be done) to exist, the agent must be well disposed toward the ends, and this depends on the rectitude of the appetite. Consequently, for prudence one must have moral virtue which rectifies the appetite.[190]

In other words, prudence, which establishes the means, presupposes the moral virtues, which incline toward the ends.[191] Yet, no sooner does Aquinas affirm the dependence of prudence on the moral virtues than he also affirms the dependence of the moral virtues on prudence.

St. Thomas explains that although every particular act of prudence depends on and presupposes some fixed end toward which the moral virtues incline, the ends of the moral virtues are themselves objects of choice. This is necessary if the moral virtues are to be human virtues. In natural things devoid of reason, inclinations are without choice. The stone does not choose its downward inclination. In rational creatures, however, the inclinations proper to the moral virtues are "with choice." Consequently, in order for these inclinations to be rightly ordered they must be subject to the guiding direction of prudence.[192] Thomas explains that the "end," which is the object of moral virtue is a mean between too much and too little. The attainment of this mean requires the right judgment of practical reason, which itself depends on the virtue of prudence.

Prudence directs the moral virtues not only in choosing that which is ordered to the end, but also by predetermining the end. Now the end of each moral virtue is to attain the mean in the proper matter of that virtue, and this mean is determined by the right reasoning of prudence.[193]

190. *ST* I-II 57.4. See also *ST* I-II 58.5 ad 3.

191. *ST* I-II 56.4 ad 4.

192. *ST* I-II 58.4 ad 1; *ST* I-II 58.2 ad 4. Aquinas frequently describes the moral virtues as directed by reason or prudence (*ST* I-II 59.4).

193. *ST* I-II 66.3 ad 3.

Hence, although on one level the moral virtues provide the ends of practical reasoning, on another level prudence establishes the ends of the moral virtues.

St. Thomas' theory of virtue leads us to the familiar issue of the ultimate foundations of human action. Once again we are confronted with an apparent circularity: "Reason, as apprehending the end, precedes the appetite for the end: but appetite for the end precedes reason's reasoning about the choice of those things that are ordered to the end, which pertains to prudence."[194] In order for prudence to determine a proper means to the end, the moral virtues must supply prudence with a proper end; yet, in order for the moral virtues to have a proper end as their object, prudence must determine this proximate end from among other candidates, all of which stand as means to some further end.

To overcome this apparent circularity, Aquinas once again appeals to natural principles that are not a matter of choice. To understand his explanation we must recognize Aquinas' view of how practical reason operates.[195] It applies a universal principle to a particular action through what Aquinas calls an "operative syllogism." The universal principle functions in the operative syllogism as the major premise, while the particular action *(particulare operabile)* is itself the conclusion of the syllogism.[196] The movement from the universal proposition to the particular action/conclusion is through a particular proposition functioning as the minor premise or middle term.[197] Practical reasoning, therefore, requires a twofold knowledge, one universal, the other particular.[198]

The key to understanding Aquinas' theory of virtue is his notion that the universal and particular knowledge employed in practical reasoning flow from different sources. The universal knowledge flows from the natural habit of first practical principles, while the particular knowledge is acquired through sense knowledge and experience.

194. *ST* I-II 58.5 ad 1. See also *ST* I-II 65.1.

195. See Westberg, *Right Practical Reason,* 158–160.

196. *ST* II-II 49.2 ad 1. The description of the reasoning process in terms of syllogistic logic is from Aristotle. For an excellent introduction into the Thomistic interpretation of Aristotelian logic, see John Oesterle, *Logic: the Art of Defining and Reasoning* (Englewood Cliffs, N.J.: Prentice-Hall, 1997).

197. *ST* I-II 76.1.

198. Ibid. and *ST* II-II 49.2 ad 1.

The reasoning of prudence terminates, as in a conclusion, in some particular operable, to which it applies universal knowledge, as stated above. Now a particular conclusion is argued from a universal and a particular proposition. Consequently, the reasoning of prudence must proceed from a twofold understanding. One is cognizant of universals and this belongs to the understanding *(intellectus)* that is an intellectual virtue: because not only universal theoretical principles are naturally known to us, but also universal practical principles, such as 'evil is to be done to no one,' as was said above. The other understanding *(intellectus)*, as is said in the *Ethics* (6.11), is cognizant of an extreme, i.e., of some primary particular and contingent operable that functions as the minor premise and which, as we have seen, must be something particular in the syllogism of prudence. This primary particular is some particular end, as was said above. Hence, the understanding presented as a part of prudence is a right estimate of some particular end.[199]

Aquinas is here reminding us that the foundation of practical reasoning, and consequently of prudence as well, is the universal moral knowledge contained in the habit of first practical principles. He here refers to this natural habit as *intellectus.* Elsewhere in his mature treatment of prudence he describes it as *"ratio naturalis"* or *"synderesis."*[200] Yet, no matter what term he employs, his meaning is clear. On the cognitive level, the foundation of the acquired human virtues is a natural virtue of the mind that contains the primary principles of practical reasoning.

As we would expect, in his analysis of the virtues Aquinas is also attentive to the appetitive foundations of the virtues. Aquinas holds that the will is naturally rightly ordered with regard to its proper object, which is the good of reason *(bonum rationis)*. Aquinas elsewhere describes the good of reason as the "good in general" *(bonum universale)*.[201] As we have seen, Aquinas maintains that included in the general notion of the good are all the particular things that reason apprehends as goods fitting to the agent him or herself.

For it is not only things pertaining to the will that the will desires, but also that which pertains to each power, and to the entire person. Hence the human person wills naturally not only the object of the will, but also other things that are appropriate to the other powers; such as the knowledge of

199. *ST* II-II 49.2 ad 1.

200. *ST* II-II 47.6 ad 1; *ST* II-II 47.6 ad 3.

201. *ST* II-II 58.5 ad 2; *ST* I-II 1.2 ad 3.

truth, which befits the intellect, and to be and to live and other like things which regard natural well-being, all of which are included in the object of the will as so many particular goods.[202]

All the goods, therefore, that collectively constitute human flourishing, reason apprehends as fitting goods, and the will—since its object is the good of reason—naturally wills them. Consequently, "the will does not need a virtue perfecting it" with regard to the "good of reason."[203] Instead, "the human person's dealings with him or herself are sufficiently rectified by the rectification of the passions by the other moral virtues."[204] In other words, just as the practical intellect naturally contains universal principles that direct us toward general human goods, so too the will naturally contains certain universal inclinations that incline us toward these same general goods. The cognitive habit of first practical principles as well as the appetitive inclination towards the goods prescribed by this natural knowledge are natural principles that are naturally rightly ordered and thus require no further acquired habits or inclinations to render them sound toward their general objects.[205]

Yet, just as the universal precepts of practical reason must be specified and embedded in certain particular precepts (in other words, just as the *intellectus* of *synderesis* must be supplemented by the *intellectus* of prudence), so too the will's universal inclinations must be specified and embedded in certain particular inclinations directed toward particular goods. Consequently, although "the will from the very nature of the power is inclined to the good of reason," nevertheless, "because this good is varied in many ways, the will needs to be inclined by means of a habit to some fixed good of reason."[206]

When Aquinas refers to the rational good as "varied in many ways," the variety he has in mind here is a variety that transcends the limits of

202. *ST* I-II 10.1.

203. *ST* I-II 56.6.

204. *ST* II-II 58.2 ad 4.

205. St. Thomas does not refer to the natural principles underlying the action of the will as a *habitus,* because he affirms that, unlike the natural *habitus* in the intellect, the appetitive powers' "inclination to their proper objects, which seems to be the beginning of a *habitus,* does not belong to the *habitus,* but rather to the very nature of the powers" (*ST* I-II 51.1).

206. *ST* I-II 50.5 ad 3; see also *ST* I-II 50.5 ad 1.

the will's natural disposition. Unlike the passions, whose motions are entirely internal to the agent, the will's act is an operation that often has external effects. Since external operations do not occur in a vacuum, but affect the entire community in head and members, to be rightly ordered, external operations must be in harmony not only with the agent's own good, but also with the good of the community, both collectively and individually. Aquinas holds, however, that these goods lie beyond the reach of the will's natural inclinations. Aquinas' point seems to be the following. Although the will is naturally inclined to the universal or common good, the agent must (a) learn what concretely is the common good and what actions promote it, and (b) the agent must acquire dispositions in the will that incline the will toward these goods. Specifically, the agent's will must become inclined toward God according to a concrete conception of him; toward the temporal common good of the human community, also according to some concrete conception of it; and toward the particular goods of the other members of this community.

On the natural level, the primary virtue that instills these inclinations in the will is justice.[207] Aquinas defines justice as "a *habitus* by which one renders to each one his due by a constant and perpetual will."[208] As a particular virtue justice inclines us to act rightly toward other individuals. Importantly, however, as a general virtue, justice directs all our actions to the common or universal good.[209] Moreover, the virtue of religion, which Aquinas considers to be "a part of justice,"[210] inclines our actions toward God as their end, where God is concretely understood as the "first principle of creation and of the government of things."[211] From the perspective of the process of practical reasoning, this means that just as prudence rightly orders the practical intellect toward those particular actions that embody the universal precepts of the natural law, so too general justice and the virtue of religion rightly incline the will toward those same actions as particular specifications of

207. *ST* I-II 56.6.
208. *ST* II-II 58.1.
209. *ST* I-II 60.3 ad 2; *ST* II-II 58.5; *ST* II-II 58.6 ad 4.
210. *ST* II-II 81.5 sc.; *ST* II-II 81.5 ad 3.
211. *ST* II-II 81.3; *ST* II-II 81.1.

the will's general object. In other words, we naturally know and love the general goods that constitute human flourishing, but we must acquire virtues that dispose us to know and love these goods in the concrete.

By placing the natural principles of the cardinal virtues on a cognitive and appetitive foundation, St. Thomas ensures the connection and interdependence of these virtues. In order for the moral virtues to incline us toward actions we freely choose, they must be ordered and specified by the right reason supplied by prudence. In order for prudence to incline practical reason to judge correctly about human actions, practical reason must be moved toward a proper end by a will rightly inclined by the moral virtues. In other words, the process of practical reasoning, if it is to lead to good actions that make the agent good as well, presupposes a virtue of right judgment in the intellect and virtues of rightly ordered love in the will and in the passions.

When we view Aquinas' theory of virtue from the perspective of his psychology of love, we discover that this theory is simply the logical development of his understanding of the relationship between knowledge and love in action. Early in the *Prima secundae* Aquinas affirms the dynamic relationship existing between knowledge and love. "Love surpasses knowledge in moving, but knowledge precedes love in attaining, 'for nothing is loved unless it be known.'"[212] Aquinas' theory of virtue confirms this insight and reveals what it implies: that as the principle of the will's motion, love is the cause of all the virtues, but as an inclination specified by its object as known, love is the product of virtue. Thus, on the one hand Aquinas affirms that "every right movement of the will proceeds from a right love;"[213] that "every virtuous affection derives from some well-ordered love;"[214] that "love moves to the act of prudence;"[215] and that,

> the conditions of virtuous operation [that the agent act voluntarily, readily, firmly and with delight] are not found in any operation unless the agent love the good for which he is working, because love is the principle of all the voluntary affective powers. . . . Therefore love of the good, for which virtue operates, is necessary for virtue.[216]

212. *ST* I-II 3.4 ad 4.
213. *ST* I-II 65.4.
214. *De malo* 11.1 ad 1.
215. *ST* II-II 47.1 ad 1.
216. *De caritate* 2.

On the other hand, Aquinas also asserts that "knowledge is the cause of love,"[217] that the will's love is "regulated by reason,"[218] that "love is set in order in us by virtue,"[219] and that "every virtue that orders some passion also orders love."[220] These two sets of affirmations all rest on Aquinas' fundamental insight that love has a certain priority on the level of exercise, but knowledge has priority on the level of specification, which is a structural and thus more fundamental priority.

St. Thomas' Psychology of Knowledge and Love: Summary

The goal of this chapter has been to show that St. Thomas in his psychology of love affirms two Augustinian principles: (a) that love depends on knowledge, because nothing is loved unless it be known, and (b) that our moral knowledge depends on love, because our loves shape how we view things. Thomas is able to resolve the tension between these two affirmations by distinguishing the types of causality exercised by knowledge and love in human action, and by grounding our knowledge and love upon the natural principles of intellect and will. Knowledge has priority in showing and attaining the beloved, while love has priority in moving toward the beloved.

At the summit of ethics, therefore, both on the human and Christian levels, there stands a vital, permanent and dynamic connection between *veritas intellectus,* and *veritas vitae* or *amoris.* The truth of the intellect illumines and directs the intentions and choices of the will, while voluntary inclinations and choices command or determine the mind's investigations, and even the judgments of the theoretical and practical intellect.[221]

217. *ST* I-II 27.2: *"cognitio est causa amoris."*

218. *Super ioannem* 21.3 [185–191]: *"amor enim est motus appetitus, et si quidem reguletur appetitus ratione, sic est amor voluntatis, qui proprie est dilectio, quia sequitur electionem."*

219. *ST* I-II 55.1 ad 4.

220. *De virtutibus in communi* 12 ad 9.

221. Carlos-Josaphat Pinto de Oliveira, *"Ordo rationis, ordo amoris:* la notion d'ordre au centre de l'univers éthique de s. Thomas," in Ordo sapientiae et amoris: *image et message de saint Thomas d'Aquin à travers les récentes études historiques, herméneutiques et doctrinales: hommage au professeur Jean-Pierre Torrell, O.P. à l'occasion de son 65e anniversaire,* edited by Carlos-Josaphat Pinto de Oliveira (Fribourg, Switzerland: Editions universitaires Fribourg, 1993), 297.

As we have seen, Thomas develops the implications of the interpenetration and mutual dependence of knowledge and love throughout the *Prima secundae.* This dynamic structure plays a role in his theology of happiness, his theory of practical reasoning, and his understanding of the virtues.

Now that we have traced these features of Thomas' psychology of love, we can turn to how Thomas elevates this psychology in his theology of grace. Thomas is acutely aware that human knowledge and love on the natural level, especially as wounded by sin, are insufficient to attain the goal of human life: the goal of knowing and loving God in a way that unites us to God and fulfills the deepest longings of the human heart. What is needed is the gift of grace and the infused virtues, especially the virtue of charity. It is to a consideration of St. Thomas' theology of grace and the theological virtues that we now turn.

CHAPTER 4

Intellect and Will in St. Thomas' Theology of Faith

At this point in our study it will be helpful to review the itinerary we have thus far traveled. We began our investigation by posing the question of charity's relationship to knowledge. According to St. Thomas Aquinas, what is charity's relationship to knowledge in human action? In our introductory remarks we saw that this question touches on charity's status as a virtue. In order to live a virtue one must have knowledge of the virtue's object and of its proper acts. Does charity as a divinely infused virtue have this same relationship to knowledge? Some scholars argue that it does not. Moreover, as we noted in chapter one, they maintain that in his later works St. Thomas recognized charity's independence from conceptual knowledge. Specifically, they hold that in St. Thomas' mature estimation, charity's act is antecedent to and independent of conceptual knowledge and practical reasoning. Yet, if this is the case, in what sense is charity anything like other human virtues? Indeed, if charity's act is antecedent to and independent of practical reasoning, in what sense is charity's love for God a freely chosen human act? Consequently, our stated purpose has been to analyze St. Thomas' theory of charity's relationship to knowledge. The first step in this analysis, however, has been to study St. Thomas' conception of the natural principles underlying charity's activity.

In chapter two we considered Thomas' theory of the will as a rational appetite. In those pages we discovered that Thomas maintains throughout his career that intellect and will together form the dual principle of human action. At every stage of practical reasoning, the intellect brings the informing light of human intelligence to bear upon the particulars of human action, while the will directs the intellect in the consideration of those particulars. The intellect specifies the will's object, while the will moves the intellect to exercise its act. We also learned that Thomas' theory avoids falling into an infinite circularity—where every act of the will depends on reason, while every act of reason depends on the will—by placing the ground of practical reasoning in nature and ultimately in God. Thomas affirms that reason specifies and commands all of the will's acts, except the will's first act which is instilled in it by nature, while the will moves the intellect to engage in all its acts except the intellect's first act which is instilled in it by nature. Since God is the author of nature, this means that "what first moves the will and the intellect is something above the will and the intellect, namely God."[1]

Next, after having established in chapter two the character of the will's relationship to intellect in practical reasoning, in chapter three we undertook a closer analysis of the will's primary act, which is love. Without undertaking a full presentation of Aquinas' psychology of love, we probed Aquinas' view of the relationship between knowledge and love in human action. We discovered that, following St. Augustine, Aquinas affirms both that love depends on knowledge (because nothing is loved unless it is known) and that our moral knowledge depends on love (because our loves shape how we view things). Aquinas resolves the tension inherent in this twin affirmation by distinguishing the types of causality exercised by knowledge and love, and by grounding our knowledge and love upon the natural principles of intellect and will: knowledge has priority in attaining the beloved, while love has priority in moving toward the beloved.

These discoveries have brought us to the threshold of our treatment of charity. They have prepared us for an analysis of Aquinas' theology of faith. A study of the Thomistic conception of faith provides an invaluable preface to our analysis of charity, because, in Aquinas' view,

1. *De malo* 6.

faith itself contains both cognitive and appetitive components. Indeed, Aquinas regards charity as perfecting the appetitive component of faith. Thus, in order to grasp the true character of Aquinas' theology of charity, it will be helpful first to consider his theology of faith. This is especially true because of the development his theology of faith undergoes. As with his general analysis of human action, Aquinas modifies his theology of faith as he begins to understand more clearly the types of causality proper to the intellect and will. Just as in his mature treatment of human action Aquinas integrates more successfully the mutual interaction of intellect and will, so too in his mature analysis of faith.

In the pages that follow, our intention is not to offer a full account of Aquinas' theology of faith.[2] Instead, our focus will be on the relationship between the cognitive and appetitive components of faith's proper act. First, however, since we can only accurately understand the theological virtues in relation to Aquinas' theology of grace, we shall begin by tracing the relevant features of this theology.

Grace and the Elevation of Human Nature

Any study of St. Thomas' theology of the virtues must begin with a consideration of his doctrine of grace. As Thomas O'Meara has noted,

> Aquinas's theological ethic of virtues flows fully and necessarily from a divine presence called grace, because the virtues of a life, even that which is the dynamic source of Christian action, must (in the perspective of Aristotelianism) like all potentialities and activities, have a ground or a "nature."[3]

In other words, every virtue, as the perfection of a capacity, is rooted in a nature. If we seek to understand this virtue, we must begin by having some understanding of the nature in which it resides. We must have some understanding of the goal toward which this nature is directed and

2. For insightful assessments of St. Thomas' theology of faith, see Benoit Duroux, *La psychologie de la foi chez s. Thomas d'Aquin* (Tournai, Belgium: Desclée, 1963), and Romanus Cessario, *Christian Faith and the Theological Life* (Washington, D.C.: The Catholic University of America Press, 1996).

3. Thomas F. O'Meara, "Virtues in the Theology of Thomas Aquinas," *Theological Studies* 58 (1997): 258.

of the activities that lead it to attain this goal. This is the case even with regard to the theological virtues, but with them the "nature" in question is the graced nature proper to the Christian life. Consequently, to understand faith, charity and the other infused virtues, we must first have some understanding of Thomas' theology of grace.

St. Thomas begins his treatment of grace by recognizing the limits of the human person's natural powers when unaided by grace. Thomas holds that humans were created in grace.[4] Nonetheless, he recognizes that a number of his contemporaries believe that humans were created in a purely natural state.[5] Hence, since it was possible for God to have created us in this way, Thomas regards it as helpful to consider how far the spiritual powers of "integral human nature" could extend without the aid of grace.[6]

First, there is the knowledge that the intellect can attain through its natural power. "The human intellect has a form, i.e., an intelligible light, that of itself is sufficient for knowing certain intelligible things, namely those things we can come to know through the senses."[7] Aquinas elsewhere maintains that among the things the human intellect in its integral natural state can know are truths about God. The unaided human intellect cannot know God's essence as it is in itself. Yet, since sensible things are creatures of God, by knowing them one can come to know something of their creator. One can know whether God exists, and one can know those things that necessarily belong to him as the transcendent first cause of all that is.[8] Second, there is the love of God that is nat-

4. *ST* I 95.1; *ST* II-II 5.1; *Quodlibet.* 1.4.3.

5. *ST* I 95.1; *ST* I-II 109.3 sc.; *ST* II-II 5.1. See, for example, Alexander of Hales, *Summa theologiae* II 91.1 ad 1 and St. Bonaventure *In sent.* II 29.2.2.

6. For example, after affirming in *Quodlibet.* 1.4.3 that humans were created in grace, St. Thomas adds that "since it was possible for God to have created man in a purely natural state *(in puris naturalibus)*, it is useful to consider how far natural love could extend."

7. *ST* I-II 109.1.

8. *ST* I 12.12. St. Thomas is here speaking in general terms of the knowledge "we" can attain by the natural light of the intellect, without distinguishing between "integral nature" before the fall, or wounded nature after the fall. Elsewhere, however, St. Thomas reveals his belief that integral human nature before the fall would be able to attain this same type of knowledge of God. Of course, since in Thomas' view our first parents were created in grace, they would also have knowledge of God that went beyond what nature could of itself attain. *ST* I 94.1: "[Adam], however, knew God by means of a higher

ural to the human will. The human will in its unwounded integrity naturally loves God above all things, loving him as "the principle of all being."[9] Moreover, in its natural integrity the human will also naturally loves all other things according to their proper relationship to God, referring them to God as the human person's ultimate end.[10]

Aquinas explains, however, that even in a person unwounded by sin, this natural knowledge and love of God is deeply limited. "Reason and will are naturally ordered to God as the principle and end of nature, but according to the proportion of nature. Yet, reason and will according to their nature are not sufficiently ordered to him as the object of supernatural beatitude."[11] The intellect can know that God exists and, among other things, that he is one, all powerful, and good, but it cannot know that he is a Trinity or that he plans for us to participate intimately in his inner trinitarian life.[12] Likewise, even though the human will unwounded by sin can love God above all things and love all other things as ordered to God, it cannot love him in a manner that merits eternal beatitude in the vision of the divine essence.[13]

Aquinas further recognizes that after the fall the limits of human knowledge and love are much greater. Even the knowledge of God that was naturally within our reach, the wounded human intellect can only attain after much labor, many years of study, and always with a mixture

---

knowledge than that by which we know him; thus his knowledge was in a certain way intermediate between the knowledge proper to our present condition and the knowledge belonging to heaven."

9. *Quodlibet.* 1.4.3 ad 1. In St. Thomas' view, this is true not only for humans, but for all things. All creatures, from angels to algae, love God above all things with the type of natural love that is proper to them (*ST* I 60.1).

10. *ST* I-II 109.3.

11. *ST* I-II 62.1 ad 3.

12. *ST* I 32.1. See also *ST* II-II 2.7.

13. *ST* I-II 109.3 ad 1; *ST* I 60.5 ad 4; *ST* I 93.8 ad 3; *Quodlibet.* 1.4.3 ad 1. Interestingly, in the *Prima pars,* St. Thomas holds that reason's subjection to God, the body's subjection to the soul, and the lower powers' subjection to reason are not natural endowments, but are the product of God's grace, "otherwise this would have remained after sin" (*ST* I 95.1). In his subsequent analysis of grace in the *Prima secundae,* however, Thomas appears to retreat from this view. Instead of presenting reason's subjection to God as a product of grace, he now affirms that the unwounded will naturally loves God above all things and orders its love for everything else toward God as to its end, needing grace only in order to desire supernatural good (*ST* I-II 109.3).

of many errors.[14] Moreover, although the wounded human will can do many particular good things and direct them to God, it cannot persevere in these good actions nor integrate them unfailingly into an ordered love of God.[15] In other words, after the fall, although one may acquire true (albeit imperfect) virtues, one cannot always act according to these acquired natural virtues. One sooner or later directs one's actions toward some lesser good. One eventually turns away from God and toward a disordered conception of oneself.[16] Thus, fallen humanity stands in need of a healing act of God's love. It stands in need of God's redemptive grace revealed in Christ.

St. Thomas' affirmation that our first parents were created in grace is an expression of his theology of providence and predestination.[17] Thomas regards providence as an aspect of God's eternal wisdom. Providence is the plan *(ratio)* in God's mind according to which he orders all things to their ultimate end.[18] Drawing on a close reading of the promises of Scripture and of the Pauline description of divine election, Thomas portrays predestination as that part of God's providence that concerns the rational creature. Predestination is the freely chosen divine plan that directs humans and angels to eternal life in the loving vision of God.[19]

Human nature is naturally ordered to God as its end, but is unable by its natural powers alone to attain this end in a way that fully actualizes these powers.[20] Although human nature has no claim on God's

14. *ST* I 1.1; *ST* II-II 2.4.

15. *ST* I-II 65.2; *ST* I-II 109.2; *ST* I-II 109.8.

16. *ST* I-II 109.3; *ST* I-II 109.2.

17. Marie-Dominique Chenu, *S. Thomas et la théologie* (Paris: Editions du seuil, 1959), 116; Thomas F. O'Meara, *Thomas Aquinas, Theologian* (Notre Dame, Ind.: University of Notre Dame Press, 1997), 103–104. See *De veritate* 14.10 ad 2.

18. *ST* I 22.2.

19. *ST* I 23.1.

20. Aquinas unequivocally proclaims that "every intellect naturally desires the vision of the divine essence" (*SCG* III 57.4), but the human intellect cannot on its own know what this is, or know that it is attainable or how it is attainable. As Kevin Staley states, "the philosopher can show *that* the human good requires an immediate relationship with an infinite and transcendent Good without being able to say much about what such happiness would be like, how it is to be achieved, or Who the Supreme Good is" (Kevin Staley, "Aristotle, Augustine, and Aquinas on the Good and the Human Good: A note on

grace and cannot even know on its own that a fuller attainment of God is possible, human nature's openness to more perfect fulfillment is part of God's providential plan. God has instilled in human nature a unique receptivity for the gift of grace.[21] "There is in the nature of the soul or of any rational creature a certain aptitude for the reception of grace."[22] The rational creature is "ordered to grace,"[23] in an ordering so intimate it is analogous to the eye's relationship to light.[24] Consequently, although the beatific vision is above the nature of the human soul *(supra naturam),* this vision is nonetheless according to the nature of the soul *(secundum naturam).*[25] Specifically, it is an activity of knowing and loving God that, although it is beyond the strength *(virtus)* of the intellect and will to attain, it is nonetheless within the capacity *(potentia)* of the intellect and will to attain through the added strength of God's grace. The spiritual powers of intellect and will render the rational creature uniquely capable of intimate union with God *(capax dei),* because these spiritual powers are uniquely capable of receiving the elevating action of grace *(capax gratiae).*[26] Consequently, in the eternal plan of his providence, God has ordained for humans to attain full union with himself through the healing and elevating action of his grace.[27]

St. Thomas recognizes the important role of grace in healing fallen human nature.[28] He is also deeply aware of the central place of Christ in mediating this healing and redeeming grace.[29] Christ is the author of

---

Summa theologiae I-II QQ. 1–3," *Modern Schoolman* 72 [1995]: 312, n. 4). See also Aertsen, *Nature and Creature: Thomas Aquinas's Way of Thought* (Leiden: E. J. Brill, 1988), 361–370; Thomas Hibbs, *Dialectic and Narrative in Aquinas: An Interpretation of the* Summa contra gentiles (Notre Dame, Ind.: University of Notre Dame Press, 1995), 109–115; 131–132.

21. *ST* I 62.6 ad 1.

22. *De malo* 2.11.

23. *ST* I 95.1 sc.

24. *De malo* 2.11 sc 4.

25. *ST* III 9.2 ad 3. Hence, grace is not "miraculous," because the human soul is *"naturaliter capax gratiae"* or *"capax dei per gratiam"* (*ST* I-II 113.10). See Aertsen, *Nature and Creature,* 369, and Joseph Wawrykow, *God's Grace and Human Action: "Merit" in the Theology of Thomas Aquinas* (Notre Dame: University of Notre Dame Press, 1995), 157–8 n. 26. See also *ST* I-II 113.10.

26. *ST* I-II 113.10; *ST* III 4.1 ad 2; *ST* I 62.7 ad 3. See J.-H. Nicolas, *Les profondeurs de la grâce* (Paris: Beauchesne, 1969), 254–255.

27. *ST* I-II 114.2 ad 1; *ST* I-II 114.2.

28. *ST* I 95.4 ad 1; *ST* I-II 109.2.

29. *ST* I-II 112.1 ad 2; *ST* I 73.1 ad 1; *ST* I-II 114.6; *ST* I-II 106.1 ad 3. Nicolas, *Profondeurs de la grâce,* 256–258.

our sanctification.[30] It is solely through the life, death and resurrection of Christ that God pours out his healing grace upon us.[31] "We receive this grace through God's son made man, whose humanity grace filled and from which it flowed out to us."[32] "We cannot of ourselves attain grace, but only through Christ."[33] Aquinas further underlines that Christ effects this sanctification in us through the action of the Holy Spirit.[34] We should recognize here that Aquinas places his theology of Christ and of redemption within his understanding of the primary function of grace, which is to make us sons and daughters of God by granting us a fuller participation in God's divine life.[35] We are to be conformed to Christ and thereby given a share in God's divine life.[36] "The mission of the divine persons brings us to [heavenly] beatitude."[37]

Aquinas describes this graced participation as a participation in God's inner trinitarian life.[38] The primary gift of grace is God himself.[39] God becomes present within us in a new way.[40] The effect of this new presence is to elevate the natural image of God reflected in our spiritual powers of intellect and will.[41] Like wood that begins to glow with the light of the fire that envelops it, the human intellect and will, immersed in the trinitarian life of God, begin to participate more fully in the spiritual acts of knowing and loving God.[42] William Hill describes this elevated participation succinctly.

30. *ST* I 43.7 See also *ST* I-II 114.6.

31. *ST* II-II 2.7: "man's way to happiness is through the mystery of the incarnation and passion of Christ."

32. *ST* I-II 108.1.

33. *ST* I-II 108.2. See also *ST* III 8.6.

34. *ST* I 43.7; *ST* I-II 108.1; *ST* III 8.1 ad 1.

35. *ST* I 95.4 ad 1.

36. Jean-Pierre Torrell, *Saint Thomas Aquinas, volume 2: Spiritual Master* (Washington, D.C.: The Catholic University of America, 2003), 140–145.

37. *ST* II-II 2.8 ad 3.

38. *ST* III 23.3.

39. *ST* I 38.1.

40. *ST* I 43.3. Aquinas is careful to note that although God becomes present in a new way, he himself does not change. The becoming occurs on the part of the creature. See, for example, his description of the incarnation (*ST* III 1.1 ad 1).

41. *ST* I 93.4.

42. *ST* I-II 62.1 ad 1.

The creature by its very existence shares in being and goodness that is found in God as in its source, yet the perfections in question remain the creature's own, proper to its own level of existence, even though derived from God. In contrast to this, the New Being by grace means entry into God's being *as it is proper to him,* i.e., entrance into the uncreated divine life of Father, Son, and Spirit—possible to the creature only as the term of its intentionality of knowledge and love.[43]

God eternally speaks a Word that breaths forth Love.[44] These eternal processions are reflected in the knowledge and love present in the rational creature. In the gift of grace, God draws these powers into a fuller participation of his knowledge and love, a participation that is inchoate in this life, but complete in the future life of glory.[45]

St. Thomas describes grace as a qualitative *"habitus"* of the soul that elevates human nature to participate in the divine nature. As Scripture states, "he has give us the most great and precious promises, so that through them you may come to participate in the divine nature" (2 Pt 1.4).[46] Moreover, just as natural powers of the soul flow from the soul and are that by which the soul acts, so too God's grace acts in the human soul as a type of "second nature" from which certain cognitive and appetitive *habitus* flow and are that by which one lives his or her graced life.[47]

Thomas explains that these infused *habitus* or dispositions are of three types. First, there are the three theological virtues that perfect the soul's spiritual powers in relation to God as the ultimate end. There is faith, which perfects the intellect, and there are hope and charity, which perfect the will.[48] Second, there are infused moral virtues that perfect the intellect and will (and the lower appetites) in relation to those things that are ordered to God as the ultimate end. In other words, these virtues perfect our spiritual powers in relation to the means toward our ultimate end.[49] Lastly, there are other infused cognitive and appetitive

43. William Hill, *The Three-Personed God: The Trinity as a Mystery of Salvation* (Washington, D.C.: The Catholic University of America Press, 1982), 276. Emphasis in the original.

44. *ST* I 43.5 ad 2.

45. Ibid.

46. *ST* I-II 50.2; *ST* I-II 110.3.

47. *ST* I-II 110.3 ad 3; *ST* I-II 110.4.

48. See *ST* I-II 62.1–3.

49. See *ST* I-II 63.3 corpus and ad 1.

habitus that perfect the intellect and will by rendering them receptive to the guiding action of the Holy Spirit.[50] These *habitus* are the gifts of the Holy Spirit, which the Fathers and the Scholastics find revealed in Isaiah 11.1–2.[51]

Throughout this psychology of grace, Aquinas portrays sanctifying grace as elevating and respecting the natural relationship between intellect and will in human action. There is, however, one important difference. In this life, the intellect does not see God directly. Grace unites us to God as to one unknown.[52] Consequently, the intellect's relationship to the will in the graced knowledge and love of God differs from the relationship between intellect and will existing in the natural knowledge and love of God. To understand the character of this new relationship, we must consider more closely Aquinas' theology of faith.

The Virtue of Faith and Its Act

The goal of God's graced action upon the intellect is to bring the intellect to the unending and unmediated vision of God. Grace effects this vision within us, however, only in heaven after we have completed our earthly journey.[53] During our earthly pilgrimage, grace effects an inchoate participation in the heavenly vision of God by placing in the intellect a disposition *(habitus)* to believe in the revealed truth about God and in the rational creature's vocation to live in loving union with him.[54] This infused disposition is the theological virtue of faith. The cognitive component of the life of grace, therefore, begins in this life as faith in God and is brought to completion as the vision of God in heaven.[55]

50. See *ST* I-II 68.1.

51. See *ST* I-II 68.4. Edward O'Connor, "The Evolution of St. Thomas' Thought on the Gifts," in *Summa theologiae,* volume 24, edited and translated by Edward O'Connor (New York: McGraw-Hill Book Co., 1973), Appendix 4, 110–130.

52. *ST* I 12.13 ad 1: *"ei quasi ignoto coniungamur."* Torrell, *Saint Thomas Aquinas: Spiritual Master,* 34–39.

53. *ST* I-II 65.5.

54. Gregory Rocca, "Analogy as Judgment and Faith in God's Incomprehensibility: A Study in the Theological Epistemology of Thomas Aquinas" (Ph.D. diss., The Catholic University of America, 1989), 319–320.

55. *Super epistolam ad hebraeos* 11.1 [54–59].

As we would expect from this description of faith, St. Thomas maintains throughout his career that God himself, considered as the first truth *(prima veritas)*, is the object of faith.[56] The knowledge of faith, however, differs from other forms of human knowing. Thomas' portrayal of this difference is shaped by the description of faith in the Letter to the Hebrews as "the substance of things to be hoped for, the evidence of things that appear not" (Heb 11.1), which Thomas maintains can be rewritten as follows: "faith is a habit of mind, whereby eternal life is begun in us, making the intellect assent to what is non-apparent."[57] To explain the implications of this description, Thomas at various places in his works compares the knowledge of faith to other types of human knowledge.[58]

First, there is the simple and clear understanding *(intellectus)* of principles, which Thomas regards as analogous to sight *(visio)*. Second, there is the knowledge of conclusions attained through deliberation and understood through first principles. The process of reasoning that leads to this knowledge is what Thomas calls science *(scientia)*. Since one knows the conclusions of science in and through one's understanding of principles, science also leads to understanding *(intellectus)* and yields a form of knowledge akin to sight. These forms of knowledge are analogous to the physical act of seeing because both render their objects evident to the intellect. Indeed, the certitude of this type of knowledge is based on its evidence. The intellect assents to its truth because the identity *(adequatio)* between mind and thing is clearly evident—the identity between what reason proposes about something and the way that thing really is.[59] A lesser type of human knowing occurs when there is not sufficient evidence to establish the relationship between thought and thing. In such cases there is either doubt or opinion *(dubitatio vel opinio)*. In opinion the mind assents to one possibility, retaining awareness, however, that the other possibility might be true. Doubt occurs when the mind withholds assent because both possibilities appear equally plausible.

56. *In sent.* III 23.1.1; *De veritate* 14.8; *ST* II-II 1.1.
57. *ST* II-II 4.1. See also *In sent.* III 23.2.1 and *De veritate* 14.2.
58. See *In sent.* III 23.2.2A; *De veritate* 14.1; *ST* II-II 2.1.
59. See *ST* I 16.2.

Aquinas describes the act of faith (i.e., belief) as a type of knowing that shares elements in common with *intellectus* and *scientia,* on the one hand, and *opinio* and *dubitatio,* on the other. Like *intellectus* and *scientia,* belief is certain. Belief, science, and understanding all generate firm and certain assent. Yet, unlike *intellectus* and *scientia,* the certitude of faith is not based on the evidence of its object. Faith is of things unseen. Consequently, belief shares in common with opinion and doubt that its object is unseen.[60] Faith is an assent without clear evidence, without vision of the object to which one is assenting. The intellect assents, but unlike *intellectus* or *scientia,* the mind remains restless. It continues to think about and mull over the truths to which it assents, striving to understand them more fully. For this reason, we can join St. Augustine in characterizing faith as "thinking with assent" *(cogitare cum assentione).*[61]

This description of faith raises the question of the origin of faith's certitude. What leads the believer to assent firmly to an object he or she does not see? Why is the assent of faith more perfect than opinion, since, as is the case with one who opines, the believer does not see the identity between thought and thing? Throughout his career, Aquinas responds to this problem with a twofold affirmation: assent is caused by the will and its certitude is caused by God who moves the will to move the intellect. "Believing is an act of the intellect assenting to divine truth by a command of the will moved by God through grace."[62] The will moves the intellect to assent firmly to the truths of faith from a motion caused by God, who is First Truth itself.

Over the years, however, Aquinas modified his description of how God moves the intellect and will in the assent of faith. This modification parallels the changes Aquinas introduces into his mature understanding of intellect and will in human action. Aquinas recognizes that faith's assent is an act of theoretical reasoning. Yet, since the will moves the intel-

60. *ST* II-II 2.1. See also *In sent.* III 23.2.2A.

61. *In sent.* III 23.2.2A; *De veritate* 14.1; *ST* II-II 2.1 sc. See Benoit Duroux, *La psychologie de la foi chez s. Thomas d'Aquin* (Tournai, Belgium: Desclée, 1963), 61–88.

62. *ST* II-II 2.9. Note that the *Catechism of the Catholic Church* (155) employs this same definition. Marie George, "'Trust Me.' 'Why Should I?' Aquinas on Faith and Reason," in *The Ever-Illuminating Wisdom of St. Thomas Aquinas* (San Francisco: Ignatius Press, 1999), 53, n. 10. See also *ST* II-II 2.1 ad 3; *ST* II-II 4.1 ad 2.

lect to make this assent, belief is analogous to an act of practical reasoning.[63] In both cases, the intellect's act is shaped by the action of the will. Not surprisingly, therefore, Aquinas' description of the act of faith develops as he develops his understanding of the relationship between intellect and will in practical reasoning.

Evolution of St. Thomas' Theology of Faith

As is the case with the other changes St. Thomas introduces into his psychology of human action, the changes he introduces into his theology of faith occur within a context of basic continuity. Consequently, to understand better the significance of these changes, it will be helpful to begin by noting the continuities existing between his earlier and later accounts of faith.

Continuities in St. Thomas' Teachings on Faith

As we noted above, St. Thomas maintains throughout his career that faith imparts a type of knowledge that shares features in common with both science and opinion, but differs from both by being the product of the will's choice. Thomas remains unwaveringly true to this insight, asserting in both his earlier and later works that faith's act proceeds from both the intellect and the will.[64] The act of faith requires some (even though limited) conceptual knowledge of God in the intellect and some motion in the will. Together they make belief a free act—an act of *liberum arbitrium*—that has moral significance.[65] (For example, unbelief

63. *De veritate* 14.4; *ST* II-II 4.2 ad 3.

64. *In sent.* III 23.2.2A: *"fides captivare dicitur intellectum, inquantum non secundum proprium motum ad aliquid determinatur, sed secundum imperium voluntatis." De veritate* 14.5: *"cum igitur fides sit in intellectu secundum quod est motus et imperatus a voluntate; id quod est ex parte cognitionis, est quasi materiale in ipsa; sed ex parte voluntatis accipienda est sua formatio." ST* II-II 2.1 ad 3: *"intellectus credentis determinatur ad unum non per rationem, sed per voluntatem. Et ideo assensus hic accipitur pro actu intellectus secundum quod a voluntate determinatur ad unum."*

65. *In sent.* III 25.2.1A: *"actus autem omnium virtutum dependet ab actu fidei, quae intentionem dirigit: unde in omni qui habet liberum arbitrium exigitur ad salutem ejus quod habeat actum fidei, et non solum habitum. Fides autem non potest exire in actum, nisi aliquid determinate et explicite cognoscendo quod ad fidem pertineat; et ideo omni ei qui habet usum liberi arbitrii,*

by one who has been offered the gift of faith is sinful precisely because one's response to the gift is a free act.)[66] Moreover, throughout his career Thomas describes the certitude of faith as resting on God as first truth.[67] Faith is certain because of the veracity of the one from whom the message of faith comes.[68]

In his *Commentary on the Sentences,* St. Thomas introduces a distinction between the formal and material objects of a power, to explain unique features of faith's act.[69] The material aspect of a power's object is *what* the power grasps or attains, while the formal aspect of the object is that *by which* the power grasps or attains its material object. Thomas offers the example of sight. "Light is what is formal in the object of sight, because it makes a colored thing actually visible, while materially color itself is the object because it is potentially visible."[70] In the case of faith, the formal aspect of faith's object functions like light in relation to the physical power of sight.

> Since faith does not assent to anything except on account of believable first truth, nothing can be actually believable except because of first truth, just as color is visible because of light. Thus, first truth is formal in the object of faith and is that from which the whole character of faith's object derives.[71]

God as first truth revealing the message of faith makes this message believable just as light makes color visible.

In the *De veritate,* Aquinas offers a similar explanation, but introduces

---

habere fidem explicitam quantum ad aliquid, est de necessitate salutis." ST II-II 2.9: *"ipsum autem credere est actus intellectus assentientis veritati divinae ex imperio voluntatis a deo motae per gratiam, et sic subiacet libero arbitrio in ordine ad deum."*

66. See *ST* II-II 10.1 and 2.

67. Duroux, *La psychologie de la foi,* 31–37.

68. *In sent.* III 23.2.2b: *"ratio enim qua voluntas inclinatur ad assentiendum his quae non videt, est quia deus ea dicit: sicut homo in his quae non videt, credit testimonio alicuius boni viri qui videt ea quae ipse non videt."* (Notice Thomas' problematic description of the will as having cognitive capacities [e.g., *assentio* and *visio*], as if the will were a miniature agent. St. Thomas will rectify this slip in his later works.) *De veritate* 14.2 ad 9; *ST* II-II 4.8 ad 2.

69. Concerning the distinction between material and formal object as it relates to St. Thomas' theology of faith, see T. C. O'Brien, "Objects and Virtues," in *Summa theologiae,* volume 31, edited and translated by T. C. O'Brien, appendix 1, (New York: McGraw-Hill Book Co., 1974), 178–185, and Cessario, *Christian Faith and the Theological Life,* 49–83.

70. *In sent.* III 24.1.1A.

71. Ibid.

two interesting clarifications. First, setting aside the distinction between the formal and material aspects of the object, he probes more deeply the analogy between first truth and light. Thomas considers an objection to the claim that first truth is the object of faith. The objector himself accepts the analogy between first truth and light, but notes that Aristotle only explicitly calls color the object of sight. Thus, since light is apparently not the proper object of sight, neither is first truth the proper object of faith. This objection forces Thomas to look more closely at how light is the object of sight.

> In one way light is the object of sight and in another way not. In so far as light is not seen by us except to the extent that it is conjoined to some determinate body—either by reflection or by some other means—light is not said to be the *per se* object of sight. Instead, this is color, which is always in a determinate body. Yet, in so far as nothing can be seen except through light, light is called the first visible, as Ptolemy also says. In this way also first truth is the first and *per se* object of faith.[72]

Aquinas is here grappling with how first truth can both be the object of faith and yet remain unseen. Like light, first truth, without itself being directly seen, is the medium by which the contents of faith are believed. In the body of the article in which the above response appears, Aquinas considers how the believer is "conjoined" to first truth. God as first truth remains unseen, but faith nonetheless unites us to him. Being united to the one who infallibly knows that the message of faith is true, we are able to assent to this message with infallible certitude. It is here that Aquinas introduces a second clarification. Since the message to which God empowers us to assent is a message that proclaims truths about God himself, God as first truth is both the "medium of faith" and its object. In other words, what Aquinas describes in the *Sentences* as the formal aspect of the object *(quod est formale in obiecto),* he now describes in the *De veritate* as the *"medium"* by which we attain that object.[73] Aquinas changes his terminology, but in both works he portrays first truth as that *by which* the truths of faith are believed.

In the *Summa theologiae,* Aquinas offers a synthesis of his earlier de-

72. *De veritate* 14.8 ad 4.

73. *De veritate* 14.8 ad 9: *"veritas prima se habet in fide et ut medium et ut obiectum."*

scriptions.[74] The certitude of faith rests on God who is the formal medium by which the believer is led to assent. Aquinas begins by establishing the distinction between the material object *(materiale obiectum)* and the formal aspect of the object *(formalis ratio obiecti)*. "The object of every cognitive habit includes two things: first, that which is known materially and functions as the material object; second, that by which it is known and which is the formal aspect of the object."[75] Aquinas offers the example of geometry. The conclusions of geometry function as the material object of that science, while the formal aspect of the object are the means *(media)* of demonstration through which the conclusions are known. Similarly, first truth as the formal aspect of faith's object is the medium of assent through which the message of faith is rendered believable. Likewise, the material object of faith is God and other things in relation to God as they relate to our salvation.

Lastly, Aquinas affirms throughout his works that although the light of faith imparts a knowledge beyond what the human intellect can naturally attain on its own, the mode by which we understand this higher knowledge is still according to the human mode of knowing, which is in and through sense images, conceptual propositions, and the judgment of reason in the act of assent. Although God is the material object of faith, faith provides only limited knowledge of God through the propositions expressed in the articles of faith. In himself, the triune God is one and simple. Yet, because of the limitations of the human intellect, in this life we know God through complex propositions.

In his *Commentary on the Sentences,* Aquinas offers the example of the Christian's faith in the Incarnation. When we believe in the Incarnation, we are not merely forming the concept of the Incarnation in our minds, otherwise anyone who thought about the Incarnation would qualify as a believer. Instead, one who believes in the Incarnation is affirming the existence of the Incarnation.[76] This affirmation arises in the mind by means of a complex judgment, because affirmations of existence "are made by the intellect composing and dividing."[77]

74. Rocca, "Analogy as Judgment and Faith," 318.

75. *ST* II-II 1.1.

76. *In sent.* III 24.1.1B.

77. Ibid.

Aquinas is here addressing an aspect of knowledge he will develop more fully in the *Summa theologiae.* There he defines truth as the *adequatio* between mind and thing, by which he means that truth exists in the mind when the form of the thing known is present immaterially in the intellect.[78] This occurs in simple apprehension, whereby the intellect comes to know *what a thing is.* Aquinas explains, however, that although at this level the mind contains truth, it does not yet know truth. It only knows truth when it judges that what the mind affirms actually exists in reality.[79] Stated in another way, the human intellect attains knowledge of truth through affirming the existence of a predicate in a subject. Throughout his career, Aquinas holds that faith retains this element of the regular human mode of knowing truth. All perfections are one and simple in God, but in our knowledge of God we express God's simple perfection through composition and division.[80]

Once again, however, we encounter here the radical difference between faith and other forms of human knowing. In scientific knowledge, reason is able to judge the truth of its knowledge because it can see how the predicate is present in the subject. Most fundamentally, the intellect sees what it knows in and through principles naturally evident to it. In faith, however, the believer affirms the truth of a proposition without *seeing* the truth of the proposition. The believer does not see how the perfections affirmed about God actually exist in God. As we noted earlier, what leads the intellect to assent is not the intellect's ability to see the identity between thought and thing, but the command of the will moving the intellect to assent.

> Faith is in the theoretical intellect to the extent that it is subject to the command of the will. . . . Hence, in believing the will commands the intellect, not only with respect to executing the act, but also with respect to the determination of its object, since the intellect assents to a determinate belief from the command of the will.[81]

It is in grappling with how God moves us to make this assent that Aquinas begins to modify his description of supernatural faith.

78. *ST* I 16.1.
79. *ST* I 16.2.
80. *ST* I 13.12.
81. *De virtutibus in commune* 1.7.

St. Thomas' Earlier and Later Theologies of Faith

The key feature in the development of St. Thomas' theology of faith is his description of how God moves the human person to make the act of faith. In his earlier works Thomas describes this cognitively. The revealed truths of faith attract the will to act. In his later works, however, after becoming aware of the Council of Orange's condemnation of Semi-Pelagianism and after discovering a crucial passage from Aristotle's *Eudemian Ethics,* Thomas develops a more balanced view. An infused cognitive light and an appetitive *instinctus* become the twin principles of faith's act, analogous to the natural light of practical reason and the natural inclination of the will that together form the twin principles of the natural human act.

Commentary on the Sentences: ratio linked to a *visio*

In the *Sentences,* St. Thomas asserts that there is a "thinking" *(cogitatio)* that precedes faith and that inclines the will toward believing.

> Faith lies at a midpoint between two acts of thinking: one of which inclines the will toward believing, and this thinking precedes faith; the other, however, seeks to understand what is already believed, and this thinking exists simultaneously with the assent of faith.[82]

Thomas describes this antecedent thinking as a *"ratio"* that functions as a motive for belief. He regards this *ratio* as one of the three elements on which faith depends.

> The act of believing depends on three things: on the intellect, which is directed to one thing; on the will, which by its command directs the intellect; and on a *ratio* that inclines the will.[83]

Aquinas goes on to explain what he means by this ratio.

> As to the *ratio* that inclines the will to the act of faith, this is to believe God *(credere deo):* for the *ratio* by which the will is inclined to assent to what it does not see is because it is God who speaks it, just as someone who does not see

82. *In sent.* III 23.2.2A ad 2.
83. *In sent.* III 23.2.2B.

certain things, will believe the testimony of a certain good man who sees the things he does not see.[84]

In the following section *(distinctio)* in his commentary, Aquinas will for the first time describe this *ratio* as the formal aspect of the object of faith *(ratio formalis obiecti)*.[85] Even in distinction 23, however, he identifies it with God himself: "the *ratio* that inclines the will toward the things that are believed is first truth itself, God, who is believed."[86]

Here, however, we encounter a difficulty. How can this *ratio* be both God himself and a "thinking" *(cogitatio)*? Aquinas, it would seem, is speaking elliptically. He will state more clearly further on that the medium of belief is God himself as the one who speaks the truths of faith. Yet here, the *ratio* implies or presupposes some sort of knowledge or sight that reveals God to be the one speaking in him who announces the faith.

With regard to what is believed, it is said to be from hearing, because the determination of what is to be believed occurs in us from God speaking to us, either from an interior speech or from an external voice. Yet, with regard to the *ratio* that induces the will to believe, this is said to be from the sight of something that reveals God to be the one who speaks in him who announces the faith.[87]

God is able to be the *ratio* or medium of our faith because something has revealed him to be speaking through those who proclaim the faith. Aquinas does not here discuss the character of this seeing. Presumably this knowledge or sight is something we learn from those who preach the faith to us or see in the context of their preaching. Either way, the important point for our discussion is that the act of faith presupposes antecedent knowledge. At this point in his career, Aquinas asserts that a thinking *(cogitatio)* about something seen *(visio)* is the sufficient motive cause of the will's act. As we shall see, in his later works, Aquinas is no longer willing to describe knowledge as the sufficient principle of the will's motion in the act of faith.

84. Ibid.

85. *In sent.* III 24.1.1A.

86. *In sent.* III 23.2.2C.

87. *In sent.* III 23.3.2 ad 2.

De veritate: praemio as a *bonum conveniens*

In the *De veritate,* St. Thomas is willing to describe faith as a sight only to express faith's certainty. To say that faith's knowledge is a type of sight is only to say that faith's assent is as certain as sight. Of itself, however, faith's object remains unseen.[88] Thomas gropes here for a cause that moves the will without also being a *visio* that simultaneously moves the intellect. He finds such a cause in the will's proper object, the good. The will's object, we are told, is sufficient to move the will, but not sufficient to move the intellect.

> Sometimes the intellect cannot be affixed to one side of a contradiction either immediately through the definition of terms (as is the case with knowledge of principles), or in virtue of the principles (as is the case with knowledge of conclusions through demonstration). Instead, it is affixed by the will, which chooses to assent precisely and fixedly to one side because of something that is sufficient to move the will, but not sufficient to move the intellect, namely, because it seems good or fitting to assent to this side. This is the disposition of the believer, since we believe what another says because it seems fitting or useful to do so.[89]

The will assents to someone's testimony because it seems good to do so. Thomas sees this dynamic at work in all types of faith, but especially in the theological virtue of faith. In the case of theological faith, however, the reason why believing God's word seems good is because of the promised reward for believing in this way.

> Thus also we are moved to assent to what God says because we are promised eternal life as a reward if we believe. And this reward moves the will to assent to what is said, although the intellect is not moved by anything it understands.[90]

The will is moved to command the intellect to assent to God's word because we are promised eternal life as the reward for this assent. Here again Aquinas' argument presupposes the presence of knowledge in the

88. *De veritate* 14.2 ad 15.
89. *De veritate* 14.1.
90. Ibid.

intellect that moves the will to assent to the articles of faith. Knowledge of our promised reward moves the will to assent.

Thomas' description of this dynamic raises a question: what can move the will without simultaneously moving the intellect? Aquinas cannot intend here to drive a wedge between the intellect's object and the will's object, between the true and the good. Instead, his intention seems to be to distinguish theoretical truth, which necessarily moves the intellect to assent, from practical truth (the good), which only moves the intellect under the direction of the will. Hence, although faith's assent is an act of the theoretical intellect, the object that moves the will to move the intellect to assent belongs to the order of practical truth, which moves the intellect only as directed by the will.[91] By the time Aquinas reconsiders the nature of faith in the *Summa theologiae,* he recognizes that it is not enough to describe the will's role in faith as generated by the attraction of a known good.

Summa theologiae: lumen fidei and *instinctus fidei*

A number of scholars have shown that St. Thomas modifies his description of faith upon discovering the Council of Orange's condemnation of Semi-Pelagianism.[92] At issue for St. Thomas is the adequacy of describing the causality of grace in the act of faith merely in cognitive terms. As we have seen, in his earlier works, Thomas is content to describe the act of faith as caused by knowledge. A *cogitatio, visio,* or *bonum cognitum* moves the will to act. It moves the will to move the intellect to assent to the articles of faith. This description implies that, although the habitual cognitive motive of faith—in other words the *habitus fidei*—is divinely infused, the act of faith is essentially generated by the will's own natural power. When, however, Aquinas begins to grasp that not only the habit of belief, but also the act of belief itself must be caused by God's graced action, he develops an account of how grace in the gift of faith also elevates the will's act.

91. *De veritate* 14.4.

92. H. Bouillard, *Conversion et grâce chez saint Thomas* (Paris: Aubier, Editions Montaigne, 1944), 92–134; Max Seckler, *Instinkt und Glaubenswille nach Thomas von Aquin* (Mainz: Mattias-Grünewald-Verlag, 1962), 90–132.

Concerning the human person's assent to the things that are of faith, we may observe a twofold cause, one of which induces externally, such as seeing a miracle or hearing someone's persuasive arguments for faith, neither of which are a sufficient cause, since of those who see one and the same miracle or hear the same preaching, some believe and some do not. Hence, we must assert another cause, which is interior and which moves the human person interiorly to assent to the things that are of faith. The Pelagians held that the sole cause of this was human *liberum arbitrium*. Consequently they argued that the beginning of faith is from us, in so far as it is from ourselves that we are ready to assent to the things that are of faith, while the consummation of faith is from God, who proposes to us the things we should believe. But this is false because when we assent to what is of faith we are elevated above our nature, which can only occur in us from a supernatural principle moving us interiorly, and this is God. Therefore, with regard to assent, which is the principal act of faith, faith is from God moving us interiorly by grace.[93]

Consequently, although belief is an act caused by the will, "the human will must be prepared by God through his grace."[94] Aquinas in his later works develops his understanding of how God moves the will to initiate this act of assent.

Edward Schillebeeckx describes well how recent scholarship understands this development in Aquinas' thought. Commenting on Max Seckler's seminal study of faith in Aquinas, Schillebeeckx states:

Seckler proceeds from Bouillard's correct finding that, during his first period in Italy (1259–1260), Aquinas, either indirectly or directly, came across the documents of the ecclesiastical condemnation of Semi-Pelagianism. From a certain point onwards (in the middle of the period in which he was writing his third book *Contra gentiles*), three ideas which are not found in Aquinas's earlier works suddenly made an appearance in his writing: greater stress was placed on God's initiative; an *auxilium divinum* was seen to be directly active in the human will; and the older doctrine of *habitus fidei*, faith as a habit, was subordinated to a more dynamic view of justification, so that the movement of God, the *motio divina*, came to occupy a central place. Bouillard, whose view was later adopted by Chenu, gave the following reasons for the appearance of these new ideas—Aquinas's increasing knowledge of the later works of Au-

93. *ST* II-II 6.1.
94. *ST* II-II 6.1 ad 3.

gustine, his more intensive study of the Bible and his discovery of Aristotle's *Eudemian Ethics.*[95]

Schillebeeckx notes that while Seckler agrees with Bouillard, he takes the analysis one step further. Seckler finds that Aquinas in his later discussions of faith begins making explicit reference to the Pelagians and links his critique of them to the key passage in the *Eudemian Ethics* where Aristotle describes God as moving the intellect and will to act. Seckler discovers that the Latin translation of the *Eudemian Ethics*—more accurately, the Latin of the *Liber de bona fortuna* that contains fragments of the *Eudemian Ethics*[96]—provides a bridge between the condemnation of Semi-Pelagianism and Aristotle's psychology of action. The bridge is the term *instinctus*. Schillebeeckx explains:

Suddenly one finds repeated references to *pelagiani* (Semi-Pelagianism), each time connected with a quotation from the *Eudemian Ethics* (for the first time in *Contra gentiles* III, c. 89, 147, 149). Bouillard, however, had not noticed that the concept *instinctus* also appeared at this very point in Thomas's works in connection with the act of faith. And it is a remarkable fact that the term *instinctus* played a part both in the Church's documents condemning Semi-Pelagianism and in the Latin translation of the *Eudemian Ethics*. The word *instinctus* is the only connection that can be established in Thomas's thought between anti-Semi-Pelagianism and these *Ethics* of Aristotle. Just as the danger of Semi-Pelagianism was averted in the writings of the Church Fathers by an appeal to the *instinctus divinus*, so too did this same term play a similar part centuries later in the works of Aquinas.[97]

95. Edward Schillebeeckx, *Revelation and Theology*, volume 2, translated by N. D. Smith (New York: Sheed and Ward, 1968), 35–36.

96. For a brief account of the fragments of the *Eudemian Ethics* in the *Liber de bona fortuna* and St. Thomas' acquaintance with them, see Th. Deman, "Le *'Liber de bona fortuna'* dans la théologie de s. Thomas d'Aquin," *Revue des sciences philosophiques et théologiques* 17 (1928): 38–45.

97. Schillebeeckx, *Revelation and Theology*, vol. 2, pp. 36–37. The passage in question from the *Eudemian Ethics* as it appears in the Latin of the *Liber de bona fortuna* reads as follows: "*Quod autem queritur hoc est: quid motus principium in anima. Palam quemadmodum in toto deus, et omne illud: movet enim aliquo modo omnia quod in nobis divinum. Rationis autem principium non ratio, sed aliquid melius; quid igitur utique erit melius et scientia et intellectu nisi deus? Virtus enim intellectus organum. Et propter hoc, quod olim dicebatur, bene fortunati vocantur qui si impetum faciant dirigunt sine ratione existentis. Et consiliari non expedit*

When we consider the discoveries of these scholars in light of our earlier analysis of Aquinas' mature psychology of action, we find that not only does *instinctus* provide a bridge between his "anti-Semi-Pelagianism" and the *Ethics* of Aristotle, it also establishes a bridge between Aquinas' mature theology of faith and his mature psychology of action. Stated in another way, granted that the catalyst for Aquinas' later theology of faith was the discovery of the Church's condemnation of Semi-Pelagianism, the way he chooses to rectify his earlier theology of faith is shaped by his growing understanding of the relationship between intellect and will in human action. Note, for example, that in order to understand that knowledge is not the sufficient cause of the will's motion, one must first recognize clearly the distinction between specification and exercise, something that Aquinas introduces in his later descriptions of human action. The word *instinctus,* used by Aristotle to describe God's role in the principles of action and by the Council Fathers to describe God's role in the act of faith, enables Aquinas to develop this parallel between the natural and supernatural principles of action.

In chapter two we saw that Aquinas in his mature thought expresses more clearly the lines of causality at work in human action. The intellect functions as the formal cause of the act, presenting the will its object and specifying the character of its action, while the will functions as the efficient cause of the act, moving the intellect and the other powers to act, even directing the intellect in the act of specification. Aquinas describes these twin natural principles as a cognitive light and an appetitive inclination. Significantly, Aquinas holds that the cognitive light is a participation in the divine light, and that the appetitive inclination of the will flows from a divine *instinctus.*

> . . . the light of natural reason, whereby we discern what is good and what is evil (which is the function of the natural law), is nothing else than an imprint on us of the divine light.[98]

---

ipsis: habent enim principium tale quod melius intellectu et consilio. Qui autem rationem, hoc autem non habent neque divinos instinctus, hoc non possunt; sine ratione enim existentes adipiscuntur."

98. *ST* I-II 91.2.

It is necessary to hold that in the first movement of the will, the will proceeds from the *instinctus* of some exterior mover.[99]

In his mature theology of faith, Aquinas regards supernatural faith as a divinely infused principle of belief that elevates both the cognitive and appetitive principles of human action. As Aquinas explains in his introductory treatment of the theological virtues in the *Summa theologiae,* this elevation occurs most fully in living faith, in other words, in faith informed by the virtue of charity elevating the action of the will.

The theological virtues direct the human person to supernatural happiness as by natural inclination humans are directed to their connatural end. This happens in two ways. First, concerning reason or intellect, in so far as it contains first universal principles known to us by the natural light of the intellect, from which reason proceeds both in speculation and in action. Second, through the rectitude of the will which naturally tends toward the good of reason. . . . Consequently, with respect to both of these the human person needs something else to be added to him supernaturally which will order him towards his supernatural end. First, concerning the intellect, the human person receives certain supernatural principles, which are grasped by means of a divine light; these are the matters of belief which pertain to faith. Second, the will is ordered to this end both as to the motion of intention, tending to this end as something attainable (and this pertains to hope), and as to a certain spiritual union, whereby the will is in a certain way transformed into the end (and this pertains to charity). For the appetite of a thing is naturally moved and tends toward its connatural end, and this motion proceeds from a certain conformity of the thing with its end.[100]

Faith elevates the intellect through an infused light, while hope and charity elevate the action of the will, empowering it to attain its end.

Nevertheless, Aquinas maintains that even lifeless faith, faith unformed by charity, contains an appetitive element that is moved to act by the graced action of God.[101] "Some act of the will is presupposed for

99. *ST* I-II 9.4. In a subsequent article, we learn that this *"exterior movens"* is God himself (*ST* I-II 9.6). See also *De malo* 6. Note that both at *ST* I-II 9.4 and *De malo* 6 Aquinas explicitly cites the passage from the *Eudemian Ethics* that contains the term *instinctus* in the Latin translation appearing in the *Liber de bona fortuna.*

100. *ST* I-II 62.3. Elsewhere Aquinas explains that the *credibilia* function as premises in which theological conclusions are known (*ST* II-II 4.8 ad 3).

101. Duroux, *La psychologie de la foi,* 201.

faith, but not an act of the will informed by charity."[102] "The faith that is a gift of grace inclines the human person to believe by giving him a certain affection for the good, even when faith is unformed by charity."[103] Just as he earlier described the will's natural motion as having its source in a divine *instinctus,* so too Aquinas describes God's action on the will in faith as an *instinctus.* Thus, in describing what God gives us in the gift of faith, Aquinas' states that "included in this giving is not only the *habitus,* which is faith, but also the interior *instinctus* to believe."[104] Moreover, in commenting on Jesus' statement in the Gospel of John that, "no one can come to me unless the Father, who sent me, draws him," Aquinas states the following.

> The Father draws us to the Son in many ways, using the different ways in which we can be drawn without compulsion. One may draw another by a persuasive reason. The Father draws us to the Son in this way by demonstrating to us that he is his Son. . . . But an object or external revelation are not the only things that draw us. An interior *instinctus* also impels and moves us to believe. Thus, the Father draws many to his Son by an *instinctus* of divine operation moving the human heart interiorly to believe: 'It is God who works in us, both to will and to accomplish' (Phil 2.13).[105]

For this reason, we are induced to believe not only by "divine teaching confirmed by miracles" but also and even more by "an interior *instinctus* to believe."[106] In Aquinas' mature theology of faith, therefore, faith both imparts a higher cognitive light, which is a fuller participation in the divine light, and a higher appetitive inclination, which is a fuller participation in the divine *instinctus.* Yet, as we have seen, for faith to merit the promise it believes, this faith must be formed by charity.[107] Before turning our attention to charity, it will be helpful to review our findings concerning the development that occurs in Aquinas' theology of faith.

102. *ST* II-II 4.7 ad 5.

103. *ST* II-II 5.2 ad 2. In *De veritate* 14.2 ad 10, Aquinas distinguishes this act from hope and charity.

104. *Super ioannem* 6.4 [241–244].

105. *Super ioannem* 6.5 [110–115, 149–156].

106. *ST* II-II 2.9 ad 3.

107. *ST* II-II 4.3.

Evolution of St. Thomas' Theology of Faith: Conclusions

We began our analysis of St. Thomas' theology of faith by recognizing the basic continuity existing between his early and later descriptions of faith. Throughout his career, Thomas portrays faith as a *habitus* existing in the intellect that disposes us to assent to the truths of faith from the command of the will. From the outset, Thomas has a keen sense of the intellect's twofold relationship to God in the act of faith. The intellect trustingly believes the infinite, unseen God, in the very act of assenting to the truth about God expressed in limited, finite propositions. The act of faith depends on these limited propositions, but assenting to these propositions is only possible because of the believer's trusting union with the God who speaks.

The limited character of faith's propositional content also leads Thomas to assert that faith depends not only on the intellect but also on the will. As we have seen, however, in his earlier works Aquinas does not sufficiently grasp the nature of the will's agency in the act of faith. He recognizes early that supernatural faith elevates the natural light of the intellect, but he is slow to grasp that grace must also elevate the will's own action. By the time he writes the *Summa theologiae,* however, Aquinas has developed a theory of how grace elevates both the natural light of the intellect and the natural inclination of the will. The light of faith is a fuller participation in the divine light, while the will's motion in faith—the *instinctus fidei*—is a fuller participation in the divine *instinctus* that moves the will. These two principles work together to enable the agent to assent to the conceptual content of faith.

When we view these developments from the perspective of Aquinas' mature psychology of action, we discover that Aquinas is applying his deepened understanding of the will's act of exercise to his theology of faith. On the level of specification, the intellect determines the propositional content of faith, while on the level of exercise, the will moves the intellect to determine the content of faith in one way as opposed to another. The *lumen fidei* empowers the intellect to do the former, while the *instinctus fidei* empowers the will to do the latter. Together, these principles enable the believer to assent to the articles of faith in a free act. "To believe is an act of the intellect assenting to divine truth from the command of the will moved by God through grace, and in this way it is subject to *liberum arbitrium* in relation to God."[108] Together, they enable us to respond freely to the invitation to trust in God and believe what he reveals to us about himself. As we noted earlier, however, on its own the *instinctus fidei* is not a sufficient agent of action. It moves the believer to assent to the truths of faith, but it does not, of itself, enable the believer to attain faith's end, which is a joyfully loving union with God. Only charity's presence in the will empowers faith to attain its end.

108. *ST* II-II 2.9.

CHAPTER 5

Charity's Relationship to Knowledge in Human Action

We have now reached the heart of our inquiry. We are now in a position to pose directly the question of charity's relationship to knowledge in human action. Does charity depend on knowledge? Specifically, does charity's act depend on the specifying action of the intellect? In the pages that follow, we shall discover that since charity is the graced elevation of the will's natural love, charity does indeed retain corc fcatures of love's relationship to knowledge. In St. Thomas' view, charity's act presupposes and depends on conceptual knowledge in the intellect. It presupposes faith's knowledge of charity's proper object, God. We shall also find, however, that because of the limited character of faith's knowledge of God, charity's relationship to knowledge differs from natural love's relationship to it in important and surprising ways. We shall discover that charity's primary act, the act of loving God above all things, is not measured by any cognitive power of the human mind. In charity, our love for God transcends the boundaries of faith's limited knowledge of God. Nevertheless, as a principle of action—as the love that underlies our love of neighbor and our love of all other things—charity not only depends on knowledge, it is specified and measured by it.

Charity as Friendship with God

St. Thomas begins his analysis of charity by defining it as a type of friendship with God. "Charity is a certain friendship *(amicitia)* of the human person toward God."[1] Thomas' definition of charity as an *amicitia* marks the culmination of over a hundred years of scholastic reflection on the nature of charity. An analysis of the history of this reflection and a full account of the contours of Thomas' description of charity as divine friendship are beyond the scope of this project.[2] We shall study charity's character as friendship only to the extent that it sheds light on charity's relationship to knowledge.

The Scriptures describe the love existing between God and his people in various ways, among which is the theme of friendship. "I no longer call your servants, but friends" (Jn 15.15).[3] St. Thomas appears to choose friendship as his preferred description of charity because of the light Aristotle's analysis of friendship can shed on our relationship with God when this analysis is applied to charity.[4] Thomas draws on Aristo-

1. *ST* II-II 23.1.

2. For early scholastic discussions concerning charity, see Wielockx, "Discussion scolastique sur l'amour." For studies of St. Thomas' theology of charity that place his theory of charity as friendship with God in its historical context, see James McEvoy, "Zur Rezeption des Aristotelischen Freundschaftsbegriffs in der Scholastik," *Freiburger Zeitschrift für Philosophie und Theologie* 43 (1996): 287–303, and "*Philia* and *Amicitia:* the Philosophy of Friendship from Plato to Aquinas," *Sewanee Mediaeval Colloquium Occasional Papers* (Sewanee, Tenn.: University Press, 1985), 1–23; G.-G. Meersseman, "Pourquoi le Lombard n'a-t-il pas concu la charité comme amitié?" *Miscellanea lombardiana* (Novara: Instituto geografico de agostini, 1957), 165–174; A. Stévaux, "La Doctrine de la charité dans les commentaires des *Sentences* de saint Albert, de saint Bonaventure et de saint Thomas," *Ephemerides theologicae lovanienses* 24 (1948): 59–97; Richard Egenter, *Gottesfreundschaft: Die Lehre von der Gottesfreundschaft in der Scholastik und Mystik des 12 und 13 Jahrhunderts* (Augsburg: Benno Filser, 1928); Franz Zigon, "Der Begriff der Caritas beim Lombarden, und der hl. Thomas," *Divus thomas (studia friburgensia)* (1924): 404–424. For general accounts of St. Thomas' theology of charity as friendship with God, see Anthony Keaty, "Thomas's Authority for Identifying Charity as Friendship: Aristotle or John 15?" *Thomist* 62 (1998): 581–601; L. Gregory Jones, "The Theological Transformation of Aristotelian Friendship in the Thought of St. Thomas Aquinas," *New Scholasticism* 61 (1987): 373–399; Fergus Kerr, "Charity as Friendship," in *Language, Meaning and God,* edited by Brian Davies (London: Geoffrey Chapman, 1987), 1–23; Joseph Bobik, "Aquinas on Friendship with God," *New Scholasticism* 60 (1986): 257–271; Louis M. Hughes, "Charity as Friendship in the Theology of Saint Thomas," *Angelicum* 52 (1975): 164–178; Leo Bond, "A Comparison between Human and Divine Friendship," *Thomist* 3 (1941): 54–94; M.-Joseph Keller and M.-Benoît Lavaud, "La charité comme amitié d'après saint Thomas," *Revue thomiste* 34 (1929): 445–475.

3. See *ST* II-II 23.1 sc.

4. See Stévaux, "La Doctrine de la charité dans les commentaires des *Sentences,*" 86–87; Keaty, "Thomas's Authority for Identifying Charity as Friendship," 594.

tle's treatment of friendship in the *Nicomachean Ethics* to affirm that friendship has the following characteristics. First, friendship entails mutual benevolence. Friendship *(amicitia)* is more than merely a solitary expression of the love that exists in friendship *(amor amicitiae* or *amor benevolentiae).*[5] Friendship requires at least two who love each other with this love, whereby they will good to each other.[6] Most fundamentally, they will their friend to be and to live, and will this for their friend's sake and not for their own sake.[7] Second, and significantly in light of Aquinas' subsequent analysis of charity's relationship to knowledge, mutual benevolence must be mutually recognized for friendship to exist.[8] Two people may wish well to each other, but they will not become friends unless they both know that the other also wishes them well. Third, the mutual love of friends breaks forth into mutual beneficence. This fact is implied in the requirement that mutual goodwill be mutually known, for the primary way we reveal our heart to another is by our actions. Hence, benevolence without beneficence "is not enough for friendship."[9] Fourth, friendship has the character of a *habitus* in that it is a semi-permanent quality that is not easily lost and that exists even when friends are apart or asleep.[10]

Lastly and perhaps most importantly, friendship is based on a certain communion in the good *(communicatio in bono),* which for Aquinas signifies both an active sharing of goods and a more basic participation in the same qualities, circumstances or origins.[11] For Aquinas, the first mean-

5. St. Thomas sometimes presents *amor amicitiae* and *amor benevolentiae* as synonymous. See *ST* I-II 27.3. Yet, later he is careful to distinguish friendship *(amicitia)* from merely benevolence *(benevolentia),* by which he means the love that is benevolence *(amor benevolentiae).* See *ST* II-II 23.1 and *ST* II-II 27.2.

6. *In ethic.* VIII 2 [9]; *ST* II-II 23.1.

7. *In ethic.* IX 4 [3]: "a friend wills for his friend to be and to live and does so not for his own sake but for the sake of his friend." *ST* II-II 25.7: "every friend first wills for his friend to be and to live."

8. *In ethic.* VIII 2 [9].

9. *In ethic.* IX 4 [2]. See also *ST* II-II 31.1.

10. *In ethic.* VIII 5 [1].

11. Scholars have brought considerable scrutiny to bear upon Thomas' use of *communicatio,* a term which has no direct English equivalent. In my analysis, I follow Joseph Bobik in arguing that Thomas has three uses of *communicatio,* the first two of which I have listed here, while the third, as we shall see, concerns that friendship which is charity. See

ing of *communicatio in bono*—the active exchange of goods and services—is rooted in the second more basic meaning. The second meaning refers to some fellowship in goodness. Two people share at least the goodness of their common humanity, but they can also be from the same country or town, have the same profession, belong to the same family, or have developed a similarly virtuous character. Each of these shared goods is a *communicatio vitae* or *communicatio in bono* upon which those who share this good can found a friendship: "all friendship is founded on some fellowship in life *(communicatio vitae)*."[12]

Aquinas believes that these characteristics of human friendship are analogously present in charity. The foundation of the analogy rests on Aquinas' understanding of grace as a type of divine "*communicatio,*" whereby God begins to share *(communicare)* his life with us.

> Since there is a *communicatio* between humans and God, inasmuch as God communicates his beatitude to us, some kind of friendship must be based upon this *communicatio*. . . . The love that is based on this *communicatio* is charity. Hence it is clear that charity is the friendship of the human person for God.[13]

Importantly for our concerns, Aquinas regards the requirements of friendship as revealing how charity presupposes the presence of faith and hope.

Joseph Bobik, "Aquinas on *Communicatio*, the Foundation of Friendship and *Caritas*," *Modern Schoolman* 64 (1988): 1–18. In this excellent article, Bobik summarizes six different Thomistic interpretations of Thomas' use of *communicatio* and then presents his own analysis. Bobik calls the first use of *communicatio* the "active sense" of the term, describing it as "the activities of friendship," while he calls the second use of *communicatio* the "passive sense," which he understands as referring to the "social relational context" (13–15). See also Guy Mansini, "*Similitudo, Communicatio,* and the Friendship of Charity in Aquinas," in *Thomistica*, edited by E. Manning (Leuven: Peeters, 1995): 1–26; Benoît-Dominique de La Soujeole, "'Société' et 'communion' chez saint Thomas d'Aquin: étude d'ecclésiologie," *Revue thomiste* 90 (1990): 587–622; L.-M. Dewailly, "*Communio-communicatio,*" *Revue des sciences philosophiques et théologiques* 54 (1970): 46–63; L.-B. Gillon, "A propos de la théorie thomiste de l'amitié: '*Fundatur super aliqua communicatione*' (II-II, q. 23, a. 1)," *Angelicum* 25 (1948): 3–17.

12. *ST* II-II 25.3. See also *De regno ad regem cypri* 1.11.

13. *ST* II-II 23.1.

Just as someone could not have friendship with another if he disbelieved in or despaired of his ability to have some sort of social or familial life together with the other, so too friendship with God, which is charity, is impossible unless one has faith, by which we believe in this society and common life with God, and unless one hopes to attain this society. Thus, charity is not in any way possible without faith and hope.[14]

Since communion with God in the good is a prerequisite for friendship with him, unless we believe that such a communion is possible and unless we hope for this good as something attainable by us through God's assistance, we will never develop a friendship with him.[15] God might indeed love us, wish us good and do good for us, but unless he makes this known to us, we will not become his friends. Knowledge of our eternal vocation, therefore, and desire for it as an absent good difficult but possible to attain by God's help, are prerequisites for the friendship which is charity.

Aquinas elsewhere reveals that friendship with God also implies other cognitive and appetitive virtues. Aquinas describes the friendship we enjoy with God as equivalent to the relationship of loving trust that ideally exists between a spiritual master and his disciples, or a craftsman and his apprentices.[16] Aquinas explains that the Holy Spirit, by whom "we are established as friends of God," reveals God's secrets to us and moves us to engage in acts of true holiness.[17] Since "it is proper to friendship to consent to a friend in what he wills," the Holy Spirit in charity moves us to fulfill God's will expressed in the commandments.[18] Yet, since we are friends of God, and not slaves, the Holy Spirit moves us freely, "inclining the will by love to the true good."[19] For this reason, Aquinas, in one of his later sermons, is even willing to describe charity

14. *ST* I-II 65.5.

15. On the role of hope in generating love, see *ST* I-II 40.7. That this description also applies to the theological virtue of hope is revealed in the *sed contra,* where Aquinas quotes the *Glossa ordinaria*'s interpretation of "Abraham begot Isaac, Isaac begot Jacob" (Mt 1.2), which sees this passage as signifying that faith begets hope, while hope begets charity.

16. *ST* II-II 2.3. Servais Pinckaers, *La vie selon l'Esprit: essai de théologie spirituelle selon saint Paul et saint Thomas d'Aquin* (Luxembourg: Editions saint-Paul, 1996), 160–163.

17. *SCG* IV 21.4.

18. Ibid.

19. *SCG* IV 22.6.

itself as a teacher that illumines the heart concerning the ways of holiness.

Frequently we do not know what we should do or desire, but charity teaches us everything that is necessary for salvation. Thus, 1 John (2.27) affirms that, 'his anointing teaches you everything.' This is because where charity is, there is the Holy Spirit, who knows all and who teaches us 'the right way' as the psalm (106.7) says. We read in Ben Sirach (2.10), therefore, that, 'you who fear the Lord, love him and your hearts will be illumined,' toward knowing what is necessary for salvation.[20]

In the *Summa theologiae,* Aquinas offers a more precise description of the Spirit's action in the soul of one who has charity. There we learn that the Spirit's action presupposes certain infused virtues and gifts.[21] Before turning our attention to them, we must first look more closely at charity's relationship to faith.

Charity and Faith

In chapter two, we saw that in St. Thomas' psychology of action the intellect enjoys a structural priority over the will. The will only acts as informed by the intellect. Yet, we also saw that on the level of exercise, the will has priority over the intellect. The intellect determines the will on the level of specification, but the will moves the intellect on the level of exercise. We also saw that St. Thomas avoids an infinite regress by grounding the first motion of the intellect and will in nature and ultimately in God. Reason commands all the will's acts, except the will's first act, which is instilled in it by nature, while the will moves the intellect to engage in all its acts except the intellect's first act, which is instilled in it by nature. Not surprisingly, Thomas establishes a similar relationship between intellect and will as elevated by grace in the theological virtues. Faith has priority in one way, charity has priority in another.

20. *Collationes in decem preceptis* 2.17–23. The reference is according to the method of citation proposed by Jean-Pierre Torrell in his critical edition. See Torrell, "Les *Collationes in decem preceptis* de saint Thomas d'Aquin, édition critique avec introduction et notes," *Revue des sciences philosophiques et théologiques* 69 (1985): 28–29.

21. See *ST* I-II 63.3 and *ST* I-II 68.2.

In his analysis of faith, Aquinas affirms the priority of faith very clearly. "Faith by its very nature is first among all the virtues."[22]

> The last end must necessarily be in the intellect before it is in the will, because the will does not move toward anything except in so far as it is apprehended by the intellect. Hence, as the last end is present in the will by hope and charity, and in the intellect by faith, the first of all the virtues must of necessity be faith.[23]

In his treatment of charity, Aquinas reaffirms this priority, while simultaneously affirming charity's greater dignity. "Since to love God is something greater than to know him, especially in this state of life, it follows that love of God presupposes knowledge of God."[24] Charity's act presupposes faith's knowledge, but goes beyond it to attain the unseen reality expressed in faith's propositions.[25] Nevertheless, faith retains a structural priority over charity by revealing charity's object, even if only partially.[26]

Charity, for its part, has priority in moving faith to its end. As we saw in the previous chapter, faith itself implies an act of the will moving the intellect to assent to the content of faith. This act, in Aquinas' judgment, functions in a manner analogous to the will's role in shaping the intellect's judgment in practical reasoning. Yet, in order for this act to be perfect it must be informed by the virtue of charity.

> Since faith is a virtue, its act must be perfect. Yet, for the perfection of an act proceeding from two active principles, each of these principles must be perfect: for something cannot be sawn well unless the sawyer possess the art and the saw is well fitted for sawing. Now, in those powers of the soul that are themselves related to opposite objects a disposition to act well is a *habitus,* as is stated above. Thus, an act that proceeds from two such powers must be per-

22. *ST* II-II 4.7.

23. Ibid.

24. *ST* II-II 27.4 ad 2. See also *Super primam ad corinthios* 13.4 [185–190].

25. *ST* II-II 27.3 ad 1; *ST* II-II 27.4; *ST* II-II 27.4 ad 1.

26. "In the final act of an adult's complete conversion from non-belief and sin to belief and grace, the infusion of grace, including charity, and the active turning to God in belief and love are simultaneous; yet there is a pattern of priority in meaning among the various elements—thus knowing before loving" (T. C. O'Brien, *Summa theologiae,* vol. 31, 142, note h). See Cessario, *Christian Faith and The Theological Life,* 99, note 32.

fected by a *habitus* in each of the powers. As we have seen, to believe is an act of the intellect moved by the will to assent, because this act proceeds from both the intellect and the will. Now, as was earlier stated, both these powers have an innate aptitude to be perfected by a *habitus*. Consequently, if the act of faith is to be perfect, there must be a *habitus* in the will as well as in the intellect.[27]

The will has priority in "moving the intellect to assent," but to do this perfectly it must contain a *habitus,* which, as we learn in the next article, is the virtue of charity.[28] "It is for this that the gift of charity is bestowed by God on each one, namely, that he may first of all direct his mind to God."[29] Charity vivifies faith, making it a virtue by directing it to its end.[30] Consequently, faith has priority in revealing the object (even if only partially), while charity has priority in moving the intellect to assent in a motion that attains faith's end, loving union with God.[31]

Two features of this initial account deserve closer scrutiny. First, we shall delineate more clearly Aquinas' distinction between the theological virtues and the acts of these virtues. This will enable us to see how Aquinas establishes a distinction on the level of grace parallel to the distinction on the level of nature between principles and acts. Second, we shall consider more carefully Aquinas' description of faith's role in presenting the object of charity to the will. Aquinas describes faith's act as "showing" the object of charity, but refuses to characterize it as an act of specification. As we shall see, Aquinas chooses his terms carefully in order to remain faithful to a unique aspect of faith's influence on the will's act of charity.

In chapter two we saw that St. Thomas grounds practical reasoning in the natural principles of the intellect and will. The intellect habitually knows certain things, while the will unfailingly inclines toward those same things. The will naturally inclines towards the goods constitutive of human flourishing, while the intellect contains both a natural habit of primary precepts of the natural law *(synderesis)* by which it perceives

27. *ST* II-II 4.2.

28. *ST* II-II 4.3.

29. *ST* II-II 26.13.

30. *ST* II-II 4.5.

31. As we saw in chapter four, faith itself has an appetitive component. Thus, stated more accurately, charity's priority consists in elevating the appetitive component of faith's own act. See *ST* II-II 4.2 and 3.

these goods as goods to be pursued, as well as a natural habit of theoretical principles *(intellectus),* whereby it reasons to conclusions about what pertains to the theoretical intellect.[32] We also noted that God is the one who instills in human nature these cognitive and appetitive principles. In chapter three we further discovered that Aquinas describes the will's natural inclination as a natural love *(amor naturalis)* that underlies the will's primary act, elective love *(dilectio). Amor naturalis* is the principle; *dilectio* is the act.

In his treatment of the theological virtues, Aquinas portrays them as infused principles that elevate our natural principles of intellect and will.

> Because [supernatural] happiness surpasses the capacity of human nature, the human person's natural principles which enable us to act well according to our capacity do not suffice to direct us to this same happiness. Hence it is necessary for us to receive from God some additional principles, whereby we may be directed to supernatural happiness, even as we are directed to our connatural end, by means of our natural principles, albeit not without divine assistance. Such like principles are called theological virtues.[33]

Faith elevates the light by which the intellect knows truth, while charity and hope elevate the will's inclination toward the good as its end.[34] We are dealing here with virtues: they are habitual dispositions that incline the intellect and will to act, but they are not themselves the acts of these powers.[35]

32. Once again, it is important to remember that Aquinas does not view these natural *habitus* as granting a priori knowledge. Instead, he maintains that the truths habitually contained in these natural dispositions are known to us *in actu* only in and through our contact with particular things in the physical world. Moreover, while knowledge of these primary truths is presupposed in every act of knowing, this does not imply that the agent him or herself has reflective understanding of them (*ST* I 2.1). For example, when a scoop of ice-cream falls off a child's ice-cream cone, the child knows that the scoop is not simultaneously on the cone and on the ground at the same time and in the same respect, even though the child could not formulate explicitly the principle of non-contradiction. Knowledge of this principle is habitually present through the habit of *intellectus,* a knowledge that is present and presupposed in every act of knowing, even though the knower is not reflexively aware of this knowledge.

33. *ST* I-II 62.1.

34. *ST* I-II 62.3. St. Thomas will later describe charity as the *"inclinatio gratiae,"* contrasting it with the *"inclinatio naturae,"* portraying both as flowing from the divine wisdom (*ST* II-II 26.6).

35. For example, in the *De caritate,* Aquinas describes the *habitus caritatis* as *"formale*

In chapter three we saw that Aquinas presents the will's act *(dilectio)* as having a twofold tendency. To love is to will good to another. Consequently, the act of love inclines toward a good and toward the person for whom we will this good. Aquinas styles love's tendency toward the good as an *amor concupiscentiae,* while he portrays love's tendency toward the person as *amor amicitiae.* These are not two acts, but one act of loving a person that contains an inclination toward the good we desire for that person. In other words, our *amor concupiscentiae* occurs within the context of an *amor amicitiae* for someone, either for ourselves or for someone else. For Aquinas, the personal aspect of love is primary. At its most basic level, even before it becomes a principle of further action, love is a freely chosen response to the goodness and value of a person. Love is a *complacentia boni,* a pleasing appetitive affinity for our beloved and his or her good.[36] As we noted in chapter three, this love occurs at the level of the will's *simplex voluntas* arising in response to reason's recognition of a person's goodness.[37] On this most basic level, the good we will for the beloved is simply the good of existence. "The first thing that one wills for a friend is that he be and live."[38] This act of love is essentially a joyful affirmation of the other's existence.

In his analysis of charity, Aquinas describes charity's act as the elevation of the will's twofold act of love.[39] Charity's primary object is God, and its primary act is to love God.[40] Like all other loves, charity's act is to will good to another. Yet, charity's act does not will good to God as

principium actus dilectionis" (*De caritate* 1). "Aquinas argues that faith, hope and charity are true virtues. That is to say, they are operative habits of the human soul, through which the human person is oriented towards her supernatural end, the direct vision of God" (Jean Porter, "The Subversion of Virtue," *Annual of the Society of Christian Ethics* 12 [1992]: 31).

36. *ST* I-II 27.1: *"amor importat quandam connaturalitatem vel complacentiam amantis ad amatum."*

37. See especially *In divinis nominibus* 4.11, where Thomas describes love as the first movement of the appetite, and thus as *"simplex."*

38. *ST* II-II 25.7.

39. *ST* II-II 25.2.

40. *ST* II-II 27.1: "to love belongs to charity as charity; for, since charity is a virtue, by its very essence it has an inclination to its proper act." Indeed, Thomas informs the reader in the prologue of *ST* II-II 27 that "the act of charity is now to be considered. First, we shall consider the principal act of charity, which is to love." See also *De caritate* 7.

something he lacks and which consequently we wish him to attain. Rather, charity's act—as the elevation of the will's most basic act of natural love (i.e., the will's *simplex voluntas*), whereby one affirms the existence of the beloved—affirms God's existence and goodness.[41] Moreover, charity's act is not merely a well-wishing *(benevolentia),* but entails a union of affection whereby we love and affirm God's goodness in an act that participates in God's own love for himself.[42] For this reason, charity's act of love is truly a *complacentia,* a pleasing affective affinity for the goodness of God. On this primary level of charity's act, we love God for himself and not because of the good he does for us, or for any other reason.[43] This is charity's proper or elicited act: the appetitive affirmation of God's goodness.[44]

In chapter three we noted that since love's act is already a certain union with the end of human action *(unio affectionis vel unio secundum quid),* it entails a certain inchoate enjoyment *(fruitio),* which becomes a perfect enjoyment only when the end is fully present *(simpliciter vel realiter).* Aquinas holds that charity entails a similar dynamic. Charity's act is perfect only in heaven, when we will enjoy *(frui)* God fully.[45] In this life, however, the act of charity is already a union of affections, and thus attains God himself. For this reason, Aquinas portrays charity's proper act *(amare)* as coming to rest in a dynamic act of enjoyment that the tradition describes as joy *(gaudium).* Joy brings charity's act of love to full fruition.[46] In this life, the beginner has an imperfect affective union with God, and therefore charity's joy is partial within him or her. In heaven,

41. *ST* II-II 31.1 ad 1.

42. *ST* II-II 27.2.

43. *ST* II-II 23.5 ad 2; *ST* II-II 23.6. See Th. Deman, "Eudémonisme et charité en théologie morale," *Ephemerides theologicae lovanienses* 29 (1953): 50.

44. Aquinas explicitly affirms that charity's elicited act is to love God: *"actus aliarum virtutum non attribuuntur caritati quasi ipsa eos eliciat, sed quia ipsa eos imperat. habet autem specialem actum quem elicit, diligere deum"* (*In sent.* III 27.2.4B ad 2); *ST* II-II 26.7 ad 3: *"caritas non solum elicit actum dilectionis secundum rationem obiecti, sed etiam secundum rationem diligentis, ut dictum est. ex quo contingit quod magis coniunctus magis amatur."* See also *ST* II-II 26.7 and *ST* I-II 6.4. Jean Porter, "A Response to Brian Linnane and David Coffey," *Philosophy and Theology* 10 (1998): 288.

45. *ST* II-II 26.13.

46. *ST* II-II 28.4 ad 1; *ST* II-II 28.4 ad 3; *ST* II-II 23.3 ad 2.

where the saints rest in perfect union with God, the joy of charity is complete.[47]

To summarize, Aquinas portrays the infused virtues of faith, hope and charity as dispositions that elevate the natural principles of intellect and will. Moreover, the acts of these virtues elevate the proper acts of intellect and will. The virtue of charity elevates the will's *amor naturalis.* Elevated in the gift of grace, through our will's proper act, we are able to love God in a way that intimately and immediately unites us to his personal goodness.

If we consider Aquinas' description of charity in light of the stages of action we traced in chapter three (see figure 1), charity, as we have thus far considered it, belongs to the stage of affirmation, whereby knowledge of the beloved (in this case, faith's knowledge of God) leads to the freely chosen affirmation of the beloved's goodness *(simplex voluntas).* In chapter three, however, we noted that knowledge and love only become principles of action when we order and intend some end through some means. From this perspective, the question arises whether, beyond the level of simple affirmation, charity also becomes the principle underlying our subsequent actions. In other words, does charity also underlie the stages of intention and decision in the process of action we sketched in chapter three? Specifically, does charity elevate the love proper to *intentio* and *electio* (see figure 3)? Further, if charity does this, what is its relationship to *ordinatio* and *judicium,* the cognitive components of intention and decision (see figure 1)? To answer these questions we must first recognize a unique feature of faith's action on charity.

Up to this point we have only studied charity's primary act, which is to love God. St. Thomas is fully aware, however, that according to the Scriptural witness, charity also extends to ourselves and to our neighbor. If charity underlies the appetitive components of intention and decision, we would expect this particularly to be the case in our actions toward our neighbor. Before turning our attention to this aspect of chari-

47. *ST* II-II 28.3. Van Ouwerkerk, in his classic study of charity (Caritas et Ratio 68–69), grasps this aspect of St. Thomas' account acutely. As we shall see, however, this seminal work suffers from several unfortunate limitations.

ty, however, we should first recognize the limited character of faith's role in shaping charity's act on the level of charity's primary act of loving God.

In his analysis of charity in the *Summa theologiae,* Aquinas asserts that charity's proper act has no mode or measure.[48] Stated in another way, charity's measure is to love God without measure.[49] On one level, when Aquinas asserts the unmeasured character of charity's act, he is simply remaining faithful to his earlier analysis of the moral virtues. Aquinas follows Aristotle[50] in affirming that in relation to the formal aspect of their object—i.e., in relation to reason itself—the moral virtues are an extreme, while in relation to their material object they are a mean between too much or too little according to the measure of reason.

> Moral virtue derives its goodness from the rule of reason, while its matter consists in passions or operations. If therefore we compare moral virtue to reason, then, in relation to reason, it has the character of one extreme, namely, conformity, while excess and defect have the character of the other extreme, namely deformity. But if we consider moral virtue in relation to its matter, then it has the character of a mean, insofar as it makes passion conform to the rule of reason. Hence, the Philosopher says (*NE* 2.6) that 'virtue, as to its essence, is a mean,' to the extent that the rule of virtue is imposed on its matter, 'but it is an extreme in relation to the best and the excellent,' namely, in its conformity to reason.[51]

Aquinas advances a parallel analysis in his treatment of charity.

> The end of all human actions and affections is the love of God, whereby principally we attain to our last end, as stated above. Thus, the mode in the love of God must not be taken as in a thing measured where we find too much or too little, but as in the measure itself, where there cannot be excess, and where the more the rule is attained the better it is, so that the more we love God the better our love is.[52]

In other words, just as in the act of adhering to reason the moral virtues

48. *ST* II-II 27.6.

49. *ST* II-II 27.6 sc: *"causa diligendi deum deus est; modus, sine modo diligere."* This phrase comes from St. Bernard (*De diligendum dei* 1 [*PL* 182, 974]).

50. *NE* 2.6 (1107a7).

51. *ST* I-II 64.1 ad 1.

52. *ST* II-II 27.6.

are an extreme without measure (for we can never adhere to the rule of reason too much), so too in the act of adhering to God charity is an extreme without measure (for we can never love God too much).[53] "The object of divine love which is God surpasses the judgment of reason, wherefore it is not measured by reason but exceeds it."[54] Aquinas offers a further comparison, this time with the arts, and once again draws on Aristotle's analysis.

According to the Philosopher (*Politics* 1.3), 'in every art, the desire for the end is endless and unlimited,' whereas there is a limit to the means: thus the physician does not put limits to health, but makes it as perfect as he possibly can; but he puts a limit to medicine, for he does not give as much medicine as he can, but according as health demands, so that if he give too much or too little, the medicine would be immoderate.[55]

In Aquinas' view, therefore, both in the arts and in the moral virtues, adherence to the formal aspect of the object—to reason and to the end—is an extreme that follows no measure. The artist and the moral agent put no limits on their desire to adhere to reason and to attain their end. In his analysis of charity, Aquinas offers an analogous principle. In relation to its proper object and end, God, charity's act is an extreme without measure.

There is this difference, however, between charity and the moral virtues. In relation to their subject matter or material object, which are passions and operations, the moral virtues do follow a mean. They follow the mean established by reason. This is not the case with charity. In relation to charity's primary object (God), even as materially considered, charity does not follow a mean. Charity remains an unmeasured extreme. This is so, Aquinas explains, because God himself is the rule and measure of the theological virtues, and God's infinite truth and goodness surpass all human power, including the power of the intellect, whether in this life or in the eternal life of heavenly beatitude.[56]

The significance of the intellect's limited power before the goodness of God becomes doubly evident when Aquinas compares charity's rela-

53. *ST* II-II 17.5 ad 2.
54. *ST* II-II 27.6 ad 3.
55. *ST* II-II 27.6.
56. *ST* I-II 64.4.

tionship to faith with the moral virtues' relationship to prudence. In this comparison, Aquinas underlines a crucial difference between prudence and faith.

> Prudence regulates the appetitive movements pertaining to the moral virtues, whereas faith does not regulate the appetitive movement tending to God, which pertains to the theological virtues. It only shows the object *(ostendit obiectum)*.[57]

Faith can do no more than show the object of charity because the knowledge of faith is limited, while the act of charity attains God himself. Thus, as St. Paul proclaims, "the charity of Christ surpasses all knowledge" (Eph 3.19).[58] Consequently, although faith shows charity its object—and thus makes the act of charity possible—faith does not measure or regulate *(moderatur)* charity's act. In relation to its proper object, God, charity is not measured by any rule: there is no limit to how much one should love God, because God is infinite goodness.[59]

57. *ST* I-II 66.6 ad 1.

58. Ibid.

59. We should note, however, that Aquinas does recognize a limit to the theological virtues in relation to us. Objectively, there is no limit placed on the acts of the theological virtues; subjectively, they do observe a limit according to the measure of our condition (*ST* I-II 64.4; *ST* II-II 17.5 ad 2). Aquinas offers the example of hope (see *ST* I-II 64.4 ad 3). Because of who we are and because of our current limited state in life, the act of hope follows a mean between presumption and despair, while in relation to God we can never hope too much. We must also be careful not to regard Aquinas' teaching concerning the subjective measure of charity's act as exactly parallel to his description of the material objects of the moral virtues. The difference at issue here is the essential difference between the material objects of these two types of virtues. The objects of the moral virtues are human acts that constitute the means to our end. They are acts *ad finem*. Consequently, they must be measured by the intellect according to a rule that considers both the end of the act and the nature of the agent. The material object of the theological virtues, on the other hand, is the ultimate end who is God himself, who is limitless and without measure. In relation to charity's proper object, therefore, the only way in which charity's act follows a measure is according to the limitations of the subject. In the moral virtues the case is clearly different. Since material objects of the moral virtues are acts of the agent, the agent himself is, in a certain sense, part of the matter of their object. Consequently, while reason measures the acts of the moral virtues in relation to their material object, reason does not measure charity's proper act in relation to its object (God), but only accidentally in relation to the (social and psychological) limitations of the agent him or herself.

Nevertheless, this limitation on faith's role in shaping the act of charity should not blind us to the fact that, for Aquinas, an act of charity is impossible without the knowledge of faith.

> Faith by its very nature is first among all the virtues. For since the end is the principle in matters of action, as stated above, the theological virtues (the object of which is the last end) must precede all the others. Moreover, the last end must necessarily be in the intellect before it is in the will, because the will does not move toward anything except in so far as it is apprehended by the intellect. Hence, as the last end is present in the will by hope and charity, and in the intellect by faith, the first of all the virtues must of necessity be faith.[60]

Thomas reminds us that "vision is a cause of love." Consequently, "the more perfectly we know God, the more perfectly we love him."[61] In heaven this charity is perfect;[62] here on earth, it is imperfect. In either case, an act of charity depends on the knowledge that precedes it.[63] As Servais Pinckaers explains, "it is in faith that we receive our initial knowledge of the mystery of Christ and that the ties of charity are bound between us and him through the action of the Holy Spirit. The entire development of the spiritual life springs from this root."[64] The act of charity springs from the root of faith, even though faith's knowledge does not measure the quantity of charity's act.

As we shall shortly see, however, faith nonetheless depends on charity's act in order to function as a true virtue and attain its end. In chapter

60. *ST* II-II 4.7.

61. *ST* I-II 67.6 ad 3.

62. In heaven, each person's charity is perfect in the sense that each person will love God with the intensity of love proper to him or her. In Aquinas' view, although all the saints in heaven love God with the same charity in the sense that they all participate in God's uncreated charity and they all celebrate God's goodness, they do not all love God with the same degree of intensity. Some love him more, others less. Likewise, these varying degrees of love occasion varying degrees of depth in one's knowledge of God. See *ST* I 12.6.

63. In the very act of denying that temporal charity has the same quantity as heavenly charity, he nonetheless affirms that in both cases charity's act follows knowledge: "the quantity of the charity of the way, which follows the knowledge of faith, is not the same as the quantity of the charity of the homeland, which follows open vision" (*ST* II-II 24.7 ad 3).

64. Pinckaers, *La vie selon l'Esprit,* 164.

four we saw that faith's act requires an act of the will. Charity elevates this voluntary component of faith and brings it to perfection. Consequently, on the one hand, faith has cognitive priority over charity by showing charity its object, while on the other hand, charity has appetitive priority over faith by exercising faith's act.[65]

Thus far we have only considered charity's primary act (the love of God) in relation to charity's proper object (God himself). As noted above, however, charity's object and act also extend to ourselves and to our neighbor. These are charity's secondary act and object. On this secondary level, charity's relationship to knowledge becomes more pronounced. On this level charity's act depends on other infused cognitive dispositions. It depends on the infused cardinal virtues and the gifts of the Holy Spirit, both of which have cognitive components. It is by studying charity's relationship to these infused virtues and gifts that we shall be able to address our earlier questions concerning charity's role in the stages of action.

Charity and the Gifts of the Holy Spirit

St. Thomas portrays the gifts of the Holy Spirit mentioned in Isaiah 11.1–8 as infused *habitus* present in all those who have sanctifying grace

65. Van Ouwerkerk's insightful study, *Caritas et Ratio,* suffers from his failure to recognize charity's priority over reason as residing on the level of exercise. Instead, he describes charity's priority in terms of law, habitually portraying charity as a law, or as functioning like a law. Although he is careful to explain that charity is a law only in the sense that it directs us to our end, and is itself ordered to this end by God's wisdom, he nonetheless poses the question of charity's role in the moral life in terms of law and answers it in the same vein: "Is charity a direct norm of the moral life, in the sense that it would not only be the motor of the moral life (being itself constituted by the exigencies of the order of secondary moral ends), but would also impose an 'order' upon the moral life, such that charity's relationship to the moral life would not consist solely in its supernatural character, but would also imply a specific type of moral conduct, its own proper way of behaving" (79–80). "Charity is the substantial norm of the supernatural moral life" (88). He wants to assert charity's priority in the moral life, but his tendency to see morality in terms of rules leads him to regard charity itself legalistically and in almost cognitive terms. His study would have been far better served if he had described charity in terms of the will's *exercitium.* Charity elevates the will's exercise, and thus has priority over faith on this level.

and as necessary for salvation.[66] Although St. Thomas' theology of the gifts is often neglected by specialists, Thomas himself assigns the gifts a central place in the moral life. Hence, his theology of the gifts of the Holy Spirit merits careful study.[67] Unfortunately, the constraints of our current project permit us to consider the gifts only to the extent that they reveal Thomas' understanding to the relationship between charity and knowledge.

We shall more easily understand the cognitive aspects of the gifts and their relationship to charity against the backdrop of Aquinas' theology of the New Law.[68] Aquinas portrays the New Law as primarily the "grace of the Holy Spirit," or simply as the Holy Spirit itself.[69] In his commentary on the Letter to the Romans, which is one of his later works,[70] after describing law as that which directs us toward the common good by inciting us to virtuous action, Aquinas asserts that, in the life of grace, the Holy Spirit Itself directs us to the ultimate common good, God, and incites us to engage in those virtuous acts that lead us to attain God. Consequently, we can call the Holy Spirit a law. The Spirit is the Law of the Gospel in the sense that it directs us to our heavenly beatitude.

Significantly, Aquinas affirms that, as the New Law, the Spirit does not induce us to virtue merely by revealing truths to us, but also by moving us to act.

66. *ST* I-II 68.2; *ST* I-II 68.3. See Porter, "Subversion of Virtue," 36.

67. See O'Connor, "Evolution of St. Thomas's Thought on the Gifts," 110–130; Cessario, *Christian Faith and the Theological Life,* 159–180; M.-M. Labourdette, "Saint Thomas et la théologie thomiste" in the article on "Don du Saint-Esprit," in *Dictionnaire de spiritualité* (Paris: G. Beauchesne et ses fils, 1957), 1610–1635; M.-J. Nicolas, "Les dons du Saint-Esprit," *Revue thomiste* 92 (1992): 141–152; Servais Pinckaers, "L'instinct et l'Esprit au coeur de l'éthique chrétienne," Novitas et veritas vitae: *Aux sources du renouveau de la morale chrétienne, mélanges offerts au professeur Servais Pinckaers à l'occasion de son 65e anniversaire,* edited by Carlos-Josaphat Pinto de Oliveira (Fribourg, Switzerland: Editions universitaires Fribourg, 1991), 216–223; J.-M. Muñoz Cuenca, "Doctrina de santo Tomás sobre los Dones del Espíritu Santo en la Suma teológica," *Ephemerides carmeliticae* 25 (1974): 157–243; A. Gardeil, "Dons," *Dictionnaire de théologie catholique* (Paris: Letouzey et Ané, 1911), 1748–1781.

68. Pinckaers, *Sources of Christian Ethics,* 177–182, 453.

69. *ST* I-II 108.1; *Super epistolam ad romanos* (henceforth cited as *Super romanos*) 8.1.

70. On the date of composition of St. Thomas' *Commentary on the Romans,* see Torrell, *Saint Thomas Aquinas: the Person and His Work,* 340.

The purpose of law is to induce people to do good. Hence, the Philosopher states that the intention of the lawgiver is to make good citizens. Human law does this only by making known what should be done. But the Holy Spirit, dwelling in the mind, not only teaches what should be done, by illuminating the intellect of the agent, it also inclines the agent's affections toward right action: 'The Holy Spirit, the Paraclete, which the Father will send in my name, will teach you (the first way) and remind you (the second way) everything I have told you' (Jn 14.26).[71]

The Spirit's motion does not violate our freedom. Instead, the Spirit moves us freely, like a guide taking us by the hand and directing us on our way.

'Those who are led by the Spirit,' are led by him as by a guide or director. The Spirit does this to us by enlightening us interiorly about what we should do: 'your good Spirit leads me in the right way' (Ps 142). Yet, since one who is led is not acting from himself, the spiritual person is not merely taught by the Holy Spirit what he should do, his heart is also moved by the Holy Spirit. Thus, this is principally how the phrase 'those who are led by the Spirit' should be understood, because those who are said to be led are moved by some higher prompting *(superiori instinctu)*. . . . Likewise, the spiritual person in a certain sense is not primarily inclined to act from the motion of his own will, but from the prompting *(instinctu)* of the Holy Spirit. Hence, Isaiah states that 'It will come like a rushing river which the Spirit of the Lord drives on' (Is 59.19), while Luke affirms that Christ was 'led out into the desert by the Spirit' (Lk 4.1). This, however, does not mean that spiritual people no longer act from their own wills and from *liberum arbitrium,* because the very motion of the will and of *liberum arbitrium* is caused in them by the Holy Spirit, as St. Paul states, 'God is the one who acts in us, both to will and to do' (Phil 2.13).[72]

In Aquinas' view, therefore, the Holy Spirit moves us to act by both illumining our intellects and inclining our wills, and does so in a way that respects and elevates our freedom.

Elsewhere he explains that in order for the Spirit to move us as a teacher and guide—in order for him to move us in a way that respects

71. *Super romanos* 8.1.

72. *Super romanos* 8.3.

our *liberum arbitrium*—the Spirit instills within us certain dispositions that render us receptive to the Spirit's action. These infused dispositions *(habitus)* are the gifts of the Holy Spirit.

It is clear that whatever is moved must be proportionate to its mover, and that the perfection of the mobile as such consists in a disposition whereby it is disposed to be well moved by its mover. Hence, the more exalted the mover, the more perfect must be the disposition whereby the mobile is made proportionate to its mover: thus we see that a disciple needs a more perfect disposition in order to receive a higher teaching from his master. . . . Consequently, the human person must receive higher perfections that dispose him to be moved by God.[73]

Just as the moral virtues render the appetitive powers receptive to the dictates of reason, so too the gifts of the Holy Spirit render us receptive to the prompting *(instinctus)* of the Holy Spirit.[74]

Aquinas portrays the gifts as perfecting the actions of the intellect and of the appetites.[75] Because of the constraints of our current project, we shall only consider the cognitive gifts and their relationship to charity. As we saw in chapter four, the intellect apprehends things, judges that its apprehensions are true,[76] and then applies this knowledge to action. Aquinas holds that there are four gifts that perfect these three activities of the intellect. *Understanding* perfects the intellect's apprehension of speculative and practical truth, while both *wisdom* and *knowledge (scientia)* perfect the intellect's judgment of theoretical and practical truth.[77] Knowledge perfects our judgment of the truths of faith as known through created things: it perfects our ability to judge what things should be believed. Wisdom, however, perfects our judgment of these divine truths through a type of spiritual union with them.[78] Lastly, the gift of *counsel* perfects the intellect's ability to reason correctly concerning the application of divine truth to action.[79]

When we study these gifts in relation to charity, we discover, as we should by now expect, that Aquinas presents charity and the intellectual

73. *ST* I-II 68.1.
74. *ST* I-II 68.4; *ST* III 75. See Pinckaers, "L'instinct et l'Esprit," 216.
75. *ST* I-II 68.4.
76. *ST* I 16.2.
77. *ST* II-II 8.6.
78. *ST* II-II 9.2 ad 1; *ST* II-II 45.3 ad 1.
79. *ST* II-II 8.6.

gifts as interdependent. On the one hand, he asserts charity's dependence on the cognitive gifts. For example, he affirms that charity presupposes and depends on the gift of understanding, whereby the Holy Spirit moves our intellects to attain a deeper grasp of the truths of faith.

In all who are in a state of grace, there must be rectitude of the will, since grace prepares the human will for good, as Augustine says. Yet, the will cannot be rightly ordered to good, unless there be already some knowledge of the truth, since the object of the will is good understood *(bonum intellectum)*, as stated in *De anima* 3.7. Thus, just as the Holy Spirit directs our will by the gift of charity, so as to move it directly to some supernatural good; so also, by the gift of understanding, he enlightens the human mind, so that it knows some supernatural truth, toward which the right will must tend.[80]

On the other hand, not only does Aquinas affirm that charity is the principle, root and cause of the gifts in general,[81] he explicitly delineates charity's role in causing the gift of wisdom. The wise person is one who knows the highest cause, and from this knowledge is able to judge human acts and to direct these acts by ordering them rightly toward our highest end.[82] Aquinas distinguishes between wisdom as a virtue and wisdom as a gift. The distinction corresponds to the two ways an intellect can engage in right judgment. "Rectitude of judgment can occur in two ways: in one way, from the perfect use of reason; in another way, from a certain connaturality with those things about which one must now judge."[83] Aquinas offers the example of right judgment concerning chastity.

Concerning those things that pertain to chastity, one who has learnt the science of morals judges rightly about them by means of rational inquiry, while one who has the habit of chastity judges rightly about such things by means of a certain connaturality with them.[84]

This example is important because it points us back to Aquinas' analysis of practical reasoning and to love's role in moral judgment. It points to

80. *ST* II-II 8.4.
81. See *ST* I-II 68.5; *ST* I-II 68.4 ad 3; *ST* II-II 139.2 ad 2; *ST* II-II 45.6 ad 2.
82. *ST* II-II 45.1.
83. *ST* II-II 45.2.
84. Ibid.

the Aristotelian insight that "as a person is, so does the end appear to him."[85]

As we have seen, Aquinas affirms that prudence and the judgment of practical reason depend on the moral virtues, which rightly order our loves.[86] This is so, Aquinas explains, because what we love becomes "connatural" to us as an end to be pursued.

> We know from experience that things appear differently to us, whether good or bad, according to whether we love or hate them. Consequently, when someone has an inordinate affection for something, that inordinate affection impedes the judgment of the intellect concerning a particular object of choice.[87]

Thus, in order to judge rightly about the means to the end of moral action, we must have moral virtue, which rightly orders our love of the end.[88]

Aquinas affirms that the human virtue of wisdom judges rightly concerning divine things in the way moral science judges rightly concerning chastity: it does so by means of rational inquiry. The gift of wisdom, however, judges them by means of connaturality, and as such it depends on a rightly ordered love. It depends on the divine love of charity.

85. *NE* 3.5 (1114a32–b1). See *ST* I-II 58.5 and *ST* II-II 24.11.

86. *ST* I-II 65.1; *ST* I-II 65.1 ad 3; *Quaestio disputata de virtutibus cardinalibus* 2.

87. *De malo* 2.3 ad 9.

88. *ST* I-II 58.5. It is important for us to remember that, according to Aquinas, the judgment of moral science described above, and even the judgment of conscience, are not enough to ensure morally good action. Even though moral science enables us to reason and judge correctly about some particular action, it does not ensure that we will judge rightly about this action when it is proposed as an action for us to do here and now. This requires the connatural judgment of practical reason rendered possible by the moral virtues and our rightly ordered love. Thus, building on Aquinas' example, we can say that, even though a young man with moral science can judge rightly that to have sexual relations with the wife of Uriah would be a sin, when he sees her bathing he may fail to judge correctly concerning what he himself should do here and now. Seeing her he may fail to see that having relations with her is sinful for him. Only the person who has the virtue of chastity and chooses to act from it (the person for whom the good of chastity is connatural as an end to be pursued) will always judge correctly, even in the particular case of a bathing Bathsheba, that such an act is sinful. This would be a case of incontinence (*ST* II-II 156); an analogous dynamic would be at work in a case of certain malice (*ST* I-II 78).

It pertains to the wisdom that is an intellectual virtue to judge rightly about divine things from the investigation of reason, while right judgment about such things arising from a certain connaturality with them pertains to the wisdom that is a gift of the Holy Spirit. Hence, Dionysius says that 'Hierotheus is perfect in divine things, for he not only learns, but also affectively experiences *(patiens)* divine things.' This sympathy *(compassio)* or connaturality for divine things occurs because of charity, which unites us to God, according to 1 Cor 6.17: 'he who adheres to God, is one spirit with him.'[89]

In the gift of wisdom, therefore, the intellect becomes receptive to the action of the Holy Spirit, moving the intellect to judge rightly about the things of God. The Spirit does not move the intellect to this right judgment through theoretical or practical reasoning, but through a certain connaturality with them generated by the virtue of charity.

The crucial feature of Aquinas' analysis is his recognition that, although the gift of wisdom is caused by charity, it is a cognitive *habitus* existing in the intellect.[90] "In this way, therefore, the wisdom that is a gift has its cause in the will, namely charity, but it has its essence in the intellect, whose act is to judge rightly."[91] Once again Aquinas offers us a pithy summation of his mature insight concerning the respective roles and mutual dependence of the intellect and will in human action. On the one hand, it belongs to the intellect to judge an act: to specify an act's moral character by determining its inner order and its order to the ultimate end. Consequently, the intellect has priority over the will on the level of specification. In other words, it has priority on the level of formal causality. Likewise, wisdom and the other cognitive gifts have priority over charity on the level of specification. Charity depends on their judgments concerning its object in order to act. On this level, wisdom is rooted in the knowledge of faith: "the beginning of wisdom as to its essence consists in the first principles of wisdom, which are the articles of faith."[92] On the other hand, it belongs to the will to move the powers of the soul to act. This includes the intellect. The will moves the intel-

89. *ST* II-II 45.2.

90. Louis Roy, "Wainwright, Maritain, and Aquinas on Transcendent Experiences," *Thomist* 54 (1990): 664–672.

91. *ST* II-II 45.2.

92. *ST* II-II 19.7. See also *ST* II-II 8.6.

lect to engage in its theoretical and practical reasoning. Indeed, on the level of practical reasoning, the will even shapes the judgment of prudence. Consequently, the will has priority over the intellect on the level of exercise. In other words, the will has priority on the level of efficient causality. Likewise, charity has priority over cognitive gifts on the level of exercise or efficient causality: charity causes wisdom to exist in the intellect. Thus, Aquinas establishes a balanced parallel between wisdom and love. As he states elsewhere, God's grace "both perfects the intellect by the gift of wisdom, and softens the affections by the fire of charity."[93] Wisdom and charity have these two interlaced roles in human action, because they each elevate the interlaced lines of moral causality proper to the intellect and will.

One final feature of Aquinas' theology of the gifts is his view of their relationship to the infused cardinal virtues. It might appear from Aquinas' description of the gifts that the gifts and the theological virtues are all one needs to live a holy Christian life. Aquinas affirms, however, that beyond these we need infused cardinal virtues, which spring from the theological virtues and the gifts as from their root principle.[94] We need these infused cardinal virtues in order to specify more particularly the knowledge and inclinations proper to the gifts and the theological virtues.

Charity and the Infused Cardinal Virtues

In his analysis of happiness, St. Thomas considers whether we must do good works in order to attain happiness. He begins by reminding us that the first requirement for attaining perfect happiness is that the will be rightly ordered toward its supernatural end.[95] This is what charity accomplishes.[96] Like the natural love in the will, which orders the will toward the good in general, charity orders the will toward the vision of the divine essence.[97] Thomas affirms, however, that right ordering toward the end is not sufficient. If we were angels it would be sufficient,

93. *ST* I-II 79.3.

94. *ST* II-II 19.9 ad 4; *ST* III 7.5 ad 1.

95. *ST* I-II 5.7.

96. *ST* I-II 65.4.

97. See *ST* I-II 4.4.

because an angel attains its end through one immediate act toward that end. In God's providence, however, humans attain their ends through movements in time—through a continuum of distinct actions, which the tradition calls "good works" or "merits."[98] This fact is crucial for understanding charity's relationship to the other virtues. Although the theological virtues order us sufficiently in relation to our supernatural end, on their own they do not sufficiently order us in relation to the good works that are the means to that end.[99]

St. Thomas' description of the theological virtues as infused principles that order the intellect and will toward a higher end is key to understanding his view of their role in human action. As we have seen, Thomas presents the theological virtues in relation to the natural principles of intellect and will. Just as the intellect naturally apprehends the goods constitutive of natural human flourishing as goods to be pursued, and the will naturally inclines toward these goods, so too the theological virtues incline the intellect toward divine truth and the will toward this truth as the perfect human good. Aquinas extends this parallel to explain the theological virtues' relationship to another set of infused virtues.[100]

Analogous Types of Principles and Virtues

In his treatment of the virtues, St. Thomas asserts that although intellect and will are naturally rightly ordered to their general object and their ultimate natural end, they need a further ordering toward the particular objects or intermediate ends that function as the means toward their ultimate end.[101] In other words, although they are rightly ordered toward natural human flourishing, they must become further ordered toward the particular actions by which one attains human flourishing.

Right reason presupposes principles from which reason proceeds. Now, reasoning about particulars must proceed not only from universal principles but

98. *ST* I-II 5.7. See Joseph Wawrykow, *God's Grace and Human Action: "Merit" in the Theology of Thomas Aquinas* (Notre Dame: University of Notre Dame Press, 1995), 177–233.

99. *ST* I-II 63.3 ad 1.

100. Cessario, *Moral Virtues and Theological Ethics,* 109–125; John Harvey, "The Nature of the Infused Moral Virtues," *Catholic Theological Society of America Proceedings* 10 (1955): 172–217.

101. *ST* I-II 58.4; *ST* I-II 56.6; see also *ST* I-II 94.2 and *ST* I 79.12.

also from particular principles. With regard to the universal principles of action, we are rightly ordered by the natural understanding of principles by which we understand that we should do no evil; or also by some practical science. But this is not sufficient in order to reason rightly about particular actions.[102]

In this passage, Aquinas considers only the cognitive principles. Elsewhere he also addresses the voluntary principles.

The human person has many and different activities because of the nobility of his active principle, the soul, whose power extends in a way to an infinity of things. Therefore, the natural desire of the good does not suffice for him, or the natural judgment for acting well, unless they be further determined and perfected. The human person is inclined by natural appetite to seek his proper good, but since this varies in many ways and because his good consists of many things, there could not be a natural appetite in him for this determinate good given all the conditions needed if it is to be good for him, since this varies widely according to the conditions of persons, times, and places and the like. For the same reason the natural judgment, which is uniform, does not suffice for the pursuit of a good of this kind.[103]

Consequently, besides the intellect's natural knowledge of the good in general and the will's natural love for this general good, the human person must become rightly ordered toward particular goods that are the means to our ultimate natural end. This is the role of the acquired cardinal virtues.

In our analysis of the virtues in chapter three, we saw that prudence perfects the practical intellect in its reasoning about the means, justice perfects the will in its inclinations toward particular ends, while courage and temperance perfect the passions in their inclination toward particular sense goods or ends. The need for these virtues becomes apparent when we remember the character of the "operative syllogism" through which practical reasoning operates. In the operative syllogism, the intellect applies a universal principle to a particular action. The universal principle functions as the major premise, while the particular action is itself the conclusion of the syllogism.[104] As we saw in chapter three, the

102. *ST* I-II 58.5.

103. *De virtutibus in communi* 6.

104. *ST* II-II 49.2 ad 1.

movement from the universal proposition to the particular action/conclusion is through a particular proposition that functions as the minor premise or middle term of the syllogism.[105] Practical reasoning, therefore, requires a twofold knowledge, one universal, the other particular.[106]

Aquinas' crucial insight is that, although we know the universal principle from the natural *habitus* of first practical principles, the particular principle becomes known to us only through the virtue of prudence.

> The reasoning of prudence terminates, as in a conclusion, in some particular operable, to which it applies universal knowledge, as stated above. Now a particular conclusion is argued from a universal and a particular proposition. Consequently, the reasoning of prudence must proceed from a twofold understanding. One is cognizant of universals and this belongs to the understanding *(intellectus)* that is an intellectual virtue: because not only universal theoretical principles are naturally known to us, but also universal practical principles, such as 'evil is to be done to no one,' as was said above. The other understanding *(intellectus)*, as is said in the *Ethics* (6.11), is cognizant of an extreme, i.e., of some primary particular and contingent operable that functions as the minor premise and which, as we have seen, must be something particular in the syllogism of prudence. This primary particular is some particular end, as was said above. Hence, the understanding presented as a part of prudence is a right estimate of some particular end.[107]

Prudence, therefore, disposes us to reason well about acts ordered toward the particular ends we pursue.

But in order for this practical disposition to exist in our intellect, our passions and our will must be rightly ordered toward these particular ends. This is the role of the moral virtues, which incline the appetites to the proper ends of the moral life.[108] Although "the will from the very nature of the power is inclined to the good of reason," nevertheless, "because this good is varied in many ways, the will needs to be inclined by means of a habit to some fixed good of reason."[109] The will needs the virtue of justice, while the passions need the virtues of courage and temperance.[110]

105. *ST* I-II 76.1.

106. Ibid.

107. *ST* II-II 49.2 ad 1.

108. *ST* I-II 58.5.

109. *ST* I-II 50.5 ad 3. See also *ST* I-II 50.5 ad 1.

110. *De virtutibus in communi* 8.

The cardinal virtues, therefore, specify and particularize the natural principles of intellect and will.[111] These natural principles orient us toward the common good of the temporal community *(civitas terrena),* and the acquired cardinal virtues specify this natural orientation by directing it toward particular actions that constitute and embody this common good. With marvelous consistency, Aquinas maintains that an analogous dynamic is present in the life of grace that orients us toward the common good of the heavenly community *(civitas caelestis).*[112]

St. Thomas begins his discussion of infused cardinal virtues by appealing to the dependence of human acts on principles and virtues, immediately establishing a parallel between natural and supernatural principles.

> All virtues, intellectual as well as moral, that are acquired by our actions arise from certain natural principles preexisting in us, as stated above. In place of these natural principles, God confers on us the theological virtues, by which we are ordered to our supernatural end, as was stated above. Hence, there must be caused in us other divine *habitus* corresponding proportionately to the theological virtues. These *habitus* are to the theological virtues what the moral and intellectual virtues are to the natural principles of virtue.[113]

Just as the natural principles of intellect and will rightly order us to our natural end, so too the theological virtues rightly order us to our supernatural end. Yet, just as our natural principles must be specified by acquired cardinal virtues, so too the theological virtues must be specified by infused cardinal virtues.[114] Even after we have received the gift of grace, the acquired cardinal virtues remain in us, but they still remain proportionate only to our temporal end. What we need are infused cardinal virtues that follow a higher measure and order us to our higher end.[115] These virtues enable us to judge rightly about the particular acts

111. "Perfected moral virtue, according to Aquinas, can thus be understood as a disposition by which the individual translates her general knowledge of that in which her good consists into specific actions" (Jean Porter, "The Unity of the Virtues and the Ambiguity of Goodness, a Reappraisal of Aquinas's Theory of the Virtues," *Journal of Religious Ethics* 21 [1993]: 144).

112. *De virtutibus in communi* 9. See also *De caritate* 2.

113. *ST* I-II 63.3.

114. *ST* I-II 63.3 ad 2.

115. *ST* I-II 63.3 ad 1.

that are the means of our ultimate supernatural end.[116] They enable us to judge rightly about which acts are truly *ad finem ultimum.*

Aquinas illustrates how the infused and acquired cardinal virtues differ by offering the example of temperance. The object of temperance is pleasurable sense goods as ordered by reason. This ordering, however, occurs differently depending on whether we are acting from infused or acquired temperance.[117]

It is evident that the measure imposed on such concupiscible pleasures is of a different nature depending on whether it is according to the rule of human reason or according to the divine rule. For instance, in the consumption of food, the measure appointed by human reason is that one should not harm the health of the body or impede the use of reason. Yet, according to the rule of the divine law, we are required to 'chastise the body, bring it into subjection' (1 Cor 9.27), through abstinence in food, drink and other such things. Hence, it is evident that infused and acquired temperance differ in species; and the same applies to the other virtues.[118]

The acquired virtues incline us to measure our actions according to the rule of reason, while the infused virtues incline us to measure our actions according to a divine rule belonging to the divine law.

116. St. Thomas is careful to explain that this knowledge extends only as far as what is necessary for salvation (*ST* II-II 8.4 ad 1, ad 2, ad 3; *ST* II-II 45.5; *ST* II-II 47.14 ad 3; *ST* II-II 52.4 ad 2). Some individuals receive special insight, such as how to govern a religious community or to proclaim the Gospel effectively, but this type of insight belongs to the charismatic gifts, given for the good of the Church, but not directly for the sanctification of the individual who receives them (*ST* II-II 52.1 ad 2; *ST* II-II 47.14 ad 1; *ST* II-II 52.1 ad 2). Indeed, as Jean Porter notes, "the prudence of the really dull saint may extend only as far as an ability to recognize that one needs to submit to the judgment of others, combined with an ability to discriminate between good and bad advice [see *ST* II-II 47.14]. In other words, infused prudence may well be manifested in an attitude of conformity to others' guidance and to the rules of one's community" (Porter, "The Subversion of Virtue," 34). As we shall see in Chapter 6, this Thomistic insight has implications for one's notion of moral development and growth in charity.

117. John Inglis, "Aquinas's Replication of the Acquired Moral Virtues: Rethinking the Standard Philosophical Interpretation of Moral Virtue in Aquinas," *Journal of Religious Ethics* 27 (1999): 16–20.

118. *ST* I-II 63.4.

Charity's Dependence on Infused Prudence

While one might be tempted to interpret St. Thomas' distinction between the rule of reason and the divine rule as signifying that infused prudence is somehow non-cognitive or, at least, non-conceptual, this would be to misinterpret St. Thomas' teaching badly. Prudence, of whatever sort, is essentially cognitive and conceptual. We see this clearly when we consider the essential components of prudence.[119] Thomas describes what he calls the "quasi-integral parts" of prudence as the dispositions necessarily present for prudence to be a complete virtue. He portrays five of them as directly cognitive and the others as indirectly cognitive, since they perfect our ability to apply our practical knowledge to action.[120] Specifically, *memory* perfects our knowledge of the past, *understanding* perfects our knowledge of the present, while in the acquisition of knowledge *docility* perfects our ability to be taught by others and *shrewdness* perfects our ability to acquire knowledge through discovery. Lastly, *reasoning* perfects our ability to move from things known to knowledge and judgment of things that were unknown. In relation to applying our knowledge to action, *foresight* perfects our ability to order things to the end, *circumspection* disposes us to take note of the circumstances that confront us, and *caution* perfects our ability to avoid obstacles.[121]

Of special interest to us are *understanding, shrewdness,* and *reasoning.* As we have seen, besides the understanding of the first universal principles of practical reasoning, prudence must have particular *understanding:* it must have a "right estimate of some particular end."[122] Moreover, in order to attain this knowledge in a timely fashion, one must have *shrewdness:* one must be able easily and rapidly to determine a particular end to serve as the middle term of the operative syllogism.[123] Presupposed in this shrewdness, is the ability to *reason* well from universals to particulars.

If we consider each of these components of prudence with care, we

119. *ST* II-II 48.1.

120. Ibid.

121. Ibid.

122. *ST* II-II 49.2 ad 1.

123. *ST* II-II 49.4.

soon discover that they are all essentially cognitive. They imply knowledge of charity's goal and of the acts that can be ordered to this goal. Indeed, it is precisely because acting toward others must be regulated by cognitive principles that Aquinas is able to demonstrate why infused prudence is necessary. If our charitable actions toward our neighbor are going to be rightly ordered toward our ultimate end, they must be specified and measured according to some cognitive scale of values *(regulam).* Since human reason of itself does not contain such a *regulam,* this cognitive *regulam* must be infused.[124]

Aquinas is able to sketch the general features of this divine *regulam* by comparing it to the rule of reason in acquired prudence. The rule of reason in acquired prudence measures our acts in relation to the hierarchy of goods in which we participate.[125] Infused prudence follows this basic regulative structure, but calibrates it according to the new fellowship in the good *(communicatio boni)* established by God's grace.[126]

The recognition that charity's act depends on reason elevated by infused prudence is evident in Aquinas' treatment of the traditional doctrine that charity's acts follow a certain order.[127] The Vulgate of the Song of Songs proclaims that "the king introduced me into the wine cellar and he set charity in order within me" (Sg 2.4).[128] What is the character of this order? In considering this, Aquinas poses an objection: the act of ordering belongs to reason and not to the will; thus, since charity resides in the will, it is improper to speak of "order" as belonging to charity. Aquinas responds by stating that the order referred to here most properly exists in things themselves. (In Aquinas' estimation, some things are inherently more lovable than others.)[129] Consequently, since the will's act tends to things themselves it is proper to refer to charity's act as nec-

124. *ST* I-II 65.3 ad 1.

125. See *ST* II-II 47.11 and 15.

126. *ST* I-II 63.4.

127. Carlos-Josaphat Pinto de Oliveira, "*Ordo rationis, ordo amoris:* La notion d'ordre au centre de l'univers éthique de s. Thomas," in Ordo sapientiae et amoris, 285–288.

128. See *ST* II-II 26.1 sc.

129. *ST* I 20.4 sc; *ST* I 20.4; *ST* II-II 26.6; *ST* II-II 26.6 ad 2; *ST* II-II 26.7. Jean Porter, "*De ordine caritatis:* Charity, Friendship, and Justice in Thomas Aquinas' *Summa theologiae,*" *Thomist* 53 (1989): 199; Stephen J. Pope, *The Evolution of Altruism and the Ordering of Love* (Washington, D.C.: Georgetown University Press, 1994).

essarily following a certain order.[130] Nevertheless, Aquinas grants that "order belongs to reason as the faculty that orders, and to the appetitive power as to the faculty that is ordered." Consequently, "it is in this way that order is said to be in charity."[131] In other words, charity's act is measured according to the real value of the objects of its love, but this ordered measure is placed in charity's acts by human reason elevated by the infused virtue of prudence. Human reason measures charity's acts according to the divine rule placed in the practical intellect by infused prudence.

In his treatment of the order of charity, Aquinas reveals that infused prudence measures both the interior and exterior components of charity's actions toward our neighbor.[132] Prudence regulates the interior act of charity *(affectio caritatis)*[133] as well as charity's exterior act of doing good to the other *(beneficentia)*.[134] Aquinas explains that charity's act of beneficence must respect the particular circumstances that surround our actions. "Since the love of charity extends to all, beneficence also should extend to all, but according as time and place require: because all acts of virtue must be delineated according to their due circumstances."[135] Aquinas sketches in detail the multiplicity of particulars the charitable person considers when ordering his or her charitable actions.

One person's proximity to another may be gauged according to the various things in which humans are able to participate *(communicare)* with each other: according to the participation of blood relatives in natural goods, of fellow citizens in civic goods, of the faithful in spiritual goods, and so forth. Different benefits should be differently dispensed according to these different types of fellowship *(communicatio)*, for we should bestow on each person more benefits according to the thing in which he is strictly speaking more fully joined to

130. *ST* II-II 26.1 ad 2.

131. *ST* II-II 26.1 ad 3.

132. See *ST* II-II 26.6 ad 1 and *ST* II-II 26.7, where Aquinas describes differences requiring order both with regard to the intensity of charity's interior act and with regard to the good we do in external acts of beneficence.

133. *ST* II-II 26.6. See also *ST* II-II 26.7 and 8.

134. Aquinas affirms clearly that *beneficentia* is an act of charity (*ST* II-II 31.4; *ST* II-II 31.1; *ST* II-II 32.5).

135. *ST* II-II 31.2.

us. Yet, this can vary according to different places, times and interactions: because in certain cases one should assist a stranger more than one's own father, if, for example, the stranger is in extreme need, while one's father suffers a lesser need.[136]

The possible complexity of these circumstances leads Aquinas to underline explicitly the role of prudence in measuring charity's act. In addressing difficult cases—for example when we are forced to decide who should receive more of our loving attention: one closer to us or one in greater need—Aquinas refuses to offer a general rule, appealing instead to the judgment of the prudent person *(prudens)*.

In the case of two people, one of whom is more closely united to us, while the other is in greater need, it is not possible by a general rule to determine whom we should assist more, for there are various degrees of need as well as of union: this requires the judgment of the prudent person.[137]

In order, therefore, for charity's love to attain its end of loving God in and through particular charitable acts toward our neighbor, it must be regulated by an infused prudence that elevates the cognitive capacities of our practical intellects.

With perfect consistency, Aquinas is here affirming the necessary priority—even on the level of grace—of the practical intellect in human action on the level of specification. Even though the intellect requires a higher measure infused by God in order for it to act according to the exigencies of the heavenly kingdom, if our graced actions are going to be human acts, this infused measure must function as a principle elevating an essentially human process of practical reasoning. Infused prudence is truly infused: it is a gift of God's grace. Yet, infused prudence is also truly prudence: it is a virtue that disposes the practical intellect of the human person to judge and command rightly about the proper means to attain our ultimate end.

This feature of infused prudence and it relationship to charity is implicit in Aquinas' description of charity as commanding the other virtues. According to Aquinas' general theory of virtue, the elicited act

136. *ST* II-II 31.3.
137. *ST* II-II 31.3 ad 1.

of a virtue is the act that most properly belongs to that virtue. It is the act the virtue directly "calls forth" *(elicitus)*. In other words, the elicited act is what we directly know and will; thus, a virtue's elicited act is what gives that virtue its general character. For example, the essence and formal object of courage is firmness of soul in bearing grave dangers.[138] Aquinas portrays this firmness as the elicited act of courage.[139] The proper elicited act of one virtue, however, can simultaneously be the commanded act of another virtue. This occurs when an agent orders the act of one virtue toward an end that is the object of another virtue. For example, if one exhibits courage so that someone else can receive what is his or her due, then one is ordering an act of courage to a further end: an act of justice. In this case, the act of firmness before grave danger is simultaneously the elicited act of courage and the commanded act of justice.

Central to Aquinas' teaching is that every commanded act presupposes an elicited act, and this in turn implies that every commanded act presupposes an act of prudence. When Aquinas refers to one virtue as commanding the act of another, this is a shorthand way of saying that the agent is commanding: the agent is ordering an act that is the proper object of one virtue to an act that is the proper object of another virtue. In other words, the agent makes the elicited act of one virtue the means of attaining the elicited act of another virtue. The agent wills the elicited act of courage as the means of attaining the elicited act of justice. The key factor to notice here is that the entire action takes place within the elicited act of justice. The agent wants to be just, and in this situation to do the just deed one must be courageous. Justice is said to command the elicited act of courage, because the virtue of justice is the principle from which the courageous act springs, and the just act is the end toward which it is directed.

Aquinas holds that the same dynamic exists in relation to charity. Charity commands the acts of the other virtues by drawing them into its own act of loving God. The act of martyrdom offers an illustrative example of a virtuous act commanded by charity.

138. *ST* II-II 123.2.

139. See *ST* II-II 124.2, corpus et ad 1.

> Charity inclines one to the act of martyrdom, as its first and principal motive, being the virtue commanding it, whereas courage inclines thereto as being its proper motive, being the virtue that elicits it. Hence martyrdom is an act of charity as commanding, and of courage as eliciting.[140]

In the case of the martyr, the elicited act of infused courage is commanded by charity's elicited act of loving God above all things.

Moreover, just as in Aquinas' other descriptions of commanded acts, when Aquinas states that "charity commands," he is speaking elliptically. In portraying charity as commanding, Aquinas is affirming that an agent who has charity wills the act of one virtue as the means of engaging in the elicited act of charity. The martyr, for example, is courageous because the martyr finds him or herself in a specific situation where to love God—to engage in charity's proper elicited act[141]—requires an act of courage.

Properly speaking, command is an act of the intellect and is the product of a process of practical reasoning informed by prudence. Thus, for example, when someone acts courageously in order to be just, this presupposes a prudential judgment that an act of courage is presently the proper means toward attaining the just end. Likewise, when the martyr courageously sacrifices his or her life, this presupposes an antecedent judgment of prudence that in the present situation this courageous act is the proper means toward loving God. Prudence is not here measuring charity's internal act of loving God: it is not measuring charity's intensity. Rather, prudence is measuring charity's exterior acts, the act in which we embody our love of God. Thus, the charity of the martyr presupposes the judgment that in the present moment this action is the way to embody in a human act one's love for God, self, and neighbor.

Aquinas nevertheless remains true to his psychology of action and balances his account of the priority of prudence on the level of specification, by affirming the priority of charity on the level of exercise. Although charity's act depends on infused prudence in order to become

140. *ST* II-II 124.2 ad 2.

141. On the love of God as charity's proper elicited act, see the texts cited in footnote 44 of this chapter.

rightly directed toward the ultimate end through particular actions, prudence and the other infused cardinal virtues depend on charity in order to be moved toward the ultimate end and toward those particular acts that are the means to this end. In other words, although infused prudence has priority on the level of specification, charity has priority on the level of exercise.[142]

Infused Virtues' Dependence on Charity

In chapter three, we saw that acquired prudence and the other moral virtues presuppose the presence of a rightly ordered love in the will. In St. Thomas' estimation, this is especially true with regard the infused cardinal virtues. They presuppose the presence of that divinely infused love which is charity.

Thomas once again distinguishes between acquired and infused cardinal virtues. The acquired cardinal virtues do not depend on the presence of charity within us. We can acquire them by our own actions, even if we do not have charity. Yet, as we have seen, the acquired virtues only produce actions proportionate to our natural end, to an end that does not transcend our natural capacity to attain. For this reason, Thomas portrays them as "true" but "imperfect" virtues, and as attainable even by non-Christians.[143] "Perfect" virtues are those that produce actions proportionate to our supernatural end. These virtues are infused within us by God and can only exist in conjunction with charity.[144]

In his explanation of why these virtues cannot exist without charity, Thomas focuses special attention on prudence.

> The other [i.e., acquired] moral virtues cannot be without prudence, and prudence cannot be without the moral virtues, because the moral virtues well order us toward the ends, from which the reasoning of prudence proceeds. Now, for the right reasoning of prudence, it is much more necessary that we be well ordered toward the ultimate end, which is the effect of charity, than that we be well ordered toward other ends, which is the effect of the moral

142. Pinto de Oliveira, *"Ordo rationis, ordo amoris,"* 296–297.

143. *ST* II-II 23.7.

144. *ST* I-II 65.2. Brian J. Shanley, "Aquinas on Pagan Virtue," *Thomist* 63 (1999): 553–577.

virtues: just as in theoretical matters right reasoning most of all needs the first indemonstrable principle, that *contradictories cannot simultaneously be true.* It is therefore clear that neither can infused prudence be without charity, nor, consequently, can the other moral virtues, since they cannot be without prudence.[145]

In order to reason well about the means to our ultimate end (which infused prudence disposes us to do), our will must incline toward this ultimate end (which charity effects in our will). Since the infused moral virtues all depend on prudence for their existence, this means that they also depend on charity.[146] Hence, for example, "whoever loses charity through mortal sin, loses all the infused moral virtues."[147]

Charity makes the infused virtues be true and perfect virtues, because it empowers them to attain their ultimate end.

The ultimate and principal good of the human person is the enjoyment of God *(dei fruitio),* as the psalm (72.28) states: 'it is good for me to adhere to God,' and to this good we are ordered by charity. . . . Therefore it is evident that integrally true virtue *(virtus vera simpliciter)* is that which is ordered to the principal good of the human person; thus the Philosopher also affirms (*Physics* 7.17) that 'virtue is a disposition of the perfect to the best.' In this way there can be no true virtue without charity.[148]

A virtue is not a virtue unless by it we attain our end. It is only as moved and animated by charity that the virtues have this character. In other words, although prudence specifies charity's acts toward our neighbor, prudence and the other virtues are moved to act and moved toward their end by charity. The will naturally has priority over the intellect on the level of exercise; this natural priority is retained and elevated in the economy of grace. Elevated by the virtue of charity, the will's act of exercise moves the powers of the soul to act, rendering these powers' infused dispositions true virtues by moving their acts toward the ultimate end.

Aquinas is careful to recognize that the cardinal virtues have their own proper character. They have their own elicited acts. As we noted

145. *ST* I-II 65.2.

146. *ST* I-II 65.4 ad 1; *ST* I-II 65.2 ad 3.

147. *ST* I-II 65.3.

148. *ST* II-II 23.7.

above, what charity does is command the acts of these virtues, drawing them into its own elicited act, which is love for the ultimate end. The feature to recognize here is that, although the virtues have their own elicited acts, they only generate these elicited acts when commanded by charity. In other words, the elicited acts of the infused cardinal virtues only exist as commanded by charity and as drawn into charity's elicited act of loving God and all things in God. Consequently, Aquinas describes charity as the efficient cause of the infused cardinal virtues. It causes them to exist. This is also how Aquinas in his mature work explains the traditional doctrine that charity is the form of the virtues.[149] Charity is the form of the virtues by being the efficient cause of their ultimate moral character as *habitus* underlying meritorious acts directed toward heavenly beatitude.[150]

Charity and the Two Rules of Action

We can now profitably consider once again St. Thomas' assertion that charity's love is regulated by two measures, reason and God. Thomas affirms that, although charity's internal act of loving God is without measure (for one can never love God too much), charity's external acts are measured by reason and by God.

> An affection whose object is subject to reason's judgment, should be measured by reason. But the object of the divine love which is God, surpasses the judgment of reason, wherefore it is not measured by reason but transcends it. Nor is there parity between the interior act and external acts of charity. For the interior act of charity has the character of an end, since man's ultimate good consists in his soul cleaving to God, according to Ps 72.28: 'it is good for me to adhere to my God,' whereas the exterior acts are ordered to the end *(sunt sicut ad finem)*, and so have to be measured both according to charity and according to reason.[151]

149. See *ST* II-II 23.8.

150. Aquinas develops his description of charity as the form of the virtues in important ways. This development offers yet more evidence that Aquinas modified his psychology of action as he reflected more deeply on the essential character of formal and efficient causality. In a later section of this chapter, we shall trace the stages of this development and probe their implications.

151. *ST* II-II 27.6 ad 3.

The external acts of charity are charity's commanded acts, whereby we love our neighbor for love of God *(propter Deum)*.[152] As actions that embody our love for God, they must be rightly ordered to God as their end. Thus, as we have seen, they are measured by reason, as aided by the infused virtue of prudence and the cognitive gifts of the Holy Spirit. Yet, since they have God as their end, and since "desire for the end is endless and unlimited," with regard to the intensity of these acts' motion toward the end, they are measured by God's infinite rule, which is another way of saying that they are without measure.[153]

Something that Aquinas does not explicitly advert to here is that in charity's love of neighbor, our love for God stands as the ultimate end intended, while our love of neighbor is the act directly willed. As such, charity's love of neighbor also contains interior components. Our love of neighbor exercised in commanded acts of charity presupposes interior elicited acts proper to charity's love of neighbor.[154] We must intend to love a particular person and choose the appropriate way of loving that person. Aquinas is clear that charity's elicited or interior acts toward our neighbor must also be measured by reason. Reason both determines the good that we will for our beloved and the intensity with which we will this good.[155] Here again, however, although what charity wills for our neighbor and the intensity with which it wills it are regulated by reason, the intensity of charity's love for the ultimate end—on account of which we love our neighbor—is measured only by the infinite wisdom of God, which the human will can never will too much.

152. On the identity between the external or exterior act and the commanded act, see David Gallagher, "Aquinas on Moral Action: Interior and Exterior Acts," *American Catholic Philosophical Quarterly* 64 (1990): 123; Pinckaers, "Notes explicatives," 184–186.

153. See *ST* II-II 27.6. In his often insightful study, Caritas et Ratio, Van Ouwerkerk fails to recognize this crucial distinction, and consequently fails to grasp Thomas' conception of infused prudence. See Van Ouwerkerk, Caritas et Ratio, 73–76.

154. *ST* II-II 25.9; *ST* II-II 26.7 sc and ad 3. *De caritate* 9: *"sic etiam secundum actum quem caritas elicit, attendendus est ordo secundum affectum in dilectione proximorum."*

155. *ST* II-II 26.6. Aquinas explains that, as to its essence, the good we will our neighbors is the same. It is the divine essence. Yet, the depth of participation of this good that we will for each is not the same. From charity we will some people (those who are holier) a deeper participation of the divine essence that others (those who are less holy) (*ST* II-II 26.7). See also *ST* II-II 26.6 ad 1, ad 2, and ad 3.

Charity and the Psychology of Action

We are now in a position to address our earlier question concerning charity's role in the stages of action. We have already discovered that charity's principal act of loving God elevates the will's most basic act. It elevates the will's act of love on the level of *simplex voluntas.* Yet, what is charity's relationship to the other stages of action? Does charity also elevate the love proper to *intentio* and *electio*? Once again, St. Thomas is not as clear on this point as we would like. In chapter three we saw that, although Thomas does not systematically address love's role in the stages of action, there are elements in his account of action that enable us to see that he does intend to integrate his theory of love into these stages. The same is true in his theology of charity. Although Thomas does not systematically delineate charity's role in the stages of action, there are places in his mature works that enable us to discern his understanding of this role and piece together an account of it.

In chapter three we noted that Aquinas integrates Augustine's primary terms for the act of love *(uti* and *frui)* into his account of action. We further noted that Aquinas recognizes that Augustine's theory of love primarily focuses on union and attainment. Enjoyment is union with the end, while use is union with what is ordered to the end. Consequently, Aquinas reserves Augustine's terms for love to what Aquinas describes as the will's second relations to its object, employing *amor* and *dilectio* to describe the love proper to the will's first relation to its object. Love is the initial proportion between the end and the means to the end generated in the will by the acts of intention and choice, respectively. In other words, love establishes the will's relation to both the end and those things that are ordered to the end, while *usus* and *fruitio* perfect love's primary acts by bringing the will to rest in its objects.

In chapter three, therefore, we described Aquinas' portrayal of the will's relationship to its object as follows. The will's first relation to the end is love of the end, while its second relation to the end is love's perfect act, enjoyment of the end. The will's first relation to the means is love of the means, while its second relation to the means is use of the means. With regard to both the end and what is ordered to the end, the second relation is the perfection of the will's love for its object. *Fruitio* or *gaudium* perfects the will's love for the end, while *usus* perfects the will's love for what is ordered to the end.

The first thing to remember in attempting to understand how charity elevates love's psychology in the stages of action is Aquinas' insistence that charity's proper act is love *(amor* or *dilectio)*. Specifically, charity's proper act is to love God. As we have seen in our analysis of the stages of action, the will's act of intention generates love of some good as an end attainable by some means. Likewise, by describing charity's love of God as love for the "ultimate end," Aquinas implies that charity's act does not remain merely on the level of affirming God's goodness (love on the level of *simplex voluntas*). It implies that charity's act, under the ordering action of the intellect, becomes a love for God as an end attainable by some means. In other words, in the stage we described as intention (see figure 1), charity's love for God becomes the principle of action. It becomes a love for God through some means, or better, it becomes a love for God, the ultimate end, through some intermediate end(s). Indeed, Aquinas' entire account of charity's relationship to the infused virtues points to this dynamic. As we have seen, infused prudence specifies charity's act by determining which actions at the present moment are the proper means toward loving God. The first step toward this determination is (a) reason's *ordinatio* that union with God is an end attainable by some means, and (b) the will's *intentio* of God as such an end. The implication of Aquinas' account is that the cognitive and appetitive components of this second stage of human action make charity's love for God a love for him as an end to be attained. They make charity's *amor dei* also an *amor finis ultimi*.

This transition from *simplex voluntas* to *intentio* implies a shift of focus in our way of viewing our relationship with God. For St. Thomas, charity's proper act is rooted in union with God. Charity's act of loving God for himself is grounded in the fellowship *(communicatio)* created in us by his grace. Charity's act on the level of affirmation, therefore, presupposes our awareness in the knowledge of faith that we are already united to God in divine friendship. When, however, we move to the stage of intentio, the focus is now on a different facet of faith's knowledge. It is the awareness that the God with whom we are already united is, nonetheless, also absent. He is an absent good attainable through some means. It is here that the virtue of hope comes into play. With the virtue of hope we begin to desire perfect union with God as an end attainable with his help. Crucial for our analysis is Aquinas' awareness that hope's desire only becomes a true act of intention when it is commanded by charity. Hence, in the transition from *simplex voluntas* to *intentio,* charity effects its act of *intentio* in and through hope's desire.

Furthermore, since Aquinas portrays *dilectio* as requiring an antecedent choice *(electionem praecedentem),* when he refers to charity's act as a *dilectio,* this would seem to imply that charity's act is further specified by a choice of means. Here again, this feature is implied by Aquinas' description of charity's relationship to the infused virtues. Just as the will's natural inclination is rightly ordered toward the ultimate end proportionate to human nature, but must be specified in relation to the many means toward this end, so too charity's inclination is rightly ordered toward God as our beatitude, but must be specified concerning the many possible means toward this ultimate end. Since on the natural level this specification occurs as the product of choice (i.e., the love of *dilectio* arises in the will as the product of our choice of the means), so too charity's specified love toward the means is generated by our choice of the means.

This fact becomes especially clear once we recognize the implications of Aquinas' doctrine concerning the order of charity. As we have seen, charity's love has an order placed in it by the ordering action of reason as elevated in infused prudence. When we read closely Aquinas' description of this cognitive ordering, we soon discover that he is not referring to the *ordinatio* proper to the stage of intention. Instead, he is speaking of the ordering that occurs at the following stage, which we have called decision (see figure 1). In other words, the *ordinatio* to which Aquinas refers in these passages is the product of the *judicium* proper to the third stage of practical reasoning. According to his psychology of action, this *judicium* is always accompanied by an *electio* in the will, which in turn generates a *dilectio.* When Aquinas speaks of charity being ordered, therefore, this ordering presupposes a choice in the will that is the proximate cause of charity's ordering.

Next, concerning the stage of execution, Aquinas recognizes a *usus* perfecting charity's love for things ordered to the end. As we have seen, *usus* properly so called signifies "the application of one thing to another,"[156] such as "applying an active principle to action."[157] Two features of Aquinas' mature theology of charity point to his recognition that charity has a *usus* that perfects it. First, Aquinas frequently refers to charity as commanding the acts of the other virtues—and in his mature analysis of command, he reveals that, properly speaking, command is an act of reason. He describes it as an act of reason presupposing an act of the will. In explaining this, he provides an account of how command is sometimes described as an act of the will.

Since the act of the will and of reason can be brought to bear on one another, in so far as reason reasons about willing and the will wills to reason, the result is that an act of reason precedes an act of the will and vice versa. And since the power of the preceding act remains in the act that follows, it happens sometimes that there is an act of the will that retains in itself something of an act of reason, as we stated in reference to use and choice; and conversely, that there is an act of reason that retains in itself something of an act of the will.[158]

Command presupposes an act of the will. Consequently, we can speak of the will or charity as commanding. Strictly speaking, however, it is reason that commands. Moreover, as we have seen, *usus* is the act of will paired with reason's command on the level of execution. Therefore, when we refer to charity as commanding, strictly speaking it is reason that commands and charity that "uses."

The second feature of Aquinas' thought that highlights charity's act of *usus* is his treatment of how the Holy Spirit is a gift. The word gift, he explains, implies in the receiver the ability to possess the thing received. In what sense, however, can someone possess the Holy Spirit? Aquinas asserts that we are said to possess only "what we can freely use or enjoy as we please."[159] This way of possessing the Holy Spirit is possible only

156. *ST* I-II 16.3.

157. *ST* I-II 16.2.

158. *ST* I-II 17.1. In his analysis of use and choice, to which he refers in this passage, he offers shorter but similar arguments (*ST* I-II 16.1 ad 3; *ST* I-II 13.1 ad 2). See also *ST* I-II 15.1 ad 3 and *ST* I-II 11.1 ad 3.

159. *ST* I 38.1. See also *ST* I 43.3.

for the rational creature in the gift of grace, whereby we participate "in the divine Word and the Love proceeding."[160] This graced participation enables us "to enjoy the divine person and to use his effects."[161] Aquinas chooses his words carefully. We enjoy the divine person himself, but we use his effects, or what he elsewhere calls "the created gift."[162] Aquinas is not referring here solely to the gifts of the Holy Spirit properly so called; he means all of the infused *habitus*, poured into our hearts by the action of the Holy Spirit. On the most general level, charity "uses" the infused virtue of prudence as it moves practical reason through the stages of action. More specifically, as an act proper to the stage of execution,[163] charity "uses" the acts of all the other virtues, and even the external components of its own act. As we noted above, *usus* is the will's act of applying the agent's powers to action, something which unites the will to the object or act ordered to the end. Consequently, the virtue of charity has an act of *usus* that moves the other virtues to act and perfects its love by uniting it to those things (objects and actions) that are ordered to its ultimate end.

Lastly, when Aquinas asserts that we enjoy the Holy Spirit, he is remaining faithful to his description of enjoyment as the perfection of love. As we have seen, Aquinas describes *fruitio* as the perfection of the will's relation to the end. When the end has been attained, the will enjoys resting in the end: so too on the level of charity. *Fruitio* or *gaudium* is the perfection of charity's act of love.[164] In heaven this *fruitio* is fully perfect.[165] In this life, however, the consummation of charity produces an enjoyment whose perfection is according to our status as wayfarers on earth. It produces the enjoyment proper to those who attain the object of their love without yet seeing their beloved.[166]

160. *ST* I 38.1: *"particeps divini verbi et procedentis amoris."*

161. *ST* I 38.1: *"frui divina persona, et uti effectu eius."* See also *ST* I 43.3.

162. *ST* I 43.3 ad 1: *"ipso dono creato."* See also *ST* I-II 16.3.

163. See *ST* I-II 16.4 and *ST* I-II 17.3.

164. *ST* II-II 28.4 ad 1; *ST* II-II 14.4; *ST* II-II 27.8; *ST* III 19.3 ad 1.

165. On the character of this perfection, see footnote 62 in this chapter.

166. *ST* II-II 28.1 ad 1. See Michael Sherwin, "'In what straits they suffered': St. Thomas' use of Aristotle to transform Augustine's critique of Earthly Happiness," in *Aquinas' Sources: The Notre Dame Symposium*, edited by Timothy L. Smith (South Bend, Ind.: St. Augustine's Press, 2005), 260–271.

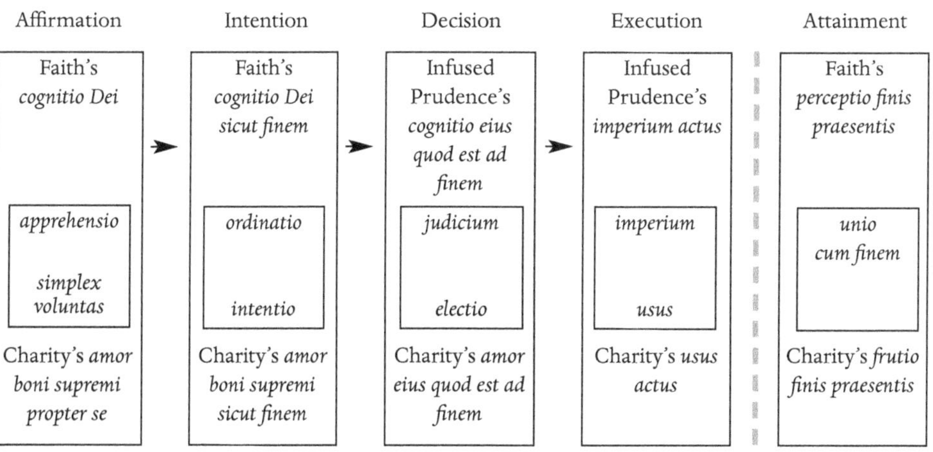

FIGURE 4. Charity and the Stages of Action

If we piece together the disparate elements of Aquinas' description of charity in the stages of action, the following picture emerges (see figure 4). Faith's knowledge of God produces charity's love for God, whereby God is loved for himself. This is an appetitive affirmation of God's own goodness as the supreme good, affirmed in and for itself. Next, faith also apprehends that, by God's wisdom and will, full and perfect union with God is *possible* for us through the grace of God. In other words, faith apprehends God (the supreme good) as an end attainable by us. In turn, charity's love, in the act of intention, begins to love the supreme good as an end attainable by us in and through some means—through actions chosen by us. Charity begins to love God this way in and through commanding hope's proper act of desiring God as an absent but attainable good. Next, in the process of practical reasoning guided by infused prudence, reason judges which acts can be ordained to our ultimate end. This judgment occurs in conjunction with the will's choice, which generates charity's love for a particular act as ordered to our ultimate end. Practical reason then commands this act in union with the will that moves the powers of the soul (i.e., it "uses" them) to execute this action. The act of *usus* perfects charity's love for what is ordered to the end (both the act and the people or things that are the object of the act) by uniting us to what is ordered to the end. Lastly, the intellect and will rest in the end attained: perfectly in the glorified vision and enjoyment of God, imperfectly in the perception of our graced communion with the ultimate end and in the will's temporal enjoyment of this end. This enjoyment is the temporal fulfillment of charity's loving union with God.

It is clear from this analysis that the synergy between knowledge and love remains constant at every stage of our graced action in this world. Infused prudence has priority on the level of specification, while charity has priority on the level of exercise. Aquinas' commitment in his later works to this balanced view of the relationship between charity and knowledge becomes even clearer when we analyze the development that occurs in his treatment of charity as the form of the virtues.

Charity as the Form of the Virtues

A full account of St. Thomas' teaching on charity as the form of the virtues is beyond the scope of our current project. His treatment of this traditional doctrine is of interest only to the extent that it sheds light on the evolution in Thomas' own thought concerning the type of causality exercised by the intellect and will—and thus also by charity and the infused cognitive virtues—in human action. In chapter three we saw that, although in his earlier works Thomas employs the language of form (*formatio, informatio, transformatio,* etc.) to describe love's causality in human action, in his later works he reserves form to the intellect and describes love as an aptitude, proportion, or *complacentia* of the appetite for the loved object. Thomas' description of charity as the form of the virtues appears to be an exception to this trend. Yet, when we study his treatment of this traditional doctrine, we discover that in his later works he modifies his earlier conclusions. While in his earlier works he portrays this doctrine as revealing charity to be the quasi-formal cause of the virtues, in his mature work he presents it as signifying merely that charity is the efficient cause of the virtues. Thus, once again, the development occurring in his teaching reveals that in his later works, Aquinas delineated more clearly the lines of causality in human action, reserving formal causality to the intellect (and its infused cognitive virtues), and efficient causality to the will (and its infused virtue of charity).

At some point in the middle ages, theologians began to describe charity's vivifying role in terms of form. Peter Lombard, for example, states that charity "informs all the virtues," explaining that without this informing action they would not be true virtues.[167] This way of describing charity's action is logical because of the analogy advanced by the Letter of James. If faith's relationship to good works—and therefore also to charity—is like that between the body and the spirit, then charity can be likened to that unique spiritual form, the soul, that gives life to the body. This analogy, however, poses problems. Granted that charity can be called a form, what type of form is it? Clearly, although it is like a soul, charity is not literally a soul. Aquinas' way of answering this question shifts over time.

In our analysis of the evolution that occurs in St. Thomas' theology of charity as the form of the virtues, we should once again avoid the temptation to exaggerate the changes that occur. As is the case with the other examples of development, these changes occur before a background of basic continuity. St. Thomas in both his early and later works describes charity's action (the action that leads charity to be called the form of the virtues) in terms of motion and perfection. Charity informs the other virtues by being the principle that moves them to act and moves them toward the ultimate end. As such, charity perfects the

167. Peter Lombard, *Libri Sententiarum* III 23.3: *"omnes informat."* The whole phrase reads as follows: *"Fides autem qua creditur, si cum caritate sit, virtus est, quia 'caritas,' ut ait Ambrosius, 'mater est omnium virtutum,' quae omnes informat, sine qua nulla vera virtus est."* When St. Thomas attributes to St. Ambrose the teaching that charity is the form of the virtues, he is doubly led astray. First, the work cited by Peter Lombard is not from Ambrose, but from an anonymous imitator of Ambrose, styled by Erasmus as "Ambrosiaster." Second, the part of the phrase that comes from Ambrosiaster refers to charity as the mother of the virtues and does not mention form or an informing action. This portion of the phrase is the Lombard's contribution and is either original to him or is drawn from some as yet unknown source. The passage from Ambrosiaster cited by Peter Lombard reads as follows: *"Dum enim caritatem, quae mater omnium bonorum est, non sectantur, non sciunt sicut oportet"* (*Comment. in epis. ad corinth. primam* 8.2 [*PL* 17, 226]). See Anthony Falanga, *Charity the Form of the Virtues according to Saint Thomas* (Washington, D.C.: The Catholic University of America, 1948), xiii, xv–xvi; Marcia Colish, *Peter Lombard* (New York: E. J. Brill, 1994), 493–506.

virtues and renders their acts meritorious toward eternal salvation.[168] Over time, however, Thomas changes his way of describing charity's causal action upon the virtues.

Charity as a *forma exemplaris*

In his *Commentary on the Sentences* of Peter Lombard, St. Thomas states that charity is the form of the virtues in three ways: by perfecting them, by being their moving principle, and by being their end. Thomas begins by explaining how forms perfect virtues. "It is evident that form perfects each virtue in its character as a virtue. For a lower power does not have the perfection of virtue unless it participate in the perfection of a higher power."[169] Next, he offers the example of how prudence perfects and informs the acquired moral virtues.

> The *habitus* that is in the irascible power does not have the character of a virtue, except to the extent that it receives understanding and discretion from reason, which prudence perfects. Accordingly, prudence places the mode and the form in all the other moral virtues.[170]

Charity is the form of the virtues in this same way: it perfects them in their character as virtues. Beyond this, however, it is also their motor and their end.

> It is not possible for a *habitus* existing in a power of the soul to have the character of virtue, with respect to the meritorious virtues about which we are now speaking, unless that power participate somewhat in the perfection of the will which charity perfects; thus, charity is the form of all the other virtues, as prudence is of the moral virtues. This is one way that charity is the form of the virtues. There are, however, two other ways that charity can be understood this way, because it is a motor and end. Just as a mover places its motion in its instrument, and just as what is *ad finem* is directed there from the character of the end, so too the mode of charity is participated by the other virtues to the extent that they are moved by charity, and to the extent that they are ordered to it as to an end.[171]

168. For a study that emphasizes the continuities, see Falanga, *Charity the Form of the Virtues.*

169. *In sent.* III 27.2.4C.

170. Ibid.

171. Ibid.

Of particular interest to us is Aquinas' description of the virtues as moved by charity and "ordered to it as to an end." Aquinas subsequently describes the perfection that prudence imparts as a type of "ordering." In explaining how higher powers inform and perfect lower powers, Aquinas states that prudence is the form of the other virtues by placing the order of reason upon them. "Just as reason is a power higher than the concupiscible power as ordering it, so, therefore, is prudence, which is the perfection of reason, the form of temperance, which is the virtue of the concupiscible power."[172] Aquinas describes charity in analogous terms. Since the will is higher than reason from the perspective of merit and voluntariness, charity is the form of prudence and of temperance.[173]

But, by drawing a parallel between prudence and charity in their roles as perfecting the virtues, does Aquinas also mean to portray charity as exercising an ordering role upon the virtues? This clearly seems to be the case when we study Aquinas' description of charity as an exemplar form.

> Charity is the exemplar form *(forma exemplaris)* of the virtues; but exemplar forms are of two types. One type serves as the representation according to which something is made. This type only requires likeness *(similitudo)* alone, as when we say that true things are the exemplar forms of pictures. The other way something is said to be an exemplar form is by being that according to whose likeness something is made and by which that something exists through participating in it: just as divine goodness is the exemplar form of all goodness and divine wisdom is the exemplar form of all wisdom.[174]

Charity is an exemplar form not merely in some static way, as when real things are the exemplars of the pictures that portray them. Rather, charity is an exemplar form in an active sense, as being that in which something participates. In other words, charity is the form of the virtues not merely because they bear the likeness *(similitudo)* of charity, but because they participate in charity's likeness in a way that causes their very existence. These virtues exist precisely because they participate in charity's own *similitudo* or *forma exemplaris.* Moreover, just as all forms have a cer-

172. *In sent.* III 27.2.4C ad 2.

173. Ibid.

174. *In sent.* III 27.2.4C ad 1.

tain measure and order, so too do the formalities of prudence and charity.[175] Just as prudence is the form of the virtues by instilling the order of prudence upon them, so too charity is the form of the virtues by instilling the order of charity upon them, directing them toward the ultimate end of the Christian life.

In the *Commentary on the Sentences,* Aquinas regards the informing action of charity as elevating the natural informing action of the will.

The powers moved by the will receive two things from it. First, they receive some form of it *(formam aliquam ipsius),* after the manner of an agent and mover that imprints its likeness *(similitudo)* upon the things it moves and changes. Now this form is either according to the form of the will itself, as all powers moved by the will participate in its freedom; or it is according to a *habitus* perfecting the will, which is charity. Thus, all the *habitus* that are in powers moved by a perfected will, participate in the form of charity *(formam caritatis).* . . . Second, they receive from the will consummation in the end. Thus, charity is called the end of the other virtues in as much as by it they are conjoined to the ultimate end.[176]

Charity elevates the will's act of informing the other powers by which these powers participate in the will's own form and likeness. This description of the will's action is consistent with Aquinas' early description of love as the form or likeness of the beloved present in the will. As we have seen, Aquinas affirms in his early theory of love (*In sent.* III 27.1 and 3) that the form of the beloved existing in the will becomes the principle of the lover's subsequent actions, moving the lover toward the beloved. In his early analysis of charity, Aquinas portrays charity as elevating this dynamic. Charity is, in some restricted sense, the form of the beloved (God) existing in the will.[177] As such, it acts as the principle of all the virtues' actions, directing them toward full union with the beloved.

In chapter three, we saw that Aquinas later abandons this way of portraying love. In his mature works, he no longer describes love as a *forma* or a *similitudo,* henceforth reserving these terms to the intellect.

175. Ibid. and *In sent.* III 27.2.4C ad 5.

176. *In sent.* III 23.3 1A.

177. *In sent.* III 27.1.1 ad 2: *"unde amor dicitur virtus unitiva formaliter: quia est ipsa unio vel nexus vel transformatio qua amans in amatum transformatur, et quodammodo convertitur in ipsum."* *In sent.* III 27.1.1 ad 5: *"amor facit amatum esse formam amantis."*

Instead, he presents love as a *complacentia* and *inclinatio* that functions as a principle of motion. Hence, the mature Aquinas reserves formal causality to the intellect and describes the will's action solely in terms of efficient causality. In his later works, Aquinas effects a similar transformation in his description of charity as the form of the virtues. He retains the traditional practice of describing charity as the virtues' form, but he now explains this solely in terms of efficient causality.

Charity as the *causa efficiens formae*

In the *Summa theologiae,* St. Thomas begins his explanation of what it means to call charity the form of the virtues by drawing attention to the meaning of form in moral analysis.

> In morals the form of an act is taken principally from the end. The reason for this is that the principle of moral acts is the will, whose object and *quasi* form is the end. Now the form of an act always follows the form of the agent. Consequently, in morals, that which gives an act its order to the end necessarily also gives the act its form. Now it is clear from what was said above that the acts of the other virtues are ordered to the ultimate end by charity. Accordingly, charity also gives form to the acts of all the other virtues; and to this extent it is said to be the form of the virtues: for these are called virtues in relation to formed acts.[178]

We can call charity the form of the virtues, because charity directs the virtues to their ultimate end. To understand Aquinas' reasoning here, we must review the treatment of moral goodness he offers in the *Prima secundae.*

Aquinas compares the moral species of an act to the species of a natural thing. The species of a thing is that which makes it be what it is. Just as natural things acquire their species from their form, so too human acts attain their moral species from their object.[179] Aquinas next explains that voluntary actions contain a twofold motion. There is the interior act of the will and the exterior act, both of which have their own proper objects. The end is the proper object of the interior act of the will, while the object of the external action is "that about which the external action

178. *ST* II-II 23.8.
179. *ST* I-II 18.2.

is." Consequently, the external act takes its species from the object about which it is, while the interior act of the will takes its species from the end, which is its proper object.[180] Aquinas explains that the will's contribution to the action is formal with respect to the external act.

That which is from the will is formal in regard to that which is from the external act: because to act, the will uses the body's members as instruments; nor do external acts have the character of moral acts except to the extent that they are voluntary. Thus, the species of human acts is considered formally with regard to the end, but materially with regard to the object of the external act.[181]

Aquinas means by this that the moral character of the external act is determined more by the interior act of the will than by the exterior act's own specific character.[182] Aquinas offers the example of one who steals in order to commit adultery. "He who steals to commit adultery, is, strictly speaking, more adulterer than thief."[183] Aquinas is here merely probing an aspect of his doctrine that one virtue (or vice) can command the act of another.[184] When one is courageous in order to be just, the commanded courageous act is drawn into the agent's elicited act of justice. The just deed is the end functioning as the object of the interior act of the will, while the courageous deed is the object of the exterior act. Consequently, the act is more an act of justice than of courage. Thus, Aquinas can state that the will's interior act "is compared to the exterior act as something formal to something material."[185] Elsewhere Aquinas explicitly states that the will's formality is rooted in its role as the efficient cause of the external action. As we saw above, Aquinas states that "the form of the act always follows the form of the agent."[186] Consequently, since the will is the efficient cause of the act, its goodness func-

180. *ST* I-II 18.6.

181. Ibid.

182. The moral character of the external act is *more* but not *solely* determined by the interior act of the will. In Aquinas' view, for the act to be morally good both the interior act (end) and the specific character of the external act (object) must be good (*ST* I-II 20.2). See Pinckaers, *Le renouveau de la morale* (Paris: Téqui, 1964), 114–143.

183. *ST* I-II 18.6. Aquinas is quoting Aristotle (*NE* 5.2 [1130a24]).

184. *ST* II-II 32.1 ad 2.

185. *ST* I-II 18.6 ad 2.

186. *ST* II-II 23.8.

tions as the form of the act. "The will is compared to the exterior action as its efficient cause. Thus, the goodness of the act of the will is the form of the exterior action as existing in the agent cause."[187] In other words, just as a natural thing attains its species from its form, so too an exterior action principally attains its moral species from the end, which is the object of the interior act of the will.

Aquinas, however, is equally clear in his mature work that the will does not order anything directly. "The will does not order, but tends to what has been ordered by reason. Hence, the word *intention* denotes an act of the will, presupposing the ordination of reason ordering something to the end."[188] The will acts as the efficient cause of the act, but as ordered to its end by reason.[189] Hence, although the goodness of the will's interior act is the form of the exterior act, properly speaking this form, as a principle of right order and proper measure, exists in the intellect.[190]

Therefore, although Aquinas can describe charity as ordering the acts of the virtues to their ultimate end, he recognizes that charity itself is ordered to this end by cognitive virtues in the intellect: "Order belongs to reason as the faculty that orders, and to the appetitive power as to the faculty that is ordered. It is in this way that order is said to be in charity."[191] Charity orders by being an act that is itself ordered to the ultimate end. The intellect orders acts to the ultimate end, while the will moves the acts of the virtues toward this ultimate end. Consequently, in his mature work Aquinas refuses to call charity an exemplar form. In fact, he reverses his earlier teaching and explicitly denies that charity is an exemplar. He now affirms instead that charity is solely the efficient cause of the virtues. "Charity is called the form of the other virtues not as being their exemplar or their essential form, but rather as being their efficient cause, in so far as it instills the form on all of them."[192]

187. *ST* I-II 20.1 ad 3.

188. *ST* I-II 12.1 ad 3; see also *ST* I-II 13.1.

189. As we saw in chapter two, the goodness of the will's intention of the end depends both on the intensity of the will's act and on its proper relation to the end as determined by reason. See *ST* I-II 19.8.

190. *ST* I-II 18.5.

191. *ST* II-II 26.1 ad 3.

192. *ST* II-II 23.8 ad 1. My thesis that St. Thomas in his later works refuses to call charity an exemplar form suggests an early date of composition for the *De caritate*. Just as in the *Commentary on the Sentences*, so too in the *De caritate* Thomas portrays charity as a *forma ex-*

emplaris and as imparting a *forma communis* upon the other virtues whereby they "participate" in the *forma caritatis.* Indeed, in the *De caritate,* Thomas even describes the *forma communis* that charity imparts as a *species communis,* a term with even stronger cognitive connotations than those implied by the term *forma.* The scholarly consensus concerning the date of the *De caritate* is that the *De caritate* should be listed among the collection commonly entitled *"Quaestiones disputatae de virtutibus"* and consequently that it is one of Thomas' later works (1269–1272). Yet, the problems involved in dating Thomas' disputed questions quickly draw even the most careful specialists into a terrible tangle, and render their conclusions tentative at best. Thus, without attempting in the limited space available to argue conclusively for an earlier date of composition, I would like to suggest that scholars reconsider the date of composition of both the *De caritate* and the *De spe,* and that they study whether internal evidence points to an earlier date of composition, such as during Thomas' first Parisian regency. In what follows I can only sketch my reasons for suggesting this. Even if we grant, as I believe is reasonable, that the evidence is overwhelming that during his second Parisian regency Thomas disputed a series of questions later gathered into a collection commonly entitled *"Quaestiones disputatae de virtutibus,"* it is not at all certain which questions the collection originally contained. Indeed, it is often listed ambiguously as *"De virtutibus et ultra."* The late dating of questions 1–5 has captivated commentators because of the happy correspondence between the subjects treated in these questions and in the questions that form the *Secunda pars,* which Thomas was composing at that time. What this argument fails to account for, however, are the differences in doctrine one encounters when one compares the accounts of charity and hope advanced in the *De virtutibus* (as it now stands) and the *Secunda pars.* The example of the term *forma exemplaris* is illustrative. If the two works are contemporaneous, how do we account for the fact that Aquinas is willing in both the *Sentences* and the *De caritate* to describe charity as a *forma exemplaris,* while in the *Secunda pars* he explicitly denies that charity is a *forma exemplaris,* describing it instead as a *forma efficiens?* Further, why no mention in the *Secunda pars* of charity imparting a *similitudo* or *forma vel species communis* that enables the other virtues to participate in the *forma caritatis,* something which Aquinas freely does in both the *De caritate* and in the *Sentences* commentary? Similar problems can be found with the *De spe.* Significantly, in the *De veritate's* first twenty questions (which principally deal with cognitive issues), St. Thomas considers faith after having analyzed the nature of truth. Might he not have followed an analogous format in questions twenty-one to twenty-nine (which principally deal with appetitive issues)? Might he not have considered charity and hope after having analyzed the good, which he does in *De veritate* 21 and 22? In other words, might not St. Thomas have disputed the questions on charity and hope during his first Parisian regency (1256–1259)? This would explain why his teaching in the *De caritate* on charity as the form of the virtues more closely resembles the teachings he advances in the *Commentary on the Sentences.* The introduction to the forthcoming Leonine edition of the *De virtutibus* promises to shed more light on this question. See also Torrell, *Saint Thomas Aquinas: the Person and His Work,* 201–207, 336; James Weisheipl, *Friar Thomas d'Aquino: His Life, Thought and Works,* second edition (Washington, D.C.: The Catholic University of America Press, 1983), 307–312, 365–366; P. Mandonnet, "Chronologie des questions disputées de saint Thomas d'Aquin," *Revue thomiste* 23 (2928): 266–287, 341–371; P. Synave, "Le problème chronologique des questions disputées de s. Thomas d'Aquin," *Revue thomiste* 31 (1926): 154–159; P. Glorieux, "Les questions disputées de s. Thomas et leur suite chronologique," *Rechereches de théologie ancienne et médiévale* 4 (1932): 5–33.

Aquinas now sees clearly that exemplar causality belongs to the intellect. This new awareness is revealed in his new way of describing divine exemplarity. In the *Commentary on the Sentences,* Aquinas explains how charity functions as an exemplar form by drawing an analogy with divine exemplarity.

> The other way something is said to be an exemplar form is by being that according to whose likeness something is made and by which that something exists through participating in it: just as divine goodness is the exemplar form of all goodness and divine wisdom is the exemplar form of all wisdom.[193]

In this passage, Aquinas is willing to describe divine goodness as an exemplar form that is participated in by creatures. In the *Summa theologiae,* Aquinas no longer refers to divine goodness in this way. The divine good is the final cause of all things, being that toward which anything inclines when they incline toward a good.[194] Aquinas recognizes that the form of a thing is also the good that is the end of the process of generation, and that, as such, this form preexists in the agent. Yet, Aquinas is now fully aware that as existing in the agent (God), the form resides in the intellect. God's will causes the form to exist in the creature, but as existing in God this form is an idea in his mind.[195] Thus, in God, exemplar forms are ideas in the divine mind.[196] They do not pertain to the divine will.[197] So too, the form that orders the virtues' acts toward the ultimate end resides in the human mind by means of infused cognitive virtues, while charity generates these virtues' acts by being their efficient cause. Not surprisingly, therefore, Aquinas in his mature work abandons any mention of the virtues participating in the will's "form" or sharing in the will's "likeness." Aquinas now considers *forma* and *similitudo* as proper only to the intellect. We call charity "the form of the virtues" only to express that charity is the efficient cause of these virtues' "ordering" toward the ultimate end. Since it is in relation to the end that an act attains its ultimate moral species, and since natural things attain their species from their form, charity can be called the form of the virtues by being that which moves them to the end, and generates their ultimate moral species.

193. *In sent.* III 27.2.4C ad 1.

194. *ST* I 44.4. See also *ST* I 44.4 ad 3.

195. *ST* I 15.1; *ST* I 15.2.

196. *ST* I 44.3.

197. St. Thomas recognizes that in God intellect and will are essentially one and the

St. Thomas' Mature Theology of Charity as *forma virtutum*

At first glance, St. Thomas' continued description of charity as the form of the virtues seems to contradict our thesis that Thomas in his mature works reserves the language of form to the intellect. The above analysis reveals, however, that in his mature presentation of this traditional doctrine, although he retains the language of form, he deeply modifies its meaning. He continues to describe charity as the form of the virtues, but denies that charity acts on the virtues as a formal or exemplar cause. Instead, he now proclaims that charity is solely the efficient cause of the virtues. Here again, Thomas remains true to his mature insight that in the genesis of human action, formal causality belongs to the intellect, while efficient causality belongs to the will. The intellect specifies the formal character of the action, while the will causes this formal character to exist in the act. Consequently, infused cognitive virtues specify the meritorious actions of the virtues by ordering them to God, while charity causes these actions to be meritorious as the principle of motion toward God as our ultimate end. In other words, the infused cognitive virtues specify the act, while charity exercises the act. Here as elsewhere we discover, therefore, that, far from separating charity's action from the intellect, St. Thomas in his mature works integrates charity's action more deeply into the action of the intellect and the infused dispositions that elevate it.

Charity's Relationship to Knowledge: Summation

We began this chapter by posing the question of charity's relationship to knowledge in human action. In answering it, we have discovered that according to St. Thomas charity does indeed depend on the informing action of the intellect. In order to love God and neighbor from the infused gift of charity, the intellect must have some knowledge of God. It must have the knowledge of God supplied by the virtue of faith and

same (*ST* I 22.1 ad 3). Nevertheless, he also holds that the cognitive and appetitive actions in God follow a certain order such that some things are more properly said to belong to the divine intellect than to the divine will (see *ST* I 27.3 ad 3, *ST* I 45.6 and *ST* I 59.2 ad 2).

perfected in the gifts of understanding and knowledge. Because this knowledge is limited, strictly speaking it does not specify or measure charity's act of loving God. Faith "shows" the object of charity, but it does not "regulate" this object.[198] Yet, charity's love for God as expressed in external actions, and its love for neighbor both on the internal and external levels, depend on knowledge even more deeply. In the infused virtue of prudence and the gifts of wisdom and counsel, the intellect specifies and measures charity's love. It places the order of God's wisdom into our love for creatures and ensures that this love is directed toward our unmeasured love of God. All of this occurs on the level of specification and according to the order of formal causality. As we have seen, on the level of efficient causality, the will has precedence over the intellect and its infused cognitive virtues and gifts. These virtues are caused by charity and their acts are moved by charity toward their ultimate end. In the *Summa contra gentiles,* St. Thomas affirms that "the goal and ultimate perfection of the human soul is by knowledge and by love to transcend the entire created order and to attain the first principle, who is God."[199] The findings of this chapter are that St. Thomas remains true to this insight in his later works. Indeed, his mature concern to integrate knowledge and love more deeply together reveals his continuing adherence to the view that "the knowledge and love of God are the principle of all good actions: extinguish the knowledge and love of God, and the good life in its entirety perishes."[200] In the next chapter we shall investigate some of the implications of St. Thomas' theology of charity for charity's status as a virtue.

198. *ST* I-II 66.6 ad 1.

199. *SCG* II 87.6: *"finis autem animae humanae et ultima perfectio eius est quod per cognitionem et amorem transcendat totum ordinem creaturarum et pertingat ad primum principium, quod deus est."*

200. *Postilla super psalmos* 52.2: *"cognitio et amor dei est principium omnis boni operis, ita sublata cognitione et amore dei omnis bona vita tollitur."*

CHAPTER 6

Charity's Status as a Virtue

We initiated our study of St. Thomas' theology of charity by posing two related questions: (1) what is the relationship between charity and knowledge in the theology of St. Thomas? and (2) what are the implications of this relationship for charity's status as a virtue? The analysis of St. Thomas' thought we pursued in chapters two through five has enabled us to answer the first of these questions. It will also enable us in this concluding chapter to suggest an answer to the second. We shall begin by retracing briefly the steps of our analysis in chapters two through five as a way of restating the conclusions that shape our answer to the first question. We shall then turn to the second question and consider some of the implications of St. Thomas' theology of charity for charity's status as a virtue.

Relationship between Charity and Knowledge: The First Question

We began our study by recognizing the Second Vatican Council's call to renew moral theology. We also outlined the response to this call offered by several Catholic moral theologians, such as Karl Rahner and Josef Fuchs, who hold that a component of the needed renewal can be found in a new understanding of charity's relationship to practical reasoning. They assert the existence of two levels of freedom and two types of moral action proper to these two freedoms. There is the level of basic freedom and the level of freedom of choice. Free choice is exercised in particular (categorical) acts. Our choices occur in response to (categorical) objects of cognition. As such, this freedom is constrained by the various psychological limitations that plague us; thus, it is often profoundly restricted or entirely absent. These theologians argue, however, that the level of basic freedom is not constrained in this way. This freedom is actualized in a way that transcends particular objects of cognition. Consequently, it is not restricted by the social and psychological limitations that constrict us on the level of free choice.

The moralists we considered, whom we have described as theologians of moral motivation, affirm that one's basic freedom is actualized through a morally significant motion in the will occurring antecedent to practical reasoning. They describe this motion as one's "self-realization in basic freedom," or "basic free option."[1] It is either "a total surrender of the self to the Absolute, or a refusal of such surrender."[2] The refusal of this self-surrender is the essence of mortal sin, while total self-surrender to the Absolute is, for these moralists, the essence of charity. Charity is a person's "basic free love of God," and consists in the "radical opening of the self to the Absolute."[3] Moreover, as we have seen, proponents of this view argue that one's self-realization in basic freedom is not exercised in any particular categorical act.[4] Rather, one's free option is a process that accompanies and underlies one's particular acts.

In our introductory chapter, we also noted that James Keenan maintains that Thomas Aquinas in his later works partially develops a theology of charity analogous to the one advanced by the theologians of moral motivation. Aquinas distinguishes between the will's act on the level of exercise *(secundum exercitium)* and the will's act on the level of specification *(secundum specificationem vel determinationem)*. In essence, Keenan argues that Aquinas' "specification" corresponds to what the theologians of moral motivation describe as the level of freedom of choice, while "exercise" corresponds to the level of basic freedom. From this perspective, when Aquinas speaks of the will's freedom on the level

1. Fuchs, "Basic Freedom and Morality," 96 and 98.
2. Ibid., 97.
3. Ibid., 105 and 99.
4. Fuchs, "Good Acts and Good Persons," 50.

of exercise he is describing what later moralists will call one's self-realization in basic freedom or one's free option. He is describing a motion in the will that is antecedent to and independent of practical reasoning and the psychological limitations that constrain it. Moreover, in Keenan's view, after establishing the distinction between specification and exercise, Aquinas portrays charity as the elevation of the will's motion on the level of exercise. In Keenan's estimation, therefore, Aquinas develops a theology of charity that portrays charity's action as antecedent to practical reason. In other words, like the theologians of moral motivation, Aquinas develops the view that charity is a purely formal willingness to surrender to God and to engage in right action.

In our introductory chapter, however, we also recognized a possible problem posed by the theology of charity advanced by Fuchs and the other proponents of a theology of moral motivation. The work of a number of moral philosophers from the tradition of analytic philosophy helps bring this problem into focus. Their work points to the connection between knowledge and virtue. Specifically, they claim that we cannot engage in an act of virtue unless we know something about the goal of that virtue and about which actions embody that virtue in the present context of our life and social situation. The insights of these moral philosophers, when viewed in the context of James Keenan's interpretation of Aquinas, pose anew a basic question of Thomistic interpretation. Our goal has not been to offer extended treatments of either Keenan's work or of the work of the moral philosophers referred to here. Instead, we have outlined their views as a means of introducing the questions that guide our analysis of Aquinas. Their views have led us to consider again the relationship between knowledge and love in the theology of Aquinas.

The primary question that has guided our analysis of St. Thomas' theology of charity concerns the relationship between knowledge and love. What is the relationship between charity and knowledge in the theology of St. Thomas? The analysis of Thomas' thought we undertook in chapters two through five provides our answer. These chapters reveal that St. Thomas in his mature thought integrates knowledge and love ever more deeply together, presenting them as the mutually dependent principles underlying any human action. The human person acts knowingly and freely through his intellect and will, and the principles of knowledge and love that underlie these powers. Charity and the infused virtues elevate this dynamic interaction, with the result that charity both depends on knowledge and is a prerequisite for the proper functioning of infused virtues that supply this knowledge, directing them to their final goal.

Far from disengaging charity and the will from practical reasoning, Aquinas in his mature thought effects a work of deeper integration at every level of the human psychology. In his later works, the changes he introduces into his description of intellect and will, knowledge and love, charity and the infused virtues, all have the same result. They enable Aquinas to explain more successfully how every human act is simultaneously an act of intellect and will, and of knowledge and love. When we act, we always act through the intellect's knowledge and the will's love. The intellect, its knowledge, and the infused virtues that elevate it, all have priority over the will in one way, while the will, its love, and the charity that elevates it, all have priority over intellect in another way, with the ultimate foundation of both being the graced nature God causes within us. Reason and its knowledge command all of the will's actions, except the will's first act which is instilled in it by God (through nature and through grace), while the will and its love move the intellect to engage in all its actions except the intellect's first act which is instilled in it by God (through nature and through grace). The core chapters of the study, therefore, offer us an answer to the first of our two questions. They enable us to answer the interpretive question concerning the relationship between knowledge and love in St. Thomas' mature theology of charity. They also prepare us to consider our second guiding question, the question of the implications of this relationship for charity's status as a virtue.

Charity's Status as a Virtue: The Second Question

In addressing the implications of St. Thomas' theology of charity for charity's status as a virtue we shall first confront the issue of intellectual and psychological determinism. As we have seen, one reason the theologians of moral motivation develop their theory of charity is to explain how the human person is free in the face of the intellectual and psychological limitations that constrain him or her. In light of this contemporary concern, we shall consider whether St. Thomas, by developing a theology of charity that affirms charity's intimate dependence on knowledge at every level of human action, proposes a theory of human action that falls prey to intellectual and psychological determinism. In what follows we shall consider these two types of determinism separately.

The argument that a psychology of action that does not develop a theory of moral motivation inevitably succumbs to intellectual determinism, depends for its force on a specific understanding of practical reasoning. It depends on a deterministic view of practical reasoning, whereby reason reaches necessary conclusions from necessary, universal premises. This conception of practical reasoning is a fundamental presupposition of the theology of moral motivation.

When theologians of moral motivation develop their theories of fundamental freedom, implicit in their accounts is a view of practical reasoning as an activity extrinsic to the agent's inner personality and freedom, a freedom which is virtually identified with the will. The will, as the core of personal moral agency, stands in radical freedom before the demands of practical reason. From this perspective, the will's basic moral act—which the theologians of moral motivation regard as charity's basic act—is a willingness to be determined by the impersonal conclusions of practical reason.[5] Thus, for example, Josef Fuchs describes charity as a "total surrender."[6] It is "a total surrender of the self to the absolute,"[7] and a "self-surrender to God."[8] As such, the will's basic free act is an act of surrendering to reason's judgments exercised in a habitual "inner readiness to behave rightly."[9] James Keenan offers a similar de-

5. The judgments of practical reason can justly be described as "impersonal" and "extrinsic" once one defines the agent's inner moral personality (one's fundamental freedom before God) as "independent" of practical reasoning.

6. Fuchs, "Basic Freedom and Morality," 105.

7. Ibid., 97.

8. Ibid., 107.

9. Josef Fuchs, *Moral Demands and Personal Obligations* (Washington, D.C.: Georgetown University Press, 1993), 157.

scription. The will's primary *exercitium* which charity elevates and which makes us morally good before God is a "willingness to be determined."[10] It is a "willingness to submit to the rule of reason."[11]

For both Fuchs and Keenan, therefore, practical reason follows a process that constrains the freedom of choice of the agent. In their view, the only way to explain human freedom is by positing the existence of a morally significant motion in the will that is antecedent to and independent of practical reasoning. Even so, however, the freedom they regard as saving us from intellectual determinism is a freedom to accept or reject reason's demands. It is the freedom to submit or refuse to submit to the dominance of reason.[12] A theory of Christian love and the moral

10. Keenan, *Goodness and Rightness*, 46.

11. Ibid., 134. See also E. Chiavacci, *Teologia morale*, volume 1 (Assisi, 1983), 96–98; 256. For an insightful analysis of Chiavacci's viewpoint, see Antonio Nello Figa, *Teorema de la Opcion Fundamental: Bases para su Adecuada Utilización en Theología Moral* (Rome: Gregorian University Press, 1995), 19–30.

12. In this regard, the moral psychology of the theology of moral motivation is remarkably similar to aspects of the moral psychology developed by dominant trends in modern philosophy. For example, Iris Murdoch contends that the defining feature of the dominant modern view of the human person is the division between thought and action. She sees this division embraced and concisely encapsulated in the work of Stuart Hampshire. Murdoch explains that for Hampshire and the modern view, thought and belief are not directly under our control. Thought is grounded on universal principles and necessarily unfolds according to the dictates of logic and the rules of reason. Action, on the other hand, is the product of the human will and is that for which one is morally responsible (Iris Murdoch, "The Idea of Perfection," in *Existentialists and Mystics*, 302). Hampshire, for example, affirms that, "It is essential to thought that it takes its own forms and follows its own paths without my intervention, that is, without the intervention of my will" (Stuart Hampshire, *Thought and Action* [London: Chatto and Windus, 1959], 153). For Hampshire, thought, even thought about practical matters, is "self-directing" (ibid.). It "begins on its own path," and is "governed by its universal rules" (ibid. 153–154). According to Murdoch, the modern deterministic view of practical reasoning stands in stark contrast to its conception of the will as radically free. The modern view may regard the process of practical reasoning as governed and guided by impersonal, necessary principles leading to necessary conclusions, but the modern view presents the will as radically free before these necessary conclusions. Murdoch explains that according to the dominant modern view, action for which we are morally responsible is uniquely the product of the human will. Indeed, the will itself becomes the locus of personal agency and identity. Hence, Hampshire can proclaim, "I identify myself with my will" (ibid. 153). Murdoch notes that from the perspective of modern philosophy what is at stake here is both (a) the objective status of reason and (b) the freedom of the individual now identified with the will. She explains that, "[in the modern view], our personal being is the movement of our overtly choosing will. Immense care is taken to picture the will

life grounded in a notion of submission has profound psychological implications that merit careful scrutiny. Here, however, we shall consider how St. Thomas offers a very different notion of practical reasoning.

It is in contrast to a deterministic conception of practical reasoning that St. Thomas' theory of action acquires new significance. St. Thomas' account of practical reasoning reveals that practical reason need not be deterministic in the way the theologians of moral motivation fear. At first glance this might not seem to be the case. Thomas' concern to ground intellect and will upon the wisdom of God might lead one to conclude that the will necessarily follows reason's judgment. Specifically, Thomas seeks to avoid moral relativism by grounding the principles of intellect and will upon the wisdom and eternal law of God. As we noted in chapter two, Thomas regards the natural principles underlying both the intellect and the will as participating in the eternal law of God.[13] As such, intellect and will become the twin sources of the natural law.[14] This description of the intellect's relationship to the eternal law might lead one to conclude that Thomas is proposing a form of in-

---

as isolated. It is isolated from belief, from reason, from feeling, and is yet the essential centre of the self. 'I identify myself with my will.' It is separated from belief so that the authority of reason, which manufactures belief, may be entire and so that responsibility for action may be entire as well. My responsibility is a function of my knowledge (which tries to be wholly impersonal) and my will (which is wholly personal)" (Murdoch, "Idea of Perfection," 304–305). Reason follows its necessary rules and reveals to us the demands of morality. The will, as the center of the freely choosing self, is responsible for its actions because it can choose to follow or reject the demands of reason. Murdoch explains that this separation is necessary in order to preserve the will's freedom. "If the will is to be totally free the world it moves in must be devoid of normative characteristics, so that morality can reside entirely in the pointer of pure choice" (ibid., 333). The agent is free from the necessary and determined conclusions of reason because "the agent, thin as a needle, appears in the quick flash of the choosing will," where it can accept or reject reason's judgment (ibid., 343). If Murdoch is correct in her interpretation of the modern view, then a fruitful area for further study would be the historical relationship between modern philosophy, the Catholic manuals of moral theology, and the theologies developed by the theologians of moral motivation.

13. *ST* I-II 93.6.

14. Strictly speaking, since law is an ordinance of reason, the natural law properly exists in the intellect. Yet, since the intellect is unable to apply itself to action unless moved by the will, the natural inclinations of the will toward the good proper to human flourishing enable reason's natural principles to function as a rule that guides our actions. They enable it to function as the natural law.

tellectual determinism. The view could be something like this: St. Thomas is affirming that the intellect reaches its conclusions necessarily from its divinely instilled principles and the will necessarily follows these judgments from an inclination instilled in it by God.[15] Even if one advanced a more voluntarist reading of the will—one that envisioned the will as remaining radically indifferent before the judgments of practical reason—an objector could still respond that the will nonetheless remains constrained to choose from within the limited horizon of practical reason: it still must choose from among the objects that practical reason offers.[16]

Aquinas, however, avoids this determinism by distinguishing clearly between theoretical and practical reasoning. As we have seen, although Aquinas establishes a powerful analogy between the principles of theoretical and practical reason, he does not regard the judgments of practical reasoning as operating like a scientific or mathematical deduction. Moral decision-making is not simply a matter of deducing conclusions from principles. This is so, Aquinas maintains, because while theoretical reason has as its object necessary things, practical reason considers contingent things: it deals with future possibles that might or might not occur.[17] This means that while the primary precepts of the natural law never change and are always applicable, the secondary and more particular precepts hold only for the most part and can change in particular situations.[18]

Moreover, as we have seen, will, unlike in theoretical reason, has a role in shaping this practical action. Although the will's inclinations are rooted in natural principles, these inclinations are general. In human action, these inclinations become particularized by being directed toward specific objects and specific actions through the specifying operation of the intellect. The will's inclinations are specified and particularized by the action of practical reason. Yet, as we saw in chapter two, the will has a role in shaping the judgments of practical reasoning. In practical rea-

15. See Keenan, *Goodness and Rightness*, 29–31, 47.

16. See, for example, Fuchs, "Good Acts and Good Persons," 48, and Keenan, *Goodness and Rightness*, 66.

17. Hibbs, "Principles and Prudence," 275.

18. See *ST* I-II 94.4 and 5.

soning, the will can both direct what reason considers and shape how reason perceives what it considers. In other words, although the will inclines toward what reason judges as good, the will has a role in shaping this judgment. Since the will moves the powers of the soul, including reason, as the agent cause of their acts, the will has a role in shaping the rational judgment that specifies the will's own act of choice.

> The human person can will and not will, act and not act; again, he or she can will this or that, and do this or that. The reason for this is found in the very power of reason. For the will can tend to whatever reason can apprehend as good. Now reason can apprehend as good not only *to will* or *to act,* but also *not to will* and *not to act.* Again, in all particular goods, reason can consider an aspect of some good, and the lack of some good, which has the aspect of evil: and in this respect, it can apprehend any single one of these goods as electable or avoidable.[19]

The will follows reason's judgment on the level of specification, but because reason can judge limited goods in numerous ways, and because reason's act of consideration is under the will's control on the level of exercise, the will can shape reason's judgments. The will, therefore, both follows reason's judgment and shapes the rational consideration that leads to this judgment. In other words, at every stage in practical reasoning intellect and will work together to shape reason's practical judgments. Stated more accurately, although the human person acts from general principles instilled in him by nature, he himself, in and through his intellect and will, directs his own practical reasoning and shapes his own conclusions about particular actions. As Jean Porter has noted, "This suggests an answer to Keenan's worry about whether Aquinas preserves genuine freedom of the will."

> Keenan is concerned about the relative priority of reason and will because he presupposes that they are sharply divided, but in fact this is not so; as Westberg repeatedly reminds us, 'Thomas Aquinas, however, emphasized the unity of thought and will in action' (50).[20]

19. *ST* I-II 13.6.

20. Jean Porter, "Recent Studies in Aquinas's Virtue Ethics: A Review Essay," *Journal of Religious Ethics* 26 (1998): 203. See Westberg, *Right Practical Reason*, 50.

As we have seen throughout our study, this balanced perspective enables St. Thomas to avoid both moral relativism and intellectual determinism. He avoids relativism by grounding the principles of intellect and will upon the eternal wisdom and law of God. He avoids intellectual determinism by recognizing that at every stage in practical reasoning intellect and will work together to shape reason's judgments.

Consequently, instead of explaining freedom by positing the existence of a motion in the will that is independent of practical reasoning, Aquinas develops a radically different view of practical reason. Since practical reasoning is shaped by our affections and our will, reason's judgments do not bind the will as an extrinsic authority. Rather, the judgments of practical reasoning are the product of reason and will, knowledge and love, together. If there is a "binding" that occurs, it is a freely chosen commitment of the self. The agent is bound by the choices he makes in and through his knowledge and love. He is bound to act according to his freely chosen judgments that are the product of both his intellect and will. The operative word here is thus not "submission," but "commitment." The moral life is the product of our freely chosen commitment to live in a certain way.

We should note how profoundly Aquinas' view of practical reason and of freedom differ from the ones held by the theologians of moral motivation. For Fuchs and Keenan, freedom stands in opposition to law and authority. They characterize freedom as the radical ability to choose indifferently between being moral (characterized as a willingness to enter into the processes of practical reasoning and to obey its findings) and being immoral (characterized as an unwillingness to enter into this process). This freedom of indifference is a freedom from constraint: freedom from the constraint of law and authority, whereby one is able to accept or reject the law's precepts and an authority's will expressed in these precepts. Once, however, we characterize both the intellect and will as having a natural orientation toward the goods of human flourishing, we no longer regard freedom as the ability to choose indifferently between morally good and evil acts. We no longer characterize it as a freedom *from* constraint. Instead, it becomes freedom *for* excellence. From this view, freedom is the radical ability to act according to one's deepest inclinations toward truth and happiness. Freedom is the ability to choose and to do those acts that lead to and participate in true human happiness.[21] Thus, while the theologians of moral motivation present practical reason as imposing exterior norms that constrain a person's freedom, something one must either accept or reject, St. Thomas presents practical reason as the expression of one's personal freedom. Practical reason is the medium through which we experience freedom. This is what *liberum arbitrium* means. It is the "free decision" made possible by the dynamic relationship between intellect and will. For Thomas, therefore, practical reason is not a threat to freedom; it is what makes freedom possible.

Granted that St. Thomas by integrating the will into the process of practical reasoning avoids intellectual determinism, is not his theory nonetheless confronted with some form of psychological determinism? It would seem so, because both experience and the results of clinical psychology reveal the myriad ways human freedom can be limited or entirely removed. One's genetic inheritance, physio-chemical makeup, as well as one's environment and early experiences, can all act to limit one's knowledge, disorder one's inclinations, and constrain one's ability to judge rightly in concrete situations. It is here that the concerns of the theologians of moral motivation attain cogency and power. These theologians often have deep insight into the subtle and varied ways that one's freedom and knowledge can be constrained or entirely removed, at least on the level of what they call the freedom of choice.

Although we cannot know with certainty how St. Thomas would respond to contemporary insights into the social and psychological constraints under which we labor, we can draw upon St. Thomas' principles to offer a Thomistic response to the issue of psychological determinism. First, his insistence that a human act is one that springs from intellect and will points to the fact that there is no way to escape entirely the limitations inherent to being human. A freedom exercised outside of practical reason and the social and psychological limitations that constrain it is simply not a human freedom. For St. Thomas, such a freedom would be

21. For the origins of these two views of freedom, see Pinckaers, *Sources of Christian Ethics*, 327–456.

an angelic freedom rooted in the angel's non-rational intellectual insight into the truth of things.[22]

Second, from St. Thomas' perspective, this does not mean, however, that freedom is not possible on the human level. It does suggest, however, that human freedom is an achievement. Although we are born with the spiritual principles of freedom (intellect and will), freedom is something we must achieve; it is something we must grow into with the aid of a community and of God's grace, and through a life of virtue. Pascal's quip that "he who wishes to become an angel becomes a beast"[23] is perhaps too harsh to be fully applicable here—yet his insight remains nonetheless apt. If our spiritual freedom is not consciously accessible to us, then the self acting in the concrete material world—which is the only self we have[24]—is conscious only of a world determined by natural and environmental forces (forces such as genetics, family history, or individual experiences). Any human attempt, therefore, to live an angelic form of freedom inevitably evaporates, leaving a residue of resigned surrender before our animal appetites. To resist this surrender requires that we face squarely both the limitations and the unique opportunities afforded human nature. To be human is to live a peculiarly amphibious existence. We are equipped to swim the murky waters of the material, but only to breathe the air of heaven. It is only when this spiritual air permeates every fiber of our animal nature that we are truly free. From this perspective, freedom is indeed an achievement. Like the trained athlete whose muscles are toned to receive the oxygen they need to perform, so too the animal nature of the virtuous person has become permeated with, and receptive to, the ordering action of his intellect and will, as well as the healing and elevating action of God's grace. Further, just as there are social aspects in the training practices of even the most solitary of athletes, so too growth in human freedom and virtue is a social reality. Like the excellence of the athlete, the freedom of the virtu-

22. See *ST* I 57.2; *ST* I 58.2; *ST* I 58.3; *ST* I 58.4; *ST* I 59.3.

23. Blaise Pascal, *Pensées*, n. 329 [427] (358).

24. On the self as the product of our activity in the world, see Thomas Hibbs, *Virtue's Splendor: Wisdom, Prudence, and the Human Good* (New York: Fordham University Press, 2001), 40; Roger Pouivet, *Après Wittgenstein, saint Thomas* (Paris: Presses universitaires de France, 1997), 31–47.

ous person is the product of dispositions developed through disciplined choices made within a supportive community. To extend the analogy, one can indeed complain that fish are limited to swimming in water, but the greater wonder is that God created a creature so marvelously fitted to living within the confines of the sea. So too, we can bemoan the limitations placed on human freedom because of chemistry and culture, but the greater wonder is that God created a creature so marvelously fitted (in this life) to living the spiritual freedom of intellect and will from within the confines of the animal world. The greater wonder is that God has created a *spiritual animal.*

Third, the experience of the divided self, where we recognize a lack of freedom in relation to actions that are contrary to our deepest commitments, points to higher and lower levels of freedom and commitment in the human psychology. St. Thomas recognizes this division.[25] This implies that even for St. Thomas there is something akin to what the theologians of moral motivation describe as a person's basic free decision exercised on the deepest level of one's free self. Yet, from the Thomistic perspective this basic free decision is not divorced from practical reason and the knowledge proper to it. Instead, it is the product of our deepest knowledge and love of God. Thus, for example, in the case of those who act from antecedent ignorance, St. Thomas explains that they are not morally culpable because if they had knowledge of the true character of their action, the act would be "contrary to the will."[26] This implies that the agent knows and loves some more general good as his or her true goal, but is ignorant in a certain context about which particular actions are truly in harmony with this goal. Of course, we can also drop to the level of the principles of intellect and will, but at this level we would then be considering the principles of our free action and not

25. In St. Thomas' view, the limitation of our freedom can occur on three progressively more profound levels: there is the inclination away from the true good that we successfully resist (this is the experience of the person who is continent but not chaste); there is the experience of those whom passion momentarily inclines to choose a particular thing that is contrary to the good they most deeply love and would choose if the passion was not present (this is the case of one who sins from incontinence); lastly, there is the experience of those who act from a passion that overcomes the judgment of reason, in which case the act ceases to be a truly human act. See *ST* II-II 155 and 156.

26. *ST* I-II 76.3.

our free acts themselves. We would be considering what underlies all our actions.

Why it matters that one's fundamental decision be a free act exercised in and through rational knowledge is best understood when we contrast the implications of Aquinas' theory of charity and the theory advanced by the theologians of moral motivation. This contrast will bring into high relief the ways Aquinas' commitment to charity's dependence on rational knowledge preserves his theology from the limitations that constrain the theologies of moral motivation. Specifically, it will bring into full view how the commitment to charity's dependence on knowledge enables Aquinas' theology of charity to escape the formalism into which charity in the theologies of moral motivation falls. We shall then be able to discern how Aquinas' theology of charity allows him to present charity as a virtue analogously like other human virtues and thus to show that our growth in charity is intelligibly like other aspects of human moral development.

In chapter one, we noted that when the theologians of moral motivation claim that charity's motion—the motion that renders us morally good—is antecedent to and independent of practical reason, these theologians are confronted with three interrelated difficulties. First, this view empties charity and moral goodness of conceptual content. As a purely formal striving, charity as an ethical concept ceases to have explanatory power. One can no longer describe the charitable life in terms of specific kinds of actions or a specific pattern of life. Secondly, this conception of charity implies that knowledge of God is of little practical importance for moral goodness as theologians of moral motivation define it. If the motions of charity's love are pre-conceptual, this love cannot depend upon conceptual knowledge of God. As a result, the role of Christ (as the revelation of God) and of the Christian community (as the place where one encounters Christ) have no essential importance for one's relationship with God. The theologians of moral motivation wish to argue that Christ and his Church have an essential role in the Christian life, but their principles do not enable them to show how this can meaningfully be the case. Thus, paradoxically, this would mean that, although right behavior and moral virtue depend upon knowledge of

God, one's relationship with God would not. Thirdly, this view of charity has specific implications for one's psychology of moral judgment. To assert that charity's motion is causally independent of practical reasoning implies that charity does not influence our judgments concerning right action. This means that what we love, at least on the level of spiritual love, does not affect what we choose to do. Each of these difficulties seems to flow inevitably from a psychology of action that locates one's response to God's grace in an action that is antecedent to and independent of practical reasoning. They each seem to flow from a theology that regards charity's act as a purely formal striving. In what follows, we shall address each of the above mentioned difficulties more closely. In doing so, we shall show that, although these difficulties necessarily plague a theology of moral motivation, St. Thomas' theology of charity escapes them. St. Thomas' theology of charity enables him to present charity as a virtue analogous in many ways to other human virtues.

Charity and Specific Kinds of Action

Theologians of moral motivation such as Josef Fuchs and James Keenan are very firm in asserting that moral goodness, as they define it, depends entirely on one's moral motivation, which they view as signifying that *from which* or *out of which* one acts.[27] Charity as the moral motivation that generates goodness is a striving that flows from union with God.[28] The decisive feature here is that this antecedent motion occurs independently of any object or intended end. Consequently, the moral goodness of the agent does not depend upon whether one loves this or that object, but solely upon whether one loves as much as one can.[29]

27. See Keenan, *Goodness and Rightness,* 14.

28. Ibid., 133: "charity resides in the will precisely as the will's self-movement, that precedes both reason and the specified actions of the will itself. The end out of which charity acts is union with God. This end is not the end that the virtues seek, the *terminus ad quem,* because all virtues are referable to God. Rather, this end is the *terminus a quo,* the end 'out of which' we act. This end is interior, already exists within us, and has the character of a principle in action and appetite."

29. Ibid., 131–132. We should note that, at least in the case of James Keenan, the theory contains an added nuance. Although charity does not strive toward any particular object, in Keenan's view, charity does, nonetheless, strive toward *something.* Most often, Keenan styles charity's motion as a striving for union with God coupled with a striving

The primary consequence of viewing charity as a striving that can accompany any concrete action is that charity ceases to be understood in terms of characteristic kinds of actions. In other words, the theologians of moral motivation offer us a theology of charity that does not enable us to recognize specific kinds of actions as emblematic of charity. As Jean Porter has noted, although they can claim that some ways of life and kinds of actions are typically associated with charity, by stressing so thoroughly the separation between the categorical and transcendental realms it is difficult to see this association as anything more than an adventitious occurrence.[30] The issue here is not the epistemic question of whether or not one can know that one is in the state of grace and has charity. The issue is rather the conceptual question of what it means to be in the state of grace and to have charity.[31] "In order to understand what it means for someone to have a certain disposition, we must be able to recognize kinds of actions which manifest that disposition."[32] In other words, what does the graced life of one who loves from charity

---

for rightness (both in one's character and in one's actions). (See, for example, ibid., 9–11, 15, 134, 137, 154 and 169.) Thus, Keenan appears to maintain that moral goodness is not merely constituted by what we strive *out of,* but also by what we strive *for.* Yet, upon closer inspection we discover that according to Keenan the goal that charity strives *for* is entirely "formal," which for Keenan means that charity's striving is ordered toward a goal that is empty of objective conceptual content. It is a "formal interior act" of voluntary self-movement (ibid., 142). Ibid., 14–15: "Only one question, the question of moral motivation, concerns the fundamental, formal self-movement of the agent. . . . Goodness, then, is descriptive of the first and most formal movement in a person." Ibid., 67: "The end as end is derived from the will. But the end is a purely formal notion. It derives its substance only when the object presented by reason is accepted by the will. The will needs the object precisely because the end is purely formal, i.e., it is simply movement without any direction or purpose. The end without the object is not inclined toward anything." Charity strives for union with God and for rightness of character and action, but antecedently and independently of any conceptual understanding of who "God" is or of what constitutes right action and a rightly ordered self. In other words, in Keenan's view, charity is not a willingness to engage in specific kinds of right actions. Rather, charity is a willingness to engage in the general process of practically rational agency. It is a willingness to engage in practical reasoning and in those actions that reason subsequently judges to be right, whether or not these actions are objectively right. According to this view, therefore, charity's striving can accompany any and all concrete actions.

30. Porter, "Response to Linnane and Coffey," 286–287.

31. Jean Porter, "Moral Language and the Language of Grace: The Fundamental Option and the Virtue of Charity," *Philosophy and Theology* 10 (1998): 177.

32. Ibid.

typically look like? Are there characteristic actions that the charitable person normally exhibits? These questions are important because, as we noted in chapter one, in order for the Christian life and the theological virtues to be intelligible to us and to shape our behavior, they must be linked to specific kinds of actions. This is true for any activity and the dispositions that underlie it. Jean Porter offers the example of fluent speech:

> we would not know what it means to have a disposition to speak fluently, unless we also had some idea of what fluent speech is, at least sufficient to recognize it when we hear it. That does not mean that a fluent speaker can never stammer, nor does it mean that one fluent speech is enough to reassure us that someone actually possesses the disposition of fluency. However, it does mean that unless we can at least recognize fluent speech, the disposition of fluency will have no meaning for us; similarly, we could not make sense of the claim that someone who never speaks, or who always stammers, is actually a fluent speaker (as opposed to *potentially* a fluent speaker).[33]

We may not know whether this or that person has fluent speech, but if we are ever to attain fluent speech ourselves we must have some notion of what fluent speech is. Granted, this knowledge is at first fragmentary and is acquired as one is introduced into the language of a community, a process that occurs in and through being initiated into the activities of that community. Nevertheless, the point here is that the acquisition of language would not occur at all without this cognitive component.

It is here that the limitations of a theology of moral motivation become apparent. Analogously the same thing would seem to be required for charity as is required for the acquisition of fluent speech or for any other virtuous activity: to engage in the virtuous act we need some understanding of the act and its object. Yet, from the perspective of the theologies of moral motivation this does not seem possible. To the extent that the theologians of moral motivation connect charity to a pattern of life, it is simply to a general moral rectitude.[34] Consequently, on the level of specific actions, from the perspective of the theologies of moral motivation, the charitable life can look like any other life. It differs from other ways of living only by being motivated from a different "pri-

33. Ibid.

34. Porter, "Response to Linnane and Coffey," 286–287.

mary *exercitium,*"[35] or "basic free option."[36] A person's life can either be motivated from a striving out of love for rightness or by a failure to strive.[37] Yet, since one's primary *exercitium,* or basic free option, is a transcendental decision present in any categorical act, the difference that charity makes cannot be explained in terms of specific categorical actions.[38] By implication, the same is true of moral evil. A mortally sinful use of one's transcendental freedom expressed in the failure to strive for rightness cannot be described as a function of specific kinds of behavior, because a bad moral motivation can accompany any categorical action.[39]

Keenan offers an example that strikingly illustrates the issues at stake. In an essay explaining his distinction between rightness and goodness, Keenan addresses two possible objections.

> The first may take the form of an equally jolting question: 'Are you saying that Hitler, because he did what he thought was right, was good?' Another may be: 'Are you saying that the dictator, who thinks himself right in oppressing people or ordering deaths, is good?' In answer to these questions, we have to ask: Do we really believe that in these instances these people were striving as much as possible to find the right? Do we really believe that in a world that has taught for centuries that injustice is wrong and has tried to elucidate the most minimal insights into justice that Hitler's activities were simply mistaken and sincere interpretations of justice? Can we really believe a scenario in which the holocaust is the thinking of a person who was striving to be right? Certainly, the access we have to any of the discussions leading to those decisions hardly support such a belief. In a word, the Hitler question only proves our insight: Hitler's actions were not only wrong, he was bad as well.[40]

35. See Keenan, *Goodness and Rightness,* 54–56.

36. Fuchs, "Basic Freedom and Morality," 98.

37. Keenan, *Goodness and Rightness,* 15.

38. Ibid., 8: "The contemporary description of goodness is antecedent to and distinct from the question of rightness. Goodness simply asks whether one strives out of love or duty to realize right activity;" ibid., 141: "[moral motivation] unites one not with one's action but with one's self-determination to goodness or to badness;" ibid., 120: "Issues concerning goodness and badness are distinguished by, and remain within, the context of an antecedent first movement of the will. In that context we can know the person before he or she wills a particular object. We do not need a description of whether a person or the actions are right or wrong."

39. Ibid., 10–11.

40. James Keenan, "Can a Wrong Action Be Good? The Development of Theological Opinion on Erroneous Conscience," *Eglise et théologie* 24 (1993): 217.

Keenan raises two issues we should clearly distinguish. First, there is the question of whether we can know a person's subjective status before God. The traditional answer to this is no. We can never know with certitude what God's grace is doing in a person, even in the case of a Hitler; nor can we know the limitations upon practical reasoning and psychological freedom under which an individual is laboring. Keenan elsewhere recognizes and embraces this traditional teaching.[41] In the above quotation, however, Keenan addresses this epistemic question with an argument based upon plausibility. Is it plausible, he asks, that Hitler was in a state of grace? Keenan's point is well taken. A person's behavior over time does seem to reveal a person's deepest commitments. We are generally justified in recognizing a *prima facie* correspondence between a person's sustained way of acting and his or her goodness before God. We generally act upon this *prima facie* evidence, always recognizing, however, that our judgments remain provisional, since the moral agent has hidden wellsprings we cannot see.

From the perspective of moral theology, however, this epistemic question is secondary. The primary question is whether the behavior of a tyrant is contrary to charity *as* charity. In other words, are these specific acts contrary to charity and, if not, are there any specific acts that are contrary to charity? Even though we cannot know with the certitude of faith whether or not a specific individual has charity, can we nonetheless know that certain kinds of acts cannot be acts of charity? The principles underlying the theology of moral motivation do not allow one to answer this question in the affirmative: they do not allow the theologians of moral motivation to affirm that certain categorical acts cannot be motivated from charity. On this account, although Hitler's acts are contrary to right reason, they are not structurally contrary to charity. According to the theology of moral motivation, therefore, there is in principle no reason why the goodness of charity cannot accompany the wrongness of Hitler's genocide. This is so because, from this perspec-

41. Keenan, *Goodness and Rightness,* 150; see also 155: "In our distinction, however, the fact that one performs disordered actions only indicates the degree to which one lacks personal freedom or suffers disorders in various dimensions of one's personality. These actions do not indicate that one fails to strive to love as much as one can."

tive, moral goodness is not the cause of rightness, nor is badness the cause of wrongness. Indeed, James Keenan even warns the reader against drawing this conclusion.

Moralists familiar with scholastic terminology may be tempted to think that goodness is the *terminus a quo* of human action, rightness the *terminus ad quem*. But there is no such direct sequence. The *terminus a quo,* or point of departure, for rightness is not goodness, but reason itself.[42]

Goodness does not cause rightness because the principle of rightness is reason, while the principle of goodness is a pre-conceptual striving present in the will. This striving, Keenan tells us, is independent of reason,[43] and "has no connection to rightness."[44] The wrong actions of a dictator, therefore, although they are contrary to reason, are not contrary to charity.

Consequently, when one regards charity's motion as antecedent to and independent of practical reasoning, the Christian life becomes strangely disembodied. If charity is not linked to any specific kinds of actions, but can accompany all actions, right or wrong, then how does one learn to engage in charity? If the starting point of right action is not charity but reason and one's psychological motivation, then how is one to know whether or not one is doing what charity requires?[45] How is one to know what it means to "strive"? Here again, the issue is not the epistemic question of whether one can know that one has charity. The issue is conceptual: on the supposition that I have charity, what must I do in order to engage in charity's act? What actions must I avoid in order not to lose charity by acting against it? The theologians of moral motivation intend to maintain the traditional teaching that charity's act is something we freely choose to do and that charity can be lost because of

42. Ibid., 15.

43. Ibid., 47: "As first mover, the will's movement is independent of and prior to reason's presentation of the object;" ibid., 55: "in questions nine through seventeen of the *Prima secundae* [Aquinas refers to an *exercitium* that] precedes and is independent of reason."

44. Ibid., 55. As a result, according to Keenan's principles, wrongness is incidental to sin (ibid., 154).

45. On reason and psychological motivation as the starting points of categorical acts, see Keenan, ibid., 15.

actions we freely choose to do. Yet, since, according to their principles, moral striving does not cause actions that are rationally accessible to us, but only accompanies these actions, these moralists are unable to explain how charity's motion can be something we freely choose. Indeed, since moral apathy can just as easily accompany our rational actions as moral striving can, how do striving and the failure to strive differ psychologically? Since they are not each linked to different kinds of actions that we can conceptually recognize and distinguish, it is difficult to see how from the perspective of a theology of moral motivation we can freely choose one over the other. The principles that underlie the theology of moral motivation, therefore, render moral agency ghostlike.[46] Moral goodness does not depend upon a willingness to embrace this or that way of living. Rather, according to the theology of moral motivation, moral goodness is the function of a non-rational willingness to be human, to be a rational creature, without requiring commitment to any specific conception of what rationality requires.[47] Moral goodness, therefore, becomes the result of an ephemeral action disembodied from any storied account of human life and the actions proper to it. It becomes the product of a charity that ceases to be a virtue in any recognizably human way.

The biblical and patristic perspectives on charity diverge sharply from the foregoing formalism of the theologies of moral motivation. St. Thomas embraces this biblical and patristic perspective and gives it a deeper theoretical foundation. In what follows, we shall sketch selectively this aspect of the theologies of charity developed in the New Testament and in the works of early church Fathers. We shall then underline how St. Thomas adopts this perspective and grounds it in his psychology of action.

That the New Testament authors eschew formalism in their treatment of charity is evident in the works of St. Paul. When St. Paul wishes to describe charity and the Christian life, he presents them in terms of

46. Alasdair MacIntyre, "How Moral Agents Became Ghosts or Why the History of Ethics Diverged from that of the Philosophy of Mind," *Synthese* 53 (1982): 309.

47. For example, Keenan describes charity's motion as a "moral self-movement antecedent to the quest for prudence" (Keenan, *Goodness and Rightness,* 107).

characteristic types of actions.[48] Paul acknowledges that not everyone who exhibits apparently virtuous actions is necessarily doing them from the love of charity.[49] This, however, does not detract from the fact that one who has charity and the other theological virtues acts in certain paradigmatic ways.[50] Recognizing this enables Paul to present Christ and

48. Rom 13.10: "Love does no wrong to a neighbor; therefore love is the fulfilling of the law;" Rom 14.15: "If your brother is being injured by what you eat, you are no longer walking in love. Do not let what you eat cause the ruin of one for whom Christ died;" 1 Cor 13.4–7; "Love is patient and kind; love is not jealous or boastful; it is not arrogant or rude. Love does not insist on its own way; it is not irritable or resentful; it does not rejoice at wrong, but rejoices in the right. Love bears all things, believes all things, hopes all things, endures all things;" Gal 5.13–25: "For you were called to freedom, brethren; only do not use your freedom as an opportunity for the flesh, but through love be servants of one another. For the whole law is fulfilled in one word, 'You shall love your neighbor as yourself.' But if you bite and devour one another take heed that you are not consumed by one another. But I say, walk by the Spirit, and do not gratify the desires of the flesh. For the desires of the flesh are against the Spirit, and the desires of the Spirit are against the flesh; for these are opposed to each other, to prevent you from doing what you would. But if you are led by the Spirit you are not under the law. Now the works of the flesh are plain: fornication, impurity, licentiousness, idolatry, sorcery, enmity, strife, jealousy, anger, selfishness, dissension, party spirit, envy, drunkenness, carousing, and the like. I warn you, as I warned you before, that those who do such things shall not inherit the kingdom of God. But the fruit of the Spirit is love, joy, peace, patience, kindness, goodness, faithfulness, gentleness, self-control; against such there is no law. And those who belong to Christ Jesus have crucified the flesh with its passions and desires. If we live by the Spirit, let us also walk by the Spirit." Commenting on this passage from Galatians, Ceslaus Spicq states, "When St. Paul enumerates eight virtues, he is only pointing out different aspects of love of neighbor: joy, peace, patience, kindness, goodness, fidelity, gentleness, self-control. One proof that these virtues are not distinct from charity but are only its modes or manifestations is the parallel text, 1 Corinthians 13:4ff. Another is that they are introduced by 'fruit' in the singular as opposed to the several 'works' of the flesh. The eight virtues are really only one virtue; their names are many, but they all mean love," Ceslaus Spicq, *Agape in the New Testament,* volume 2 (St. Louis: B. Herder Book Co., 1965), 43. See also 1 Jn 2.3–6; 1 Jn 3.16–18: "By this we know love, that he laid down his life for us; and we ought to lay down our lives for the brethren. But if any one has the world's goods and sees his brother in need, yet closes his heart against him, how does God's love abide in him? Little children, let us not love in word or speech but in deed and in truth." Pinckaers, *Sources of Christian Ethics,* 122–125. Jeffrey Stout notes the difference between the method of St. Paul and the method proper to Kant and modern philosophy since Descartes. See Jeffrey Stout, *The Flight From Authority: Religion, Morality and the Quest for Autonomy* (Notre Dame: University of Notre Dame Press, 1981), 233–234.

49. 1 Cor 13.1–3.

50. See William C. Spohn, *What Are They Saying About Scripture and Ethics?* (Mahwah, N.J.: Paulist Press, 1995), 94–102; 116–120.

himself as models of the Christian life for the disciples to imitate.[51] Jesus and the apostles become types of the Christian life, and the theological virtues become traits of character that dispose the Christian to act in ways that conform to these types. By associating the theological virtues with specific kinds of actions, these actions and the lives that exhibit them become the pattern against which one can judge other actions in new situations. They become the primary guides for Christian living.[52]

The theologians of the early church adopt a similar perspective on charity and the Christian life. They regard the life of charity as something one learns through the virtuous example of others. They describe charity by means of specific characteristic types of action. Robert Wilken offers a description of this early Christian perspective.

> Of the several paths that lead to virtue, the broadest and the most obliging is the way of imitation. By observing the lives of holy men and women and imitating their deeds, we become virtuous. Before we can become doers, we first must be spectators. . . . Without examples, without imitation, there can be no human life or civilization, no art or culture, no virtue or holiness. The elementary activities of fashioning a clay pot or constructing a cabinet, learning to speak or sculpting a statue have their beginning in the imitation of what others do. This atavistic truth is as old as humankind, but in the West it was the Greeks who helped us understand its place in the moral life.[53]

In Wilken's view, Plutarch summarizes concisely the Greek perspective on the role of imitation in moral development.

> Our senses apprehend the things they encounter simply because of the impact they make upon us. For this reason the senses must receive everything

51. 1 Cor 4.16; 1 Cor 11.1; Eph 5.1–2; Phil 3.17; Phil 4.9; 1 Thes 1.6; 1 Thes 2.14; 2 Thes 3.7–10. See also Heb 6.12; Heb 13.7; 1 Jn 2.5; 1 Jn 4.17; 3 Jn 11. Spicq, *Agape in the New Testament,* 73–76; Linda L. Belleville: "'Imitate Me, Just as I Imitate Christ': Discipleship in the Corinthian Correspondence," in *Patterns of Discipleship in the New Testament,* edited by Richard N. Longenecker (Grand Rapids, Mich.: Eerdmans, 1996), 120–142; Gerald F. Hawthorne, "The Imitation of Christ: Discipleship in Philippians," in *Patterns of Discipleship in the New Testament,* 163–179; Frank J. Matera, *New Testament Ethics: The Legacies of Jesus and Paul* (Louisville, Ky.: Westminster John Knox Press, 1996), 174–183; Pinckaers, *Sources of Christian Ethics,* 120–122; *La vie selon l'Esprit,* 91–99.

52. Spohn, *What Are They Saying About Scripture and Ethics?* 106–121.

53. Robert Wilken, *Remembering the Christian Past* (Grand Rapids, Mich.: William B. Eerdmans, 1995), 121–122.

that presents itself whether it be useful or useless. The mind, however, has the power to turn itself away if it wishes, and readily fasten on what seems best. It is proper, then, that it pursue what is best, so that it may not only behold it but also be nourished by beholding it. . . . Our spiritual vision must be applied to such objects that by their charm invite it to attain its proper good. . . . Such objects are to be found in *virtuous deeds;* for these implant in those who search them out a zeal and yearning that leads to imitation. . . . [V]irtue disposes a person so that as soon as one admires the works of virtue one strives to emulate those who performed them. The good things of fortune we love to possess and enjoy, those of virtues we love to perform. . . . The good creates a stir of activity towards itself and implants at once in the spectator an impulse toward action.[54]

These Greek insights were quickly incorporated into the preaching of the early church, but they were made to conform to the deeper insight of the Gospel message that Christ is the true model of virtue, the true way to eternal life: "I have given you an example that you also should do as I have done" (*Jn* 13.15).[55] Thus, Ignatius of Antioch exhorts his readers "to imitate Jesus Christ as he imitated the Father."[56] Similarly, Clement of Alexandria states, "our tutor Jesus exemplifies the true life and trains the one who is in Christ. . . . He gives commands and embodies the commands that we might be able to accomplish them."[57] Origen, for his part, recognizes the saints in the Scriptures, who were conformed to Christ, as models of virtue as well: "Genuine transformation of life comes from reading the ancient Scriptures, learning who the just were and *imitating* them."[58]

St. Thomas embraces the biblical and patristic perspective and por-

54. Plutarch, *Life of Pericles* 1–4. Wilken, *Remembering the Christian Past,* 122–123.

55. Henri Crouzel, "L'Imitation et la 'suite' de Dieu et du Christ dans les premiers siècles chrétiens, ainsi que leur sources gréco-romaines et hébraïques," *Jahrbuch für Antike und Christentum* 21 (1978): 7–14.

56. Ignatius of Antioch, *Letter to the Philippians* 7.12. Wilken, *Remembering the Christian Past,* 127.

57. Clement of Alexandria, *Paed.* 1.12.98.1–3. Wilken, *Remembering the Christian Past,* 127.

58. Origen, *Homilies on Jeremiah* 4.5; Wilken, *Remembering the Christian Past,* 121; Peter Brown, "The Saint as Exemplar in Late Antiquity," in *Saints and Virtues,* edited by John Stratton Hawley (Berkeley: University of California Press, 1987), 4.

trays charity in similarly paradigmatic ways. As Jean Porter has noted,[59] Thomas affirms in his account of justice that we can only understand a virtue in terms of certain characteristic acts.[60] Thomas also adds that in order to exercise a virtue's act, we must do this act knowingly, from choice and for a due end.[61] This implies that we must know what acts of that virtue look like (so we can know whether or not we are engaging in them); we must choose those acts; and we must in some way know the end toward which the virtue is directed (in order to know whether or not the end is a "due end").

In St. Thomas' estimation each of these necessary features of a virtue is true of charity. The charitable person knows what charity's acts look like, chooses them freely, and knows the end toward which they are directed. As we saw in the previous chapter, St. Thomas makes this very explicit. The primary elicited act of charity is to love: to love God and to love our neighbor (and, indeed, all things) in God or on account of God *(propter Deum)*.[62] Moreover, charity's interior elicited act is exemplified in specific external actions, such as beneficence, works of mercy, and fraternal correction.[63] Further, although as a virtue charity is an infused habit, as an act it is something we freely choose. Hence, another word for charity's act is *"dilectio,"* or spiritual affection rooted in choice.[64] Lastly, the proper object and ultimate end of every act of charity is God himself.[65] Thus, here too, to engage in charity's act—to know whether this act has its due end—we must know something of who God is. We shall have more to say about this last feature of charity in the following subsection. We note it here to show that St. Thomas' portrayal of charity fulfills his own stated requirements for knowledge of a virtue and for the ability to engage in that virtue's act: by knowing its paradigmatic acts, we can know what charity is: we can formulate a definition of it. We can engage in acts of charity because (a) we know which kinds of

59. Porter, "Moral Language and the Language of Grace," 184.

60. *ST* II-II 58.1.

61. Ibid. He adds that it must also be done unwaveringly *(immobiliter)*.

62. See *ST* II-II 25.1–12.

63. See *ST* II-II 31–33. Porter, "Moral Language and the Language of Grace," 185.

64. *ST* I-II 26.3.

65. *ST* II-II 25.1.

acts embody charity; (b) we freely choose them; and (c) we know something of charity's due end, God.

Once again, however, we should take care to recognize that these insights into charity do not enable us with the certitude of faith to know that we have charity, nor do they enable us with complete certainty to recognize charity's presence in others. When St. Thomas describes charity's acts, his goal is more modest.

> The point of identifying these acts [of charity] is not to provide an infallible test for determining whether an individual has charity; apart from the theological problems that this would raise, Aquinas is aware that any action which is typical of a virtue can be performed by someone who lacks the virtue (*ST* I-II 63.2).[66]

One who lacks justice, for example, can nonetheless do what justice objectively requires. Moreover, one who loves another may be acting from a naturally good human love without the virtue of charity. Once again, therefore, the issue is not the epistemic question of whether we can know if we have the virtue of charity. Rather, the issue is the conceptual question of what charity looks like so that we may engage in its acts. For St. Thomas, to engage in a virtue requires that we know what acts embody that virtue. Charity is no exception. Thus, Thomas identifies "certain kinds of actions as being paradigmatically acts of charity, because these kinds of actions provide a picture, so to speak, of what is distinctive about the charitable person and the way of life that she or he enjoys."[67]

St. Thomas also recognizes the pedagogical importance of imitating those who are proficient in living charitable lives, especially of imitating the charity of Christ.[68] For St. Thomas, all the actions of Christ are for our instruction.[69] The way Christ lived gives us an "example of perfection concerning all those things which of themselves relate to salva-

66. Porter, "Moral Language and the Language of Grace," 185.

67. Ibid., 185.

68. Torrell, *Saint Thomas Aquinas: Spiritual Master,* 116–124; 366–369.

69. *Super ioannem* 11.6 [274–275]. *ST* III 40.1 ad 3. See Richard Schenk, "*Omnis christi actio nostra est instructio.* The Deeds and Sayings of Jesus as Revelation in the View of Thomas Aquinas," in *La doctrine de la révélation divine, Studi tomistici* 37 (Rome, 1990), 103–131.

tion."[70] St. Thomas sees this especially to be the case in Christ's passion. Thomas regards the crucifixion as the place where Christ revealed the fullness of charity and of the other virtues.[71]

He willed to die, so that his death could be for us a perfect example of virtue: of charity, because 'greater charity no one has than to lay down one's life for one's friends' (Jn 15.13). For the more and graver the things are that one is willing to suffer for one's friend, the more one shows that he loves [that friend]. Now the gravest of all human evils is death, by which human life is removed. Hence, there is no greater sign of love than that a man truly expose himself to death for a friend.[72]

No example of virtue is absent from the cross. If, therefore, you seek an example of charity, 'greater charity no one has than to lay down one's life for one's friends' (Jn 15.13); and Christ did this on the cross.[73]

Calvary is the school of charity, where Christ hangs from the cross like a master professor sitting in his chair.[74]

Like St. Paul and the early Fathers of the Church, therefore, St. Thomas regards charity as analogously like the other virtues. It is something we only understand in relation to characteristic acts that embody it, and it is something we learn by imitating the charitable actions of Christ and his saints. Consequently, by treating charity in this way, St. Thomas' theology of charity escapes the formalism into which charity in the theologies of moral motivation falls. By escaping this formalism, Thomas is able to portray charity as a virtue analogously like the other human virtues.

Charity and Specific Knowledge of God

The thesis of the theology of moral motivation—that charity's act is independent of reason—further implies that one's rational knowledge of God cannot shape one's love for God. Theologians of moral motiva-

70. *ST* III 40.2 ad 1.

71. *ST* III 46.3; *ST* III 46.4.

72. *Compendium theologiae* 1 227 [38–50].

73. *Collationes in Symbolom Apostolorum* 4 [162–178].

74. *Super ioannem.* 19, *lect.* 4, no. 2441. See Michael Sherwin, "*Christus Magister:* Christ as the Teacher in St. Thomas' Commentary on John's Gospel," in *Reading St. John with St. Thomas,* edited by Matthew Levering and Michael Dauphinais (Washington, D.C.: The Catholic University of America Press, forthcoming).

tion do at times describe charity's striving as a response to God's grace, which would imply that striving presupposes knowledge of God: it would presuppose the cognitive awareness that God is one who establishes us in right relationship with himself through an unmerited gift of his love.[75] What type of knowledge is this? Is it conceptual knowledge or is it what these moralists often call "a-thematic" knowledge? If it is "a-thematic," which for Josef Fuchs means "not conceptual and not reflectively conscious,"[76] how does such knowledge become the medium by which we freely choose something? Even proponents of the theology of moral motivation recognize that the non-reflexive character of this "a-thematic" knowledge renders our basic freedom "somewhat obscure, elusive and difficult to identify."[77] The problem is that this freedom becomes so elusive and difficult to identify that it ceases to be recognizable as freedom. By grounding transcendental freedom on a knowledge that has no connection to any particular concrete categorical object, this perspective "severs the conceptual links between freedom and action which could alone give concrete meaning to the concept of freedom."[78] In other words, how am I free to choose something if there are no objects—at least not as known by me—from which to choose? If I am able to respond freely to God's love by an act of choice, this would seem to require some knowledge of God and of the love he is offering me. This apparently necessary dependence of freedom on knowledge is something that the theologians of moral motivation would do well to consider more deeply. Doing so might lead them to reassess this aspect of their theory. As the theory now stands, however, if there is a type of knowledge that influences charity's striving, this knowledge is not a conceptual knowledge as St. Thomas understands this term: it is not knowledge

75. See, for example, Fuchs, "Basic Freedom and Morality," 106–107; Keenan, *Goodness and Rightness,* 142; James Keenan, "The Problem with Thomas Aquinas's Concept of Sin," *Heythrop Journal* 35 (1994): 413–414; "History, Roots, and Innovations: A Response to the Engaging Protestants," in *Ecumenical Ventures in Ethics: Protestants Engage Pope John Paul II's Moral Encyclicals,* edited by Reinhard Hütter and Theodor Dieter (Grand Rapids, Mich.: Eerdmans, 1998), 272–273.

76. Fuchs, "Good Acts and Good Persons," 48.

77. William Cosgrave, "Basic Choice and Basic Stance: Explaining the Fundamental Option," *Furrow* 35 (1984): 512.

78. Porter, "Moral Language and the Language of Grace," 175.

of an object known to the intellect through a *species* existing within it and understood with the aid of the products of sensation *(phantasma)*.[79] For example, Timothy O'Connell in an influential moral textbook affirms that "like all the other aspects of human-as-person, the fundamental option is not something we can directly see or consciously analyze. At most, it is something of which we can be nonreflexly *[sic]* aware."[80] Consequently, this a-thematic knowledge does not contain specific objects that one can freely choose. This means, therefore, that, from the perspective of the theology of moral motivation, one's rational reflection upon who God is does not influence how we love him nor influence what else we love in the loving of him.

The claim that our knowledge of God does not shape our love for him seems puzzling when we compare it to the dynamics present in natural human relationships. On the level of a person's natural human psychology, rational knowledge clearly influences one's love for another. We do not begin to love a person until we know something about that person. Moreover, as we grow to know that person more deeply, by rationally interacting with that person and by rationally reflecting upon our experiences with that person, we begin to love that person either more or less deeply. Since grace elevates and perfects nature, we would expect rational knowledge of God also to influence and shape charity's love for God and neighbor. This is, in fact, exactly what St. Thomas affirms.

St. Thomas asserts that "vision is a cause of love." Thus, as we noted in chapter five, Thomas maintains that "the more perfectly we know God, the more perfectly we love him."[81] Thomas is keenly aware of the limitations of our knowledge of God.[82] Nevertheless, although our

79. There are, however, some theologians of moral motivation who describe fundamental option as presupposing explicit knowledge of God and at least some knowledge of the salvific action of Christ. See, for example, Fidel Herraez Vegas, *La Opcion Fundamental: Estudio de una Realidad Constitutiva de la Existencia Cristiana* (Salamanca: Sigueme, 1978), 135–153.

80. Timothy E. O'Connell, *Principles for a Catholic Morality,* revised edition (San Francisco: Harper, 1990), 73.

81. *ST* I-II 67.6 ad 3: *"visio enim est quaedam causa amoris, ut dicitur in ix ethic . . . deus autem quanto perfectius cognoscitur, tanto perfectius amatur."*

82. St. Thomas explains that our knowledge of God is always by way of analogies

knowledge of God is limited, we do know something about him. Rational reflection, revelation, and the gift of faith all provide us with true knowledge of God, and this knowledge enkindles our love for him. As we saw in the previous chapter, St. Thomas affirms that the knowledge of faith makes the friendship of charity possible.

> Just as someone could not have friendship with another if he disbelieved in or despaired of his ability to have some sort of social or familial life together with the other, so too friendship with God, which is charity, is impossible unless one has faith, by which we believe in this society and common life with God, and unless one hopes to attain this society. Thus, charity is not in any way possible without faith and hope.[83]

Since communion with God is a prerequisite for friendship with him, unless we believe that such a communion is possible and unless we hope for this good as something attainable by us through God's assistance, we will never develop a friendship with him. Consequently, Thomas can affirm that the love of God "presupposes" knowledge of God.[84] Since this knowledge is mediated to us by faith, this means that in this life charity depends on faith for its very existence.[85]

St. Thomas discerns a mutual interaction here between knowledge and love: the contemplation of spiritual good enkindles love within us, while the love of God moves us to contemplate him more deeply.[86] Thus, unlike the theologians of moral motivation who portray charity as a purely formal striving divorced from any concrete object or act, St. Thomas locates charity within the web of concrete human relationships. This enables him to develop a theology of charity that portrays one's growth in love for God as analogous to growth in human friend-

---

with creatures (*ST* I 13.5). We know the perfections of created things and we know that, since God is the cause of these perfections, they must exist in God in a preeminent way. Yet, we do not know these perfections according to their preeminent way of existing in God. Thus, for example, we know that God is wise and good. Yet, when we predicate wisdom and goodness of God, the reality signified *(res significata)* by these terms "remains incomprehended, and exceeds the signification of the term," since the mode of these terms' signification is according to the goodness and wisdom of creatures, which the goodness and wisdom of God infinitely transcends (*ST* I 13.5 and 6).

83. *ST* I-II 65.5.

84. *ST* II-II 27.4 ad 2.

85. *ST* II-II 4.7.

86. See *ST* I-II 27.2 and *ST* II-II 180.1.

ship: our love for God deepens as we grow to know and understand him more deeply, while our increasing love for him enkindles in us a desire to know him more deeply. This perspective renders both charity and our growth in the Christian life humanly intelligible even to the most humble of Christians. Anyone who has been loved by another and has loved in return can come to understand what it means to love God.

We should note as well that St. Thomas regards love's relationship to knowledge as pointing to the appropriateness of the incarnation of Christ. Christ's incarnation reveals to us the extent of God's love. Once again, Thomas sees Christ's passion as the summit of this revelation. It was fitting for God to save us by means of Christ's passion, because by it we come to know the depth of God's love for us, which "provokes" us to love him in return.[87]

There are important implications here for Thomas' theology of salvation. Thomas advances the traditional Catholic doctrine of the centrality of Christ in the work of salvation: all people are saved through Christ. Yet, in the context of Aquinas' teaching on the role of knowledge in one's love for God, does this mean that to be saved one must have explicit knowledge of Christ? At first glace this would seem to be Aquinas' view, because he affirms not merely that all people are saved through Christ, but that they are also saved through *faith* in Christ.[88] Aquinas' position, however, is more nuanced than this. He recognizes, for example, that those who lived before Christ were saved by merely having an "implicit" or "veiled" knowledge of Christ.[89] Yet, what about those who, although born after Christ, still have no knowledge of him? The Second Vatican Council affirms that "Since Christ died for all, and since all people are in fact called to one and the same destiny, which is divine, we must hold that the Holy Spirit offers to all the possibility of being made partners, in a way known to God, in the paschal mystery."[90] The challenge for the theologian is to construct a theology of grace that explains how this offer is given by the Spirit and freely responded to by the individual.

87. *ST* III 46.3.

88. *ST* II-II 2.7.

89. *ST* II-II 2.8.

90. *Gaudium et spes* n. 23; see also *Lumen gentium* 16.

We cannot know for certain how Aquinas would respond to the Council's teaching. From his principles, however, we can affirm that such persons' response to the grace, if it is to be a human response lived in charity, requires some conceptual, even if limited, understanding of God's love revealed to us in Christ. This conclusion appears necessary once we grasp the relationship between knowledge and love in the act of living faith. It would, no doubt, be an "implicit" and "veiled" knowledge of Christ. Yet, from the Thomistic perspective, the Holy Spirit's veiled offer would nevertheless entail a colloquy between God and the rational creature, a colloquy of knowledge and love, offer and response. St. Thomas' understanding of charity's relationship to knowledge of God, therefore, raises questions for both soteriology and missiology that merit further reflection.

Charity and Practical Reasoning

One further implication of a motivational theory of charity concerns charity's influence on practical judgment. In the previous sections we have seen that if charity's motion is independent of reason, then rational knowledge cannot shape our love. By the same token, this also implies that our love cannot shape our knowledge. If charity's motion is independent of reason, then charity does not influence practical reason's judgments concerning human action. Thus, from the perspective of the theologies of moral motivation, charity's striving does not make our actions right or wrong. Only reason and one's psychological motivation do this: they alone shape our judgments concerning the rightness of our actions.

Once again the work of James Keenan is illustrative. Keenan recognizes that the emotions and appetites can influence human reason and affect the judgment of prudence.[91] Keenan implicitly recognizes the influence of one's emotions—of the love that Aquinas describes as a passion—upon one's psychological motivation. In Keenan's view, however, charity only concerns our striving. It does not determine what we do or attain.[92] Curiously, this assertion implies that although emotional love

91. Keenan, *Goodness and Rightness*, 101–102.

92. Ibid., 105: "Simply put, the moral virtues concern attainment, not striving. They concern only the question of rightly ordered acts and rightly ordered lives; the question

can shape our moral judgments, spiritual love cannot.[93] In other words, from the perspective of moral motivation, our love for God in no way shapes our priorities or influences the choices we make.

St. Thomas provides a profoundly different view of charity's role in practical reasoning. As we saw in chapter five, Thomas portrays charity and the infused cognitive virtues as mutually dependent. On the one hand, charity depends on faith for its object and ultimate end, while it depends on infused cognitive virtues and gifts for it to be rightly regulated toward this ultimate end. This twofold dependence is what Thomas means to convey when he describes faith and the other infused cognitive virtues and gifts as having priority over charity on the level of specification. On the other hand, Thomas portrays these cognitive virtues and gifts as depending on charity for their very existence.[94] Charity is the efficient cause of these cognitive *habitus,* having priority over them on what Thomas calls the level of exercise.

The character of these virtues' and gifts' dependence on charity is especially evident in St. Thomas' account of wisdom. St. Thomas recognizes that there is both a gift and a virtue of wisdom, corresponding to the two ways that the intellect can form judgments. "Rectitude of judgment can occur in two ways: in one way, from the perfect use of reason; in another way, from a certain connaturality with those things about

---

of goodness in the contemporary sense is not raised in this context;" ibid., 120: "[the inference that if the object willed is "bad," the agent is "bad"] can only be made in issues concerning rightness or wrongness; that is, if an object willed is wrong, the agent is wrong. If the question is whether the agent is good or bad, we must ask not whether the object accepted and willed is right or wrong, but whether the agent is striving. Issues concerning goodness and badness are distinguished by, and remain within, the context of an antecedent first movement of the will. In that context we can know the person before he or she wills a particular object. We do not need a description of whether a person or the actions are right or wrong. Rather, we must have a description of whether one strives 'out of' *(ex)* or 'on account of' *(propter)* love in order to realize 'right order.'"

93. Indeed, Keenan also seems to minimize the importance of emotional love in the formation of moral judgment. The moral virtues seem to do little more than supply the matter which prudence informs (ibid., 101–103).

94. *ST* I-II 65.2; *ST* I-II 68.4 ad 3; *ST* I-II 68.8 ad 3. Of course, as we have seen, faith can exist "after a fashion" *(aliqualiter)* (*ST* I-II 65.4) without charity, but in this case it will be "dead faith" (*ST* II-II 4.4).

which one must now judge."[95] Thomas is here pointing to the Aristotelian insight that "as a person is, so does the end appear to him."[96]

> We know from experience that things appear differently to us, whether good or bad, according to whether we love or hate them. Consequently, when someone has an inordinate affection for something, that inordinate affection impedes the judgment of the intellect concerning a particular object of choice.[97]

Conversely, when we have "ordinate" affections from the love of charity, our love for God shapes our practical judgments, rendering the true good connatural to our intellects in the gift of wisdom.

> It pertains to the wisdom that is an intellectual virtue to judge rightly about divine things from the investigation of reason, while right judgment about such things arising from a certain connaturality with them pertains to the wisdom that is a gift of the Holy Spirit. Hence, Dionysius says that 'Hierotheus is perfect in divine things, for he not only learns, but also affectively experiences *(patiens)* divine things.' This sympathy *(compassio)* or connaturality for divine things occurs because of charity, which unites us to God, according to 1 Cor 6.17: 'he who adheres to God, is one spirit with him.'[98]

In the gift of wisdom, therefore, the intellect becomes receptive to the action of the Holy Spirit—moving the intellect to judge rightly about the things of God—through the connaturality with them generated by the virtue of charity. Once again, St. Thomas summarizes charity's relationship to wisdom in a pithy phrase: "the wisdom that is a gift has its cause in the will, namely charity, but it has its essence in the intellect, whose act is to judge rightly."[99] The intellect specifies our acts, but it is moved to engage in this specifying activity by the charity present in the will.

Aquinas paints a similar portrait of charity's relationship to infused prudence. On the one hand, charity depends on infused prudence in order to be "rightly ordered." On the other hand, however, infused prudence depends on charity for its very existence.[100] This prudence exists

95. *ST* II-II 45.2.
96. *NE* 3.5 (1114a32–b1). See *ST* I-II 58.5 and *ST* II-II 24.11.
97. *De malo* 2.3 ad 9.
98. *ST* II-II 45.2.
99. Ibid.
100. *ST* II-II 23.7.

only because charity is present inclining the will toward intimate union with God as the end of all our actions. In the presence of this loving inclination, a prudence exists that disposes the intellect to reason rightly about those things that are ordered to the end.[101] In other words, unlike the theologies of moral motivation, Aquinas' theology of charity is able to show how our love for God shapes our practical judgments about our actions here on earth. Reason is able to judge rightly about the actions that lead us to our eternal harbor, because charity elevates and inclines our wills toward that harbor.

Charity's Status as a Virtue: Conclusions

In this section we have considered how St. Thomas' commitment to the view that charity and knowledge are mutually dependent enables his theology of charity to avoid the formalism into which the theologies of moral motivation fall. This consideration has also revealed the ways in which this commitment enables St. Thomas to portray charity as a virtue analogously like other human virtues and charity's act as a love analogously like other human loves. Like other virtues, charity is characterized by certain paradigmatic kinds of action embodied for our imitation in the lives of those who are the recognized models of this virtue: Christ and his saints. Unlike other virtues, charity is infused into our hearts by the action of God's grace. Nevertheless, like other virtues, we learn to exercise this infused theological virtue in and through the example and instruction of others in a community that lives charity. Moreover, like other human loves, charity is enkindled by our knowledge of God, and this love, in turn, shapes our priorities: it shapes how we judge the good things of this life and our actions in the midst of them. These aspects of St. Thomas' theology of charity all underscore how his commitment to charity's deep interconnection with knowledge enables Thomas to present charity as a love and a virtue that we learn to live in ways analogous to how we learn to live natural love and the human virtues.

101. *ST* I-II 65.2.

Conclusion

By Knowledge and By Love

At the outset of this study we noted that one of the reasons the theologians of moral motivation undertake their effort at renewal is their legitimate concern to offer a more adequate account of those who struggle with either moral blindness or moral weakness. Is the moral status of these individuals before God best understood in relation to their external actions, or is there something about their relationship with God that the standard manualist focus on acts fails to convey? This is an important and legitimate question. The results of our study of Thomas Aquinas' theology of charity, however, suggest that the answer to this question will not be found by asserting the will's radical autonomy from reason. Instead, the mature insights of St. Thomas' theology suggest that any adequate portrayal of the moral life will respect the dynamic relationship between intellect and will, knowledge and love, in human action.

Every human act, if it is truly a human act, is done from knowledge and with love. Far from implying intellectual or psychological determinism, love's relationship to knowledge ensures that, even for the hardened sinner, moral growth is always possible. The dynamic relationship existing between the uniquely intellectual love and voluntary knowledge that are proper to human agency is precisely what enables us to overcome the psychological and social constraints (as well as our past sins) that limit our freedom. Our freedom may be deeply restricted and our knowledge may be profoundly limited. Yet, because our acts flow from the spiritual principles of intellect and will, these acts are always the product of some measure of knowing freedom. Because of this, they offer the promise of growth. No matter how faulty our judgments, since we always act from the spiritual power of the intellect, our judgments can be corrected. No matter how disordered our loves, since we always act from the spiritual power of the will, our loves can be reordered. Nonetheless, social and psychological factors can limit or even remove a person's freedom. These factors exist and are often devastating. Contemporary insights into the genetic, biochemical and environmental components of mental health far outstrip anything known to St. Thomas about the factors that can limit freedom. Even in the face of these new insights, however, a core Thomistic principle remains true: when grace elevates and heals wounded human nature, it does so in a way that respects that nature. If one is to attain mature moral freedom in Christ, it will be as a human being and not as an angel. It will be because the spiritual knowledge and love proper to the human person has—with the help of God's grace and the support of a mentoring community—been able to permeate and rightly order the bodily and animal components of our nature. In other words, the mature moral freedom of charity is lived by knowledge and by love.

Bibliography

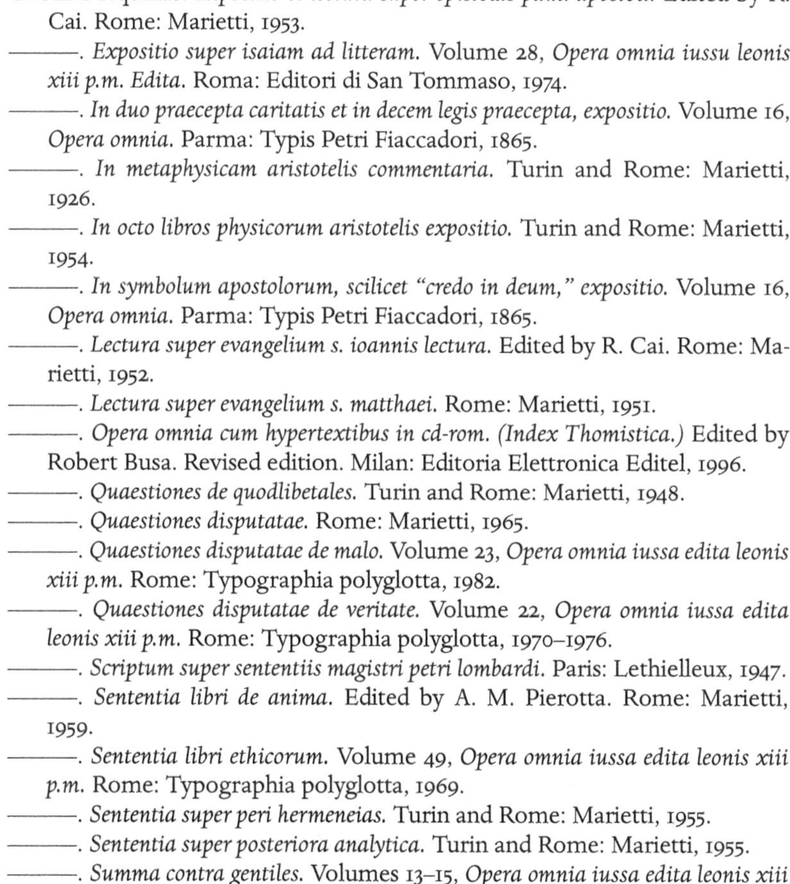

Works of Thomas Aquinas

Thomas Aquinas. *Expositio et lectura super epistolas pauli apostoli*. Edited by R. Cai. Rome: Marietti, 1953.

———. *Expositio super isaiam ad litteram*. Volume 28, *Opera omnia iussu leonis xiii p.m. Edita*. Roma: Editori di San Tommaso, 1974.

———. *In duo praecepta caritatis et in decem legis praecepta, expositio*. Volume 16, *Opera omnia*. Parma: Typis Petri Fiaccadori, 1865.

———. *In metaphysicam aristotelis commentaria*. Turin and Rome: Marietti, 1926.

———. *In octo libros physicorum aristotelis expositio*. Turin and Rome: Marietti, 1954.

———. *In symbolum apostolorum, scilicet "credo in deum," expositio*. Volume 16, *Opera omnia*. Parma: Typis Petri Fiaccadori, 1865.

———. *Lectura super evangelium s. ioannis lectura*. Edited by R. Cai. Rome: Marietti, 1952.

———. *Lectura super evangelium s. matthaei*. Rome: Marietti, 1951.

———. *Opera omnia cum hypertextibus in cd-rom. (Index Thomistica.)* Edited by Robert Busa. Revised edition. Milan: Editoria Elettronica Editel, 1996.

———. *Quaestiones de quodlibetales*. Turin and Rome: Marietti, 1948.

———. *Quaestiones disputatae*. Rome: Marietti, 1965.

———. *Quaestiones disputatae de malo*. Volume 23, *Opera omnia iussa edita leonis xiii p.m.* Rome: Typographia polyglotta, 1982.

———. *Quaestiones disputatae de veritate*. Volume 22, *Opera omnia iussa edita leonis xiii p.m.* Rome: Typographia polyglotta, 1970–1976.

———. *Scriptum super sententiis magistri petri lombardi*. Paris: Lethielleux, 1947.

———. *Sententia libri de anima*. Edited by A. M. Pierotta. Rome: Marietti, 1959.

———. *Sententia libri ethicorum*. Volume 49, *Opera omnia iussa edita leonis xiii p.m.* Rome: Typographia polyglotta, 1969.

———. *Sententia super peri hermeneias*. Turin and Rome: Marietti, 1955.

———. *Sententia super posteriora analytica*. Turin and Rome: Marietti, 1955.

———. *Summa contra gentiles*. Volumes 13–15, *Opera omnia iussa edita leonis xiii p.m.* Rome: Typographia polyglotta, 1918–1930.

———. *Summa theologiae.* Volumes 4–12, *Opera omnia iussa edita leonis xiii p.m.* Rome: Typographia polyglotta, 1888–1906.

———. *Super librum dionysii de divinis nominibus.* Edited by C. Pera. Rome: Marietti, 1950.

Other Primary Sources

Alexander of Hales. *Summa theologica.* Florence: College of St. Bonaventure, 1924–1948.

Alphonsus Liguori. *Theologia moralis.* Rome: Typographia vaticana, 1905.

Ambrosiaster. *Commentarius in epistulas paulinas.* Volume 81, parts 1–3, *Corpus scriptorum ecclesiasticorum latinorum.* Vindobonae: Hoelder, Pichler, Tempsky, 1966–1969.

Aristotle. *On the Soul.* Volume 1, *The Complete Works of Aristotle.* Edited by Jonathan Barnes. Princeton: Princeton University Press, 1984, 641–692.

———. *Metaphysics.* Volume 2, *The Complete Works of Aristotle.* Edited by Jonathan Barnes. Princeton: Princeton University Press, 1984, 1552–1728.

———. *Nicomachean Ethics.* Volume 2, *The Complete Works of Aristotle.* Edited by Jonathan Barnes. Princeton: Princeton University Press, 1984, 1729–1867.

———. *Physics.* Volume 1, *The Complete Works of Aristotle.* Edited by Jonathan Barnes. Princeton: Princeton University Press, 1984, 315–446.

Augustine. *Confessiones.* Volume 32, *Corpus christianorum, series latina.* Turnholti: Typographi Brepols, 1981.

———. *De doctrina christiana.* Volume 32, *Corpus christianorum, series latina.* Turnholti: Typographi Brepols, 1972.

———. *De trinitate.* Volume 50, *Corpus christianorum, series latina.* Turnholti: Typographi Brepols, 1968.

Bernard of Clairvaux. *De diligendo deo.* In *L'Amour de Dieu: la grâce et le libre arbitre.* Volume 393, Sources Chrétiennes. Paris: Editions du cerf, 1993.

Boethius. *De consolatione philosophiae.* Bibliotheca scriptorum graecorum et romanorum teubneriana. Munich: K. G. Saur, 2000.

Bonaventure. *Commentaria in quatuor libros sententiarum.* Volumes 1–4, *Opera omnia.* Florence: College of St. Bonaventure, 1882–1889.

Marcus Tullius Cicero. *Letters to his Friends.* Volume 1. Translated by W. Glynn Williams. Loeb Classical Library. Cambridge, Mass.: Harvard University Press, 1979.

Peter Lombard. *Libri iv sententiarum.* Florence: College of St. Bonaventure, 1916.

Philip the Chancellor. *Summa de bono.* Corpus philosophorum medii aevi. Opera philosophica mediae aetatis. Bern: Francke, 1985.

William de la Mare. *Correctorium fratris thomae.* In *D. thomae aquinatis summae theologiae partis i questiones 75–77 de essentia et potentiis animae in generali: una cum Guilelmi de la mare correctorii articulo 28.* Bonn: P. Hanstein, 1920.

William of Auxerre. *Summa aurea.* Paris: Centre national de la recherche scientifique, 1985.

Secondary Sources

Aertsen, Jan. *Medieval Philosophy and the Transcendentals: the Case of Thomas Aquinas.* New York: E. J. Brill, 1996.

———. *Nature and Creature: Thomas Aquinas's Way of Thought.* Leiden: E. J. Brill, 1988.

Anscombe, G. E. M. "Modern Moral Philosophy." *Philosophy* 33 (1958): 1–19.

Ashley, Benedict. "Fundamental Option and/or Commitment to Ultimate End." *Philosophy and Theology* 10 (1998): 113–141.

Aumann, Jordan. "Thomistic Evaluation of Love and Charity." *Angelicum* 55 (1978): 534–556.

Belleville, Linda L. "'Imitate Me, Just as I Imitate Christ': Discipleship in the Corinthian Correspondence." In *Patterns of Discipleship in the New Testament.* Edited by Richard N. Longenecker. Grand Rapids, Mich.: Eerdmans, 1996, 120–142.

Belmans, Theo. "Au croisement des chemins en morale fondamentale." *Revue thomiste* 89 (1989): 246–278.

———. "Le 'jugement prudentiel' chez saint Thomas, réponse à R. McInerny." *Revue thomiste* 91 (1991): 414–420.

———. "le 'volontarisme' de saint Thomas d'Aquin." *Revue Thomiste* 85 (1985): 181–196.

Bobik, Joseph. "Aquinas on *Communicatio,* the Foundation of Friendship and *Caritas.*" *Modern Schoolman* 64 (1988): 1–18.

———. "Aquinas on Friendship with God." *New Scholasticism* 60 (1986): 257–271.

Bond, Leo. "A Comparison between Human and Divine Friendship." *Thomist* 3 (1941): 54–94.

Bouillard, H. *Conversion et grâce chez saint Thomas.* Paris: Aubier, Editions Montaigne, 1944.

Bourke, Vernon J. *Will in Western Thought: an Historico-Critical Survey.* New York: Sheed and Ward, 1964.

Bradley, Dennis. *Aquinas on the Twofold Human Good: Reason and Human Happiness in Aquinas's Moral Science.* Washington, D.C.: Catholic University of America Press, 1997.

Brock, Stephen L. *Action and Conduct: Thomas Aquinas and the Theory of Action.* Edinburgh: T and T Clark, 1998.

———. "What is the Use of *Usus* in Aquinas's Psychology of Action." In *Moral and Political Philosophies in the Middle Ages.* Edited by B. Carlos Bazán, Eduardo Andújar, Leonard G. Sbrocchi. Volume 2. Ottawa: Legas, 1995, 654–664.

Brown, Peter. "The Saint as Exemplar in Late Antiquity." In *Saints and Virtues.* Edited by John Stratton Hawley. Berkeley: University of California Press, 1987, 3–14.

Catholic Church. *Catechism of the Catholic Church.* Mahwah, N.J., 1994.

———. *Decree on the Training of Priests (Optatam totius).* In *Vatican Council II:*

the Conciliar and Post Conciliar Documents. New Revised Edition. Edited by Austin Flannery. New York: Costello Publishing Company, 1984, 707–724.

———. *Dogmatic Constitution on the Church (Lumen gentium).* In *Vatican Council II: the Conciliar and Post Conciliar Documents.* New Revised Edition. Edited by Austin Flannery. New York: Costello Publishing Company, 1984, 350–426.

———. *Pastoral Constitution on the Church in the Modern World (Gaudium et spes).* In *Vatican Council II: the Conciliar and Post Conciliar Documents.* New Revised Edition. Edited by Austin Flannery. New York: Costello Publishing Company, 1984, 903–1001.

Cessario, Romanus. *Christian Faith and the Theological Life.* Washington, D.C.: Catholic University of America Press, 1996.

———. *The Moral Virtues and Theological Ethics.* Notre Dame: University of Notre Dame Press, 1991.

———. "Toward Understanding Aquinas' Theological Method: the Early Twelfth-Century Experience." In *Studies in Thomistic Theology.* Edited by Paul Lockey. Houston: Center for Thomistic Studies, 1995, 17–89.

Chenu, Marie-Dominique. *Faith and Theology.* Translated by Denis Hickey. New York: Macmillan, 1968.

———. *S. Thomas et la théologie.* Paris: Editions du seuil, 1959.

———. *Toward Understanding Saint Thomas.* Translated by A.-M. Landry and D. Hughes. Chicago: Regnery, 1964.

Chiavacci, Enrico. *Teologia morale.* Volume 1. Assisi: Cittadella, 1983.

Colish, Marcia. *Peter Lombard.* New York: E. J. Brill, 1994.

Cosgrave, William. "Basic Choice and Basic Stance: Explaining the Fundamental Option." *Furrow* 35 (1984): 508–518.

Crisp, Roger, and Michael Slote, eds. *Virtue Ethics.* Oxford: Oxford University Press, 1997.

Crouzel, Henri. "L'imitation et la 'suite' de Dieu et du Christ dans les premiers siècles chrétiens, ainsi que leur sources gréco-romaines et hébraïques." *Jahrbuch für Antike und Christentum* 21 (1978): 7–14.

Crowe, Frederick E. "Complacency and Concern in the Thought of St. Thomas." *Theological Studies* 20 (1959): 1–39; 198–230; 343–382.

Curran, Charles E. *The Origins of Moral Theology in the United States: Three Different Approaches.* Washington, D.C.: Georgetown University Press, 1997.

D'Avenia, Marco. *La conoscenza per connaturalità in s. Tommaso d'Aquino.* Bologna: Edizioni Studio Domenicano, 1992.

Deman, Th. "Eudémonisme et charité en théologie morale." *Ephemerides theologicae lovanienses* 29 (1953): 38–47.

———. "Le *'Liber de bona fortuna'* dans la théologie de s. Thomas d'Aquin." *Revue des sciences philosophiques et théologiques* 17 (1928): 38–45.

Denifle, H., and A. Chatelain, eds. *Chartularium universitatis parisiensis.* Paris: Friars Delalain, 1889.

Dewailly, L.-M. "Communio-communicatio." *Revue des sciences philosophiques et théologiques* 54 (1970): 46–63.

Dewan, Lawrence. "St. Thomas and the Causes of Free Choice." *Acta philosophica* (Rome) 8 (1999): 87–96.

———. "St. Thomas and the First Cause of Moral Evil." In *Moral and Political Philosophies in the Middle Ages.* Edited by B. Carlos Bazán, Eduardo Andújar, and Leonard G. Sbrocchi. Volume 3. Ottawa: Legas, 1995, 1223–1230.

———. "St. Thomas, James Keenan, and the Will." *Science et esprit* 47 (1995): 153–175.

Doig, James C. "The Interpretation of Aquinas's *Prima secundae.*" *American Catholic Philosophical Quarterly* 71 (1997): 171–195.

Doorley, Mark J. "Resting in Reality: Reflections on Crowe's 'Complacency and Concern.'" *Lonergan Workshop* 13 (1997): 33–55.

Doran, Robert M. "'Complacency and Concern' and a Basic Thesis on Grace." *Lonergan Workshop* 13 (1997): 57–78.

Duroux, Benoit. *La psychologie de la foi chez s. Thomas d'Aquin.* Tournai, Belgium: Desclée, 1963.

Egenter, Richard. *Gottesfreundschaft: Die Lehre von der Gottesfreundschaft in der Scholastik und Mystik des 12 und 13 Jahrhunderts.* Augsburg: Benno Filser, 1928.

Falanga, Anthony. *Charity the Form of the Virtues according to Saint Thomas.* Washington, D.C.: Catholic University of America, 1948.

Flannery, Kevin. *Acts Amid Precepts: the Aristotelian Logical Structure of Thomas Aquinas's Moral Theory.* Washington, D.C.: Catholic University of America Press, 2001.

Forest, A. "Connaissance et amour." *Revue thomiste* 48 (1948): 113–122.

Frank, Philip. *Das Kausalgesetz und seine Grenzen.* Vienna: Springer, 1932.

Fuchs, Josef. "Basic Freedom and Morality." In *Human Values and Christian Morality.* Dublin: Gill and Macmillan, 1970, 92–111.

———. "Good Acts and Good Persons." In *John Paul II and Moral Theology: Readings in Moral Theology No. 10.* Edited by Charles E. Curran and Richard A. McCormick, S.J. New York: Paulist Press, 1998, 47–51.

———. *Moral Demands and Personal Obligations.* Washington, D.C.: Georgetown University Press, 1993.

Gallagher, David. "Aquinas on Goodness and Moral Goodness." In *Thomas Aquinas and His Legacy.* Edited by David Gallagher. Washington, D.C.: Catholic University of America Press, 1994, 37–60.

———. "Aquinas on Moral Action: Interior and Exterior Acts." *American Catholic Philosophical Quarterly* 64 (1990): 118–129.

———. "Free Choice and Free Judgment in Thomas Aquinas." *Archiv Für Geschichte Der Philosophie* 76 (1994): 247–277.

———. "Thomas Aquinas on the Causes of Human Choice." Ph.D. dissertation, Catholic University of America, 1988.

Gallagher, Raphael. "The Fate of the Moral Manual Since Saint Alphonsus." In *History and Conscience: Studies in Honour of Sean O'Riordan.* Edited by Raphael Gallagher and Brendan McConery. Dublin: Gill and Macmillan, 1989.

———. "The Manual System of Moral Theology Since the Death of Alphonsus." *Irish Theological Quarterly* 51 (1985): 1–16.

Gardeil, A. "Dons." In *Dictionnaire de théologie catholique.* Paris: Letouzey et Ané, 1911, 1748–1781.

George, Marie. "'Trust Me.' 'Why Should I?' Aquinas on Faith and Reason." In *The Ever-Illuminating Wisdom of St. Thomas Aquinas.* San Francisco: Ignatius Press, 1999, 31–58.

Gillon, L.-B. "A propos de la théorie thomiste de l'amitié: *'Fundatur super aliqua communicatione'* (II-II, q. 23, a. 1)." *Angelicum* 25 (1948): 3–17.

Glorieux, P. "Les questions disputées de s. Thomas et leur suite chronologique." *Rechereches de théologie ancienne et médiévale* 4 (1932): 5–33.

———. *Les premières polémiques thomistes: I.—Le* Correctorium corruptorii "quare." *Bibliothèque thomiste.* 9 Kain, Belgium: Le Saulchoir, 1927.

Gury, Jean-Pierre. *Compendium theologiae moralis.* Ratisbon: Georg Josef Manz, 1874.

Hallett, Garth. *Greater Good: the Case for Proportionalism.* Washington, D.C.: Georgetown University Press, 1995.

Hampshire, Stuart. *Thought and Action.* London: Chatto and Windus, 1959.

Hawthorne, Gerald F. "The Imitation of Christ: Discipleship in Philippians." In *Patterns of Discipleship in the New Testament.* Edited by Richard N. Longenecker. Grand Rapids, Mich.: Eerdmans, 1996, 163–179.

Harvey, John. "The Nature of the Infused Moral Virtues." *Catholic Theological Society of America Proceedings* 10 (1955): 172–217.

Herraez Vegas, Fidel. *La Opcion Fundamental: Estudio de una Realidad Constitutiva de la Existencia Cristiana.* Salamanca: Sigueme, 1978.

Hibbs, Thomas. "Against a Cartesian Reading of *Intellectus* in Aquinas." *Modern Schoolman* 66 (1988): 55–69.

———. *Dialectic and Narrative in Aquinas: An Interpretation of the* Summa contra gentiles. Notre Dame, Ind.: University of Notre Dame Press, 1995.

———. "Principles and Prudence: The Aristotelianism of Thomas's Account of Moral Knowledge." *New Scholasticism* 61 (1987): 271–284.

———. "Transcending Humanity in Aquinas." *American Catholic Philosophical Quarterly* 66 (1992): 191–202.

———. *Virtue's Splendor: Wisdom, Prudence, and the Human Good.* New York: Fordham University Press, 2001.

Hill, William. *The Three-Personed God: the Trinity as a Mystery of Salvation.* Washington, D.C.: Catholic University of America Press, 1982.

Hittinger, Russell. "When It Is More Excellent to Love than to Know: the Other Side of Thomistic 'Realism.'" *Proceedings of the American Catholic Philosophical Association* 57 (1983): 171–179.

Hoose, Bernard. *Proportionalism: the American Debate and its European Roots.* Washington, D.C.: Georgetown University Press, 1987.

Hughes, Louis M. "Charity as Friendship in the Theology of Saint Thomas." *Angelicum* 52 (1975): 164–178.

Ilien, Albert. *Wesen und Funktion der Liebe bei Thomas von Aquin.* Freiburg im Breisgau: Herder, 1975.

Inglis, John. "Aquinas's Replication of the Acquired Moral Virtues: Rethinking the Standard Philosophical Interpretation of Moral Virtue in Aquinas." *Journal of Religious Ethics* 27 (1999): 16–20.

Jones, L. Gregory. "The Theological Transformation of Aristotelian Friendship in the Thought of St. Thomas Aquinas." *New Scholasticism* 61 (1987): 373–399.

Jonsen, Albert R., and Stephen Toulmin. *The Abuse of Casuistry: A History of Moral Reasoning.* Berkeley: University of California Press, 1988.

Jordan, Mark. "The *Pars moralis* of the *Summa theologiae* as *scientia* and as *ars.*" In *Scientia und Ars im Hoch- und Spätmittelalter, Miscellanea Mediaevalia.* 22/1. New York: Walter de Gruyter, 1994, 468–481.

Kant, Emmanuel. *Critique of Practical Reason.* Translated by T. K. Abbott. New York: Prometheus Books, 1996.

Keaty, Anthony. "Thomas's Authority for Identifying Charity as Friendship Aristotle or John 15?" *Thomist* 62 (1998): 581–601.

Keenan, James. "A New Distinction in Moral Theology: Being Good and Living Rightly." *Church* 5 (1989): 22–28.

———. "Being Good and Doing Right in Saint Thomas' *Summa theologiae.*" Th.D. dissertation. Gregorian University, 1988.

———. "Can a Wrong Action Be Good? The Development of Theological Opinion on Erroneous Conscience." *Église et théologie* 24 (1993): 205–219.

———. "Distinguishing Charity as Goodness and Prudence as Rightness: A Key to Thomas's *Secunda pars.*" *Thomist* 56 (1992): 407–426.

———. *Goodness and Rightness in Thomas Aquinas's Summa theologiae.* Washington, D.C.: Georgetown University Press, 1992.

———. "History, Roots, and Innovations: A Response to the Engaging Protestants." In *Ecumenical Ventures in Ethics: Protestants Engage Pope John Paul II's Moral Encyclicals.* Edited by Reinhard Hütter and Theodor Dieter. Grand Rapids, Mich.: Eerdmans, 1998, 262–288.

———. "The Problem with Thomas Aquinas's Concept of Sin." *Heythrop Journal* 35 (1994): 401–420.

———. Review of *Right Practical Reason: Aristotle, Action, and Prudence in Aquinas.* By Daniel Westberg. *Theological Studies* 56 (1995): 802–805.

Keenan, James F., and Thomas A. Shannon, eds. *The Context of Casuistry.* Washington, D.C.: Georgetown University Press, 1995.

Keller, M.-Joseph, and M.-Benoît Lavaud. "La charité comme amitié d'après saint Thomas." *Revue thomiste* 34 (1929): 445–475.

Kent, Bonnie. "Transitory Vice: Thomas Aquinas on Incontinence." *Journal of the History of Philosophy* 27 (1989): 199–223.

———. *Virtues of the Will: the Transformation of Ethics in the Late Thirteenth Century.* Washington, D.C.: Catholic University of America Press, 1995.

Kerr, Fergus. "Charity as Friendship." In *Language, Meaning and God.* Edited by Brian Davies. London: Geoffrey Chapman, 1987, 1–23.

Kopfensteiner, Thomas R. "Science, Metaphor, and Moral Casuistry." In *The Context of Casuistry.* Edited by James F. Keenan and Thomas A. Shannon. Washington, D.C.: Georgetown University Press, 1995, 123–134.

La Soujeole, Benoît-Dominique de. "'Société' et 'communion' chez saint Thomas d'Aquin: étude d'ecclésiologie." *Revue thomiste* 90 (1990): 587–622.

Labourdette, M.-M. "Dons du Saint-Esprit: iv. Saint Thomas et la théologie thomiste." In *Dictionnaire de spiritualité.* Edited by Charles Baumgartner and M. Olphe Galliard. Paris: G. Beauchesne et ses fils, 1957, 1610–1635.

Latourelle, René. *Theology of Revelation.* New York: Alba House, 1966.

Lewis, Charlton, Charles Short. *A Latin Dictionary.* Oxford: Clarendon Press, 1962.

Lonergan, Bernard. "St. Thomas's Thought on *Gratia operans.*" *Theological Studies* 2 and 3 (1942): vol. 2, 289–324; vol. 3, 69–88; 375–402; 533–578.

Lottin, Odon. "Liberté humaine et motion divine de s. Thomas d'Aquin à la condamnation de 1277." *Recherches de théologie ancienne et médiévale* 7 (1935): 52–69, 156–173.

———. *Morale fondamentale.* Tournai, Belgium: Desclée, 1954.

———. *Psychologie et morale aux xiie et xiiie siècles.* Louvain: Abbaye du Mont César, 1942.

McEvoy, James. "*Philia* and *Amicitia:* the Philosophy of Friendship from Plato to Aquinas." *Sewanee Mediaeval Colloquium Occasional Papers.* Sewanee, Tenn.: University Press, 1985, 1–23.

———. "Zur Rezeption des Aristotelischen Freundschaftsbegriffs in der Scholastik." *Freiburger Zeitschrift für Philosophie und Théologie* 43 (1996): 287–303.

McGinnis, Raymond. *The Wisdom of Love: A Study in the Psycho-Metaphysics of Love according to the Principles of St. Thomas.* Rome: Officium libri catholici, 1951.

McInerny, Ralph. "Prudence and Conscience." *Thomist* 38 (1974): 291–305.

———. "The Right Deed for the Wrong Reason: Comments on Theo Belmans." In *Aquinas on Human Action: A Theory of Practice.* Washington, D.C.: Catholic University of America Press, 1992, 220–239.

MacIntyre, Alasdair. *After Virtue: A Study in Moral Theory.* Second edition. Notre Dame, Ind.: University of Notre Dame Press, 1984.

———. "How Moral Agents Became Ghosts or Why the History of Ethics Diverged from that of the Philosophy of Mind." *Synthese* 53 (1982): 295–312.

———. *Three Rival Versions of Moral Enquiry.* Notre Dame, Ind.: University of Notre Dame Press, 1990.

Maggi de Gandolfi, María Celestina Donadío. *Amor y Bien: Los Problemas del Amor en Santo Tomás de Aquino.* Buenos Aires: Universidad Catolica Argentina, 1999.

Mahoney, John. *The Making of Moral Theology: A Study of the Roman Catholic Tradition.* Oxford: Clarendon Press, 1987.

Mandonnet, P. "Chronologie des questions disputées de saint Thomas d'Aquin." *Revue thomiste* 23 (1928): 266–287, 341–371.

Mansini, Guy. "*Duplex amor* and the Structure of Love in Aquinas." In *Thomistica*. Edited by E. Manning. Leuven: Peeters, 1995, 137–196.

———. "*Similitudo, Communicatio,* and the Friendship of Charity in Aquinas." In *Thomistica*. Edited by E. Manning. Leuven: Peeters, 1995, 1–26.

Manteau-Bonamy, H. M. "La liberté de l'homme selon Thomas d'Aquin (la datation de la Q. Disp. *DE MALO*)." *Archives d'histoire doctrinale et littéraire du moyen âge* 46 (1979): 7–34.

Matera, Frank J. *New Testament Ethics: The Legacies of Jesus and Paul.* Louisville, Ky.: Westminster John Knox Press, 1996.

Meersseman, G.-G. "Pourquoi le Lombard n'a-t-il pas conçu la charité comme amitié?" *Miscellanea lombardiana.* Novara: Instituto geografico de agostini, 1957, 165–174.

Michel, Elsbeth. Nullus potest amare aliquid incognitum: *ein Beitrag zur Frage des Intellektualismus bei Thomas Von Aquin.* Fribourg, Switzerland: Editions universitaires de Fribourg, 1979.

Moreno, Antonio. "The Nature of St. Thomas' Knowledge *'Per connaturalitatem.'*" *Angelicum* 47 (1970): 44–62.

Muñoz Cuenca, J.-M. "Doctrina de santo Tomás sobre los Dones del Espíritu Santo en la Suma teológica." *Ephemerides carmeliticae* 25 (1974): 157–243.

Murdoch, Iris. *Existentialists and Mystics, Writings on Philosophy and Literature.* Edited by Peter Conradi. New York: Penguin, 1998.

———. *The Sovereignty of Good.* London: Routledge, 1970.

Nello Figa, Antonio. *Teorema de la Opcion Fundamental: Bases para su Adecuada Utilización en Theología Moral.* Rome: Gregorian University Press, 1995.

Nicolas, J.-H. *Les profondeurs de la grâce.* Paris: Beauchesne, 1969.

Nicolas, M.-J. "Les dons du Saint-Esprit." *Revue thomiste* 92 (1992): 141–152.

Nussbaum Martha. *Love's Knowledge: Essays on Philosophy and Literature.* Oxford: Oxford University Press, 1990.

O'Brien, T. C. "Faith and the Truth About God." In *Summa theologiae.* Edited and translated by T. C. O'Brien. Volume 31. New York: McGraw-Hill Book Co., 1974, appendix 3, 195–204.

———. "Faith and the Truth Who is God." In *Summa theologiae.* Edited and translated by T. C. O'Brien. Volume 31. New York: McGraw-Hill Book Co., 1974, appendix 2, 186–194.

———. "Objects and Virtues." In *Summa theologiae.* Edited and translated by T. C. O'Brien. Volume 31. New York: McGraw-Hill Book Co., 1974, appendix 1, 178–185.

O'Callaghan, John. *Thomist Realism and the Linguistic Turn: Toward a More Perfect Form of Existence.* Notre Dame, Ind.: University of Notre Dame Press, 2003.

O'Connell, Timothy E. *Principles for a Catholic Morality.* Revised edition. San Francisco: Harper, 1990.

O'Connor, Edward. "The Evolution of St. Thomas' Thought on the Gifts." Volume 24, *Summa theologiae.* Edited and translated by Edward O'Connor. New York: McGraw-Hill Book Co., 1973, appendix 4, 110–130.

O'Connor, William Riordan. "The *Uti/Frui* Distinction in Augustine's Ethics." *Augustinian Studies* 14 (1983): 45–62.

O'Donovan, Oliver. "*Usus* and *Fruitio* in Augustine, *De doctrina christiana I.*" *Journal of Theological Studies* 33 (1982): 361–397.

Oesterle, John. *Logic: the Art of Defining and Reasoning.* Englewood Cliffs, N.J.: Prentice-Hall, 1997.

O'Meara, Thomas F. *Thomas Aquinas, Theologian.* Notre Dame, Ind.: University of Notre Dame Press, 1997.

———. "Virtues in the Theology of Thomas Aquinas." *Theological Studies* 58 (1997): 254–285.

O'Neil, Charles J. *Imprudence in St. Thomas Aquinas.* Aquinas Lecture Series. Milwaukee, Wis.: Marquette University Press, 1955, 103–107.

———. "Is Prudence Love?" *Monist* 58 (1974): 119–139.

Pascal, Blaise. *Pensées.* In *L'oeuvre de Pascal.* Text established and annotated by Jacques Chevalier. Volume 34, *Bibliotèque de la Pléiade.* Paris: Editions de la nouvelle revue française, 1936.

Pesch, Otto. "Philosophie und Theologie der Freiheit bei Thomas von Aquin in *Quaest. disp. 6 De malo:* ein Diskussionsbeitung." *Münchener Theologische Zeitung* 13 (1962): 1–25.

Pieper, Josef. *About Love.* Translated by Richard and Clara Winston. Chicago: Franciscan Herald Press, 1972.

———. *Faith, Hope, Love.* San Francisco: Ignatius Press, 1997.

Pinckaers, Servais. "A propos du 'volontarisme' dans le jugement moral." *Revue Thomiste* 85 (1985): 508–511.

———. "L'acte humain suivant saint Thomas." *Revue thomiste* 55 (1955): 393–412.

———. "L'instinct et l'Esprit au coeur de l'éthique chrétienne." In Novitas et veritas vitae: *Aux sources du renouveau de la morale chrétienne, mélanges offerts au professeur Servais Pinckaers à l'occasion de son 65e anniversaire.* Edited by Carlos-Josaphat Pinto de Oliveira. Fribourg, Switzerland: Editions universitaires Fribourg, 1991, 216–223.

———. *Morality: the Catholic View.* Translated by Michael Sherwin. South Bend, Ind.: St. Augustine's Press, 2001.

———. "Notes explicatives." In *Somme théologique: les actes humains, tome deuxième (1a–2ae, questions 18–21).* Paris: Editions du cerf, 1997, appendix 1, 155–214.

———. *Le renouveau de la morale.* Paris: Téqui, 1964.

———. *The Sources of Christian Ethics.* Washington, D.C.: Catholic University of America Press, 1995.

———. "La structure de l'acte humain suivant saint Thomas." *Revue thomiste* 55 (1955): 393–412.

———. *La vie selon l'Esprit: essai de théologie spirituelle selon saint Paul et saint Thomas d'Aquin.* Luxembourg: Editions saint-Paul, 1996.

Pinto de Oliveira, Carlos-Josaphat. "*Ordo rationis, ordo amoris:* la notion d'ordre au centre de l'univers éthique de s. Thomas." In Ordo sapientiae et amoris: *image et message de saint Thomas d'Aquin à travers les récentes études historiques, herméneutiques et doctrinales: hommage au professeur Jean-Pierre Torrell, O.P. à l'occasion de son 65e anniversaire.* Edited by Carlos-Josaphat Pinto de Oliveira. Fribourg, Switzerland: Editions universitaires de Fribourg, 1993, 285–302.

Plantinga, Alvin. *Faith and Rationality.* Notre Dame: University of Notre Dame Press, 1985.

Pope, Stephen J. *The Evolution of Altruism and the Ordering of Love.* Washington, D.C.: Georgetown University Press, 1994.

Porter, Jean. "A Response to Brian Linnane and David Coffey." *Philosophy and Theology* 10 (1998): 285–292.

———. "*De ordine caritatis:* Charity, Friendship, and Justice in Thomas Aquinas' *Summa theologiae.*" *Thomist* 53 (1989): 197–213.

———. *Moral Action and Christian Ethics.* Cambridge: University of Cambridge Press, 1995.

———. "Moral Language and the Language of Grace: The Fundamental Option and the Virtue of Charity." *Philosophy and Theology* 10 (1998): 169–198.

———. "Recent Studies in Aquinas's Virtue Ethics: A Review Essay." *Journal of Religious Ethics* 26 (1998): 191–215.

———. *The Recovery of Virtue: The Relevance of Aquinas for Christian Ethics.* Louisville, Ky.: Westminster/John Knox Press, 1990.

———. "The Subversion of Virtue." *Annual of the Society of Christian Ethics* 12 (1992): 19–41.

———. "The Unity of the Virtues and the Ambiguity of Goodness, a Reappraisal of Aquinas's Theory of the Virtues." *Journal of Religious Ethics* 21 (1993): 137–163.

———. "What the Wise Person Knows: Natural Law and Virtue in Aquinas' *Summa theologiae.*" *Studies in Christian Ethics* 12 (1999): 57–69.

Pouivet, Roger. *Après Wittgenstein, saint Thomas.* Paris: Presses universitaires de France, 1997.

Rahner, Karl. "The 'Commandment' of Love in Relation to the Other Commandments." In *Theological Investigations.* Volume 5. New York: Crossroad, 1966, 439–459.

———. *Foundations of Christian Faith: an Introduction to the Idea of Christianity.* New York: Crossroad, 1985.

———. "Freedom: iii. Theological." In *Sacramentum Mundi.* Volume 2. New York: Herder, 1969, 361–362.

———. "Guilt—Responsibility—Punishment Within the View of Catholic Theology." In *Theological Investigations.* Volume 6. New York: Seabury Press, 1974, 197–219.

———. "Justified and Sinner at the Same Time." In *Theological Investigations.* Volume 6. New York: Seabury Press, 1974, 218–230.

———. *The Love of Jesus and the Love of Neighbor.* New York: Crossroad, 1983.

———. "On the Question of a Formal Existential Ethics." In *Theological Investigations.* Volume 2. Baltimore: Helicon Press, 1963, 217–234.

———. "Reflections on the Unity of the Love of Neighbor and the Love of God." In *Theological Investigations.* Volume 6. New York: Seabury Press, 1974, 231–249.

———. "Theology of Freedom." In *Theological Investigations.* Volume 6. New York: Seabury Press, 1974, 178–196.

Riesenhuber, Klaus. "The Bases and Meaning of Freedom in Thomas Aquinas." *Proceedings of the American Catholic Philosophical Association* 48 (1974): 99–111.

Rocca, Gregory. "Analogy as Judgment and Faith in God's Incomprehensibility: A Study in the Theological Epistemology of Thomas Aquinas." Ph.D. dissertation, Catholic University of America, 1989.

Ross, W. D. *The Right and the Good.* Oxford: Clarendon Press, 1930.

Rossner, William L. "An Inclination to an Intellectually Known Good: the Question of the Existence of Intellectual Love." *Modern Schoolman* 52 (1974): 65–92.

———. "The Process of Human Intellectual Love, or Spirating a *Pondus.*" *Thomist* 36 (1972): 39–74.

Rousselot, Pierre. *The Intellectualism of Saint Thomas.* Translated by J. E. O'Mahony. New York: Sheed and Ward, 1935.

———. "Pour l'histoire du problème de l'amour du moyen age." In *Beiträge zur Geschichte der Philosophie des Mittelalters. Text und Untersuchungen* 6/6 (1908): 1–104.

Roy, Louis. "Wainwright, Maritain, and Aquinas on Transcendent Experiences." *Thomist* 54 (1990): 664–672.

San Crostobal-Sebastian, A. *Controversias acerca de la Voluntad desde 1270–1300.* Madrid: Editorial y Libreria Co. Cul., 1958.

Schenk, Richard. "*Omnis christi actio nostra est instructio.* The Deeds and Sayings of Jesus as Revelation in the View of Thomas Aquinas." In *La doctrine de la révélation divine. Studi tomistici* 37 Edited by Leo Elders. (Rome, 1990), 103–131.

Schillebeeckx, Edward. *Revelation and Theology.* Translated by N. D. Smith. Volume 2. New York: Sheed and Ward, 1968.

Seckler, Max. *Instinkt und Glaubenswille nach Thomas von Aquin.* Mainz: Mattias-Grünewald—Verlag, 1962.

Sertillanges, A. D. *La philosophie morale de saint Thomas d'Aquin.* Paris: F. Alcan, 1916.

Shanley, Brian J. "Aquinas on Pagan Virtue." *Thomist* 63 (1999): 553–577.

Sherwin, Michael. "*Christus Magister:* Christ as the Teacher in St. Thomas' Commentary on John's Gospel." In *Reading St. John with St. Thomas.* Edited by Matthew Levering and Michael Dauphinais. Washington, D.C.: Catholic University of America Press, forthcoming.

———. "'In what straits they suffered': St. Thomas' use of Aristotle to transform Augustine's critique of Earthly Happiness." In *Aquinas' Sources: The Notre Dame Symposium,* Edited by Timothy L. Smith. South Bend, Ind.: St. Augustine's Press, 2005, 260–271.

Simon, Yves. *Freedom of Choice.* Edited by Peter Wolff. New York: Fordham University Press, 1969.

Simonin, H. D. "Autour de la solution thomiste du problème de l'amour." In *Archives d'histoire doctrinale et littéraire du moyen âge* 6 (1931): 174–272.

———. "La Primauté de l'amour dans la doctrine de saint Thomas d'Aquin." *Vie spirituelle* 53 (1937), suppl.: 129–143.

Spicq, Ceslaus. *Agape in the New Testament.* Translated by Marie Aquinas McNamara and Mary Honoria Richter. St. Louis, Mo.: B. Herder Book Co., 1965.

Spohn, William C. *What Are They Saying About Scripture and Ethics?* Fully revised and expanded edition. Mahwah, N.J.: Paulist Press, 1995.

Staley, Kevin. "Aristotle, Augustine, and Aquinas on the Good and the Human Good: A note on *Summa theologiae* I-II QQ. 1–3." *Modern Schoolman* 72 (1995): 311–322.

Stévaux, A. "La Doctrine de la charité dans les commentaires des *Sentences* de saint Albert, de saint Bonaventure et de saint Thomas." *Ephemerides theologicae lovanienses* 24 (1948): 59–97.

Stout, Jeffrey. *The Flight From Authority: Religion, Morality and the Quest for Autonomy.* Notre Dame: University of Notre Dame Press, 1981.

Synave, P. "Le problème chronologique des questions disputées de s. Thomas d'Aquin." *Revue thomiste* 31 (1926): 154–159.

Thesaurus linguae latinae. Leipzig: Teubneri, 1900.

Titus, Craig Steven. "The Development of Virtue and 'Connaturality' in Thomas Aquinas' Works." Licentiate thesis, University of Fribourg, Switzerland, 1990.

Torrell, Jean-Pierre. "Les *Collationes in decem preceptis* de saint Thomas d'Aquin, édition critique avec introduction et notes." *Revue des sciences philosophiques et théologiques* 69 (1985): 5–40.

———. *Saint Thomas Aquinas, volume 1: the Person and His Work.* Washington, D.C.: Catholic University of America, 1996.

———. *Saint Thomas Aquinas, volume 2: Spiritual Master.* Washington, D.C.: Catholic University of America, 2003.

Van Ouwerkerk, C. A. J. Caritas et Ratio: *étude sur le double principe de la vie morale chrétienne d'après s. Thomas d'Aquin.* Nijmegen: Drukkerij Gebr. Janssen, 1956.

Van Steenberghen, Ferdinand. *La philosophie au xiiie siècle.* Louvain: Publications universitaires: Béatrice Nauwelaerts, 1966.

Vereecke, Louis. "Le concile de Trente et l'enseignement de la théologie morale." *Divinitas* 5 (1961): 361–374.

———. *De Guillaume d'Ockham à saint Alphonse de Ligouri.* Rome: Collegium S. Alfonsi de urbe, 1986.

———. "Histoire et morale." *Studia moralia* 12 (1974): 81–95.

———. "Préface à l'histoire de la théologie morale moderne." *Studia moralia* 1 (1963): 87–120.

———. "La théologie morale du concile de Trente à saint Alphonse de Liguori." *Studia Moralia* 25 (1987): 7–25.

Wawrykow, Joseph. *God's Grace and Human Action: "Merit" in the Theology of Thomas Aquinas.* Notre Dame: University of Notre Dame Press, 1995.

Weisheipl, James. *Friar Thomas d'Aquino. His Life, Thought and Works.* Second edition. Washington, D.C.: Catholic University of America Press, 1983.

Westberg, Daniel. "Did Aquinas Change his Mind About the Will?" *Thomist* 58 (1994): 41–60.

———. "The Relation of Law and Practical Reason in Aquinas." In *The Future of Thomism.* Edited by Deal W. Hudson and Dennis W. Moran. Notre Dame: University of Notre Dame Press, 1992.

———. *Right Practical Reason, Aristotle, Action, and Prudence in Aquinas.* Oxford: Clarendon Press, 1994.

Wielockx, Robert. "La discussion scolastique sur l'amour d'Anselme de Laon à Pierre Lombard d'après les imprimés et les inédits." Ph.D. dissertation, Catholic University of Louvain, 1981.

Wilken, Robert. *Remembering the Christian Past.* Grand Rapids, Mich.: William B. Eerdmans, 1995.

Wippel, John F. "The Condemnations of 1270 and 1277 at Paris." *Journal of Medieval and Renaissance Studies* 7 (1977): 169–201.

Wippel, J., and A. Wolter. *Medieval Philosophy from St. Augustine to Nicholas of Cusa.* New York: Free Press, 1969.

Wohlman, Avital. "Amour du bien propre et amour de soi dans la doctrine thomiste de l'amour." *Revue thomiste* 81 (1981): 204–234.

———. "l'élaboration des éléments aristotéliciens dans la doctrine thomiste de l'amour." *Revue thomiste* 82 (1982): 247–269.

Woods, Walter J. *Walking with Faith: New Perspectives on the Sources and Shaping of Catholic Moral Life.* Collegeville, Minn.: Michael Glazier Press, 1998.

Zigon, Franz. "Der Begriff der Caritas beim Lombarden, und der hl. Thomas." *Divus thomas (Studia friburgensia)* (1924): 404–424.

Index of Names

Index of Subjects

CPSIA information can be obtained
at www.ICGtesting.com
Printed in the USA
BVHW072012060819
555254BV00001B/21/P

9 780813 218717